THEEGOBOOM

THE EGO BOOM

WHY THE WORLD
REALLY DOES REVOLVE
AROUND YOU

BY STEVE MAICH AND LIANNE GEORGE

KEY PORTER BOOKS

Copyright © 2009 by Steve Maich and Lianne George

All rights reserved. No part of this work covered by the copyrights hereon may be reproduced or used in any form or by any means—graphic, electronic or mechanical, including photocopying, recording, taping or information storage and retrieval systems—without the prior written permission of the publisher, or, in case of photocopying or other reprographic copying, a licence from Access Copyright, the Canadian Copyright Licensing Agency, One Yonge Street, Suite 1900, Toronto, Ontario, M6B 3A9.

Library and Archives Canada Cataloguing in Publication

Maich, Steve
    The ego boom : why the world really does revolve around you / Steve Maich and Lianne George.

ISBN 978-1-55263-975-7

    1. Self—Social aspects. 2. Identity (Psychology)—Social aspects. 3. Self-actualization (Psychology)—Social aspects. 4. Self-perception—Social aspects. 5. Popular culture. I. George, Lianne II. Title.

HM1051.M25 2008   302'.1   C2008-901752-8

THE CANADA COUNCIL | LE CONSEIL DES ARTS
FOR THE ARTS | DU CANADA
SINCE 1957 | DEPUIS 1957

ONTARIO ARTS COUNCIL
CONSEIL DES ARTS DE L'ONTARIO

The publisher gratefully acknowledges the support of the Canada Council for the Arts and the Ontario Arts Council for its publishing program. We acknowledge the support of the Government of Ontario through the Ontario Media Development Corporation's Ontario Book Initiative.

We acknowledge the financial support of the Government of Canada through the Book Publishing Industry Development Program (BPIDP) for our publishing activities.

Key Porter Books Limited
Six Adelaide Street East, Tenth Floor
Toronto, Ontario
Canada M5C 1H6

www.keyporter.com

Text design and electronic formatting: Alison Carr

Printed and bound in Canada

09 10 11 12 13 5 4 3 2 1

ACKNOWLEDGMENTS

First and foremost, we would like to thank Ken Whyte— without his generous support and encouragement, there would be no book. Also, a special thank you to Mark Stevenson, and everyone at *Maclean's* who pitched in to pick up our slack during our absences from the newsroom; our agent Michael Levine and our editor Jonathan Schmidt, for their guidance, thoughtfulness and patience; Jordan Fenn, Martin Gould, Gillian Scobie, Alison Carr, Daniel Rondeau, Jennifer Fox and everyone else at Key Porter who lent their time and effort to this project; Peter Bregg, Carmen Dunjko, Jenny Armour, and Brian Rea for putting together a brilliant cover design.

We are extremely grateful to the dozens of experts who shared their perspectives and insights with us.

We would also like to thank all of our friends and colleagues who offered their support and feedback, especially Sarmishta Subramanian, John Intini, Adam Sternbergh, Lorenzo Savoini, Derek DeCloet, David Thomas, Susie Lindsay, Murray Foster, Michael and Nat George, Gene Hayden, Greig Dymond, Max Valiquette, Jane Tattersall, and Sinclair Stewart.

Finally, we'd like to thank our families for keeping us always on track, Vivian George, Paul and Gail Maich, and Erin Maich.

CONTENTS

INTRODUCTION

I n December of 2006, we had just set out to write a book
about the ascendancy of You in our culture. Then, as if on cue,
Time's Person of the Year issue landed on our desks. We had won.
Or rather, You had. Only four months earlier, You had topped *Business
2.0's* list of most influential business leaders. Not to be outdone, *Advertising Age* bestowed upon You, the consumer, the honour of 2006's Ad
Agency of the Year. Clearly, You were having a moment.

This book is about that. About You. The Royal You. But also the
particular you, with your individual thoughts and needs, your unique
likes and dislikes, your preferred Starbucks blend, your signature BK
burger, your personal ringtone, your political blog, your custom Adidas,
your Facebook friends, your à la carte medical insurance plan, your
designer condo, your pick 'n mix brand of spirituality, and your kid's
American Girl doppelgänger. More specifically, it is about how all of
those things are symptoms of something much bigger: a force that is
reshaping our economies, our communities, and the way we relate to
the world around us. We call it *The Ego Boom*.

If individuality—your inherent right to self-expression, self-
actualization, and self-fulfillment—is the highest ideal of a free society,
then it would seem we're living in a golden age. Never before have You
had so many tools for expressing your unique personality at your

disposal—everything from custom health care to custom denim. The inclination to doing it your way is akin to patriotism in Western countries. It permeates our art and literature, and it underpins all the seminal philosophies upon which our democratic society is premised: John Stewart Mill and Ralph Waldo Emerson; feminism and the civil rights movement; the sixties' "find your bliss" ethos; the seventies' *Free To Be You and Me* self-esteem movement; the eighties' "me" generation; the arrival of the Internet in the nineties; and the consumer tsunami marketers call "mass customization." But at what point does self-regard become self-defeating?

By the autumn of 2008, some of the astonishing costs of the Ego Boom began to come into focus. The credit collapse that started in the United States and quickly spread around the world had its roots in an environment where marketers and salesmen of all kinds equated consumption and luxury with personal expression and self-esteem. Why should only the rich be able to afford a nice four-bedroom house in a gated community? Hell, why should such benefits accrue only to the *employed*? Hundreds of thousands of consumers literally bought into the image of themselves as homeowners with flat-screen TVs and a nice car or two in the driveway—even if they didn't have a penny of savings in the bank—and Wall Street and the banking industry were only too happy to dispense mountains of credit to underwrite the illusion. Billions were made and then lost, and pretty soon the crisis spread, subsuming every maxed-out credit card and overdue car loan in the country and beyond. Every one of those collapsing debts is rooted in a marketplace where the cultivated narcissism of the buyer is the driving force.

This book is the product of the two years two journalists spent scouring countless news reports, academic studies, and marketing campaigns about the wonders of "personal democracy," customized public policy, and music services that, say, allow you to insert your name into a Jessica Simpson song. It's not an academic study but an attempt to describe an ideology which has come to dominate the billions of daily transactions that make up modern life. This ideology is communicated all around us, every day, through something we call "The You Sell"—marketing messaging that announces indiscriminately: You're special! You deserve the best! Nothing less!

The astonishing pervasiveness of the You Sell has shifted the nature of marketing from the aspirational to the affirmational.

But the You Sell has done much more than that. It has engendered a way of thinking—an ethos of entitlement—that has seeped into the relationships we form, the homes we make, the societies we build, and the governments we elect. In the process, the You Sell has become the jet fuel behind the Ego Boom. If the pro forma flattery of the You Sell sounds less than revolutionary, that's because it has become so deeply encompassing. Like the proverbial frog that can't tell the water temperature is slowly rising, we simply can't remember a time when "You" were not the centre of the universe. But, according to the books, anyway, that world did exist.

Almost a century ago, Theodore Roosevelt wrote in his autobiography that "unrestricted individualism spells ruin to the individual himself. But so does the elimination of individualism, whether by law or custom." There it was: self-actualization is either (as the American psychologist Abraham Maslow would later convince an entire generation) the only thing worth living and dying for, or it's that which is sure to destroy us.

Of course, there is nothing inherently wrong with wanting to express yourself through your stuff. The question is, what happens when a me-centred mindset becomes the dominant filter through which we learn to see the world.

The economic consequences are already painfully evident in a generation of insatiable consumers who lived well beyond their means for too long. The social consequences are more subtle, but no less serious. As Harvard professor Robert Putnam has warned, in our race toward ever-greater heights of self-indulgence we've witnessed the accelerated decline of cultural, political, and religious institutions that used to make our societies coherent and cohesive. Whatever sense of belonging might have come from membership in a community group, even something as simple as voting has been eroded as we retreat into our ever-more-insular existence. We operate first and foremost as consumers, and as such, we've convinced ourselves that we know best. And so traditional authorities must bend to our whims just as consumer brands do, or they face obsolescence. Schoolteachers, for instance, aren't so much educators anymore as service providers, charged with dispensing self-esteem pellets and passing grades indiscriminately. The news media shift their focus from informing an engaged populace to indulging our desire to escape from daily life. Religious institutions must soften their message to stay alive and relevant, shifting away from their traditional role as a beacon in troubled times and heavy-handed promoter of virtue. In place of traditional churches and temples, the infinitely flexible concept of "spirituality" serves as a source of constant pandering reassurance.

We can't help but love this sense of control, and, even when it is illusory, we'll pay a premium to feel empowered. As a result, for those who've mastered the You Sell—the purveyors of custom computers, cars, interior designs, even vitamins "just for you"—the windfalls are enormous and growing bigger all the time. But there is an increasing body of evidence to suggest that the costs go far beyond the demise of church suppers and Lion's Club picnics.

We are inhabiting an amplified, hyper-speed version of the "culture of narcissism" predicted by Christopher Lasch in 1979, in which self-actualization—on ever more insignificant scales—is sold to us as each person's number one priority. The explosion of the consumer culture has yielded an enormous degree of control over our personal space and a staggering range of choices in the marketplace. It has also propelled a standard of living unprecedented in human history. Luxury has become the dominion of the masses. But the triumph of radical individualism has come at a cost, and, on the whole, the consequences are rarely, if ever, considered.

What does it mean, for instance, that for the first time in history, there are more people living alone in North America than in any other household configuration? Or that college students in the U.S. as a group have never scored so high on the Narcissistic Personality Inventory scale? Or that we have created billion-dollar industries dedicated to reinforcing a fragile, mythical notion of our own uniqueness: custom sneakers, dolls that look like us, and even avatars, virtual versions of ourselves, on whom we spend real money to buy virtual clothing and real estate—without pausing to consider whether any of this actually contributes to an authentic sense of self?

We've gained enormously from the economic, social, and personal benefits of the Ego Boom. But it is also now clear that in the pursuit of those benefits, we accrued debts that threaten to take much of it away. What's more, we may have eroded many of the instincts that help us survive tough times together. But in the past, society's great challenges were overcome through sacrifice and collective action—both instincts that seem inconsistent with the individualistic ideology behind the Boom. How will we manage the challenges of domestic economic meltdown, international global poverty, the AIDS crisis, climate change, and the West's demographic time bomb when "here" and "now" and "me" are the central preoccupations of our world?

This is the story of how we got here—how we've benefited, what we've lost, how to recognize the You Sell when we see it, and why we just might be ready to move in a new direction. At the root of the story is the promise of "self-actualization"—a noble and natural goal that has been repackaged into a wildly profitable illusion that millions of us buy into every day. It may be only an inch deep, but it's infinitely wide.

CHAPTER ONE

THE YOU SELL:
"Everything we do is a celebration of You!"

I t's just after lunchtime on a perfect June day in downtown
Chicago. A crowd of approximately 135 girls, mothers, and grand-
mothers—punctuated by the odd bewildered dad—is packed into
the plush plum- and eggplant-coloured theatre on the bottom floor of
American Girl Place. The three-storey doll store, flanked by such elite
establishments as Ralph Lauren and the Ghirardelli Chocolate Shop, is
set just steps from the posh shops of the city's Magnificent Mile. Each
member of the audience has shelled out $28—about the price of an
average American Girl doll outfit—to witness the store's Broadway-style
stage show, the *American Girls Revue*. It's an hour-long musical whirl-
wind through time and space, in which the fictional characters of
American Girl's outrageously successful line of historical dolls and
books—eight of the bravest imagined tween girls in the history of the
United States—will recount tales of overcoming adversity to a range of
original show tunes.

Inside the theatre, the air is crackling with girl power. Girl tri-
umphalism, even. It really is no wonder parents seem as eager as the
kids to devour the empowerment message: they're delighted that their
girls have embraced a toy line that's ostensibly as much about learning as it is about fashion. American Girl is billed as the anti-Barbie—
wholesome and artfully crafted, while Barbie is flimsy and morally

vapid. And while Barbie and her nemeses, the Bratz dolls, spend their time shopping, gossiping, wearing too much makeup, and loitering at the mall, American Girl teaches girls ages seven to twelve about history, friendship, courage, and individuality. The historical characters include Kaya (who dates back to 1764), American Girl's own "daring, adventurous, Nez Perce girl" who "respects nature." Then there's Addy (1864), an African-American slave girl who escapes a Southern plantation with her mother; Samantha (1904), a wealthy Victorian, caught between her Grandmary's old-fashioned values and her Aunt Cornelia's "new-fangled ideas" about women's suffrage; and Molly (1944), who does her best to be sunny and helpful while her dad is far away, fighting for the American way of life.

The dolls and their requisite gear are considerably more expensive (a doll costs about $84, compared to a Barbie, which will run you as little as $10). But the quality of the product, like the message it's imbued with, is high enough to justify the cost. Parents, worried about ubiquitous talk of girls growing up too fast, wearing too much makeup, and expressing their sexuality too young, are happy to pay the price to keep their little girls little a bit longer. Mattel, the maker of Barbie, must've seen this wave of "age compression" anxiety coming when it purchased American Girl, formerly called the Pleasant Company, for an impressive $700 million in 1998. It was a smart bet. In 2005 alone, with the opening of the third American Girl Place in Los Angeles, the company raked in a record $436.1 million in sales, up 15 percent over 2004.

The history of American Girl is one of those high-fibre tales that warms the heart's cockles and, not incidentally, situate the brand in its particular fortress of wholesomeness. The company was founded in 1986 by a headstrong woman with the serendipitous name of Pleasant Rowland. As legend has it, Ms. Rowland, a former teacher and writer with a thing for Colonial Williamsburg, was searching high and low for birthday presents for her nieces that were an alternative to the sexed-up, hyper-materialistic, bubbleheaded dolls lining the shelves. Alas, she could find none. So she determined to create her own—a line of high-quality dolls with educational value that would teach girls about history, perseverance, and the American way.

Headquartered in Middleton, Wisconsin, the Pleasant Company was initially a mail-order business. The catalogues were the only show-case for the six original eighteen-inch dolls—all representative of key eras in American history—each of which came with a series of books detailing their adventures and what life would've been like for a young girl at that time. By 1999, the Pleasant Company had sold 5 million dolls and over 50 million books and opened its first mega-store in Chicago. Around that time, marketers were just beginning to recognize the astonishing spending power of tweens (as a group, they are estimated to drop $51 billion a year on their own, and have influence over another $170 billion spent on them by family and parents). By 2007, the empire of American Girl—as it was officially renamed by Mattel in 2004—expanded to include three big-box American Girl Place locations (Manhattan, Los Angeles, and Chicago), American Girl Boutique and Bistro stores in Dallas and Atlanta, with more than 19 million visitors, 117 million books, and 13 million dolls sold, awards for leading the industry in "experiential retail," and untold millions of preadolescent brand loyalists.

As the *American Girls Revue* winds up, the preternaturally gifted tween actors—future Broadway stars who collectively mirror the rainbow of hair and skin colours reflected in the product line—come out for bows and sugary smiles to enthusiastic applause. Then, the audience is invited to stand to sing the anthem. Not the American anthem, the American Girls Anthem.

On the surface, what we, the audience, have learned from this show is that girls count. Not only that, they've always counted. Girls have played a powerful role in history, even though—Joan of Arc and Anne Frank aside—you don't read about them in the history books. It's a deeply emotional and empowering message for girls and their parents, one that marketing experts know makes mothers weepy. "There are so many messages out there that are negative, and that are swaying girls in the wrong direction: to be overly materialistic, to be fast and slutty, to favour things that are superficial," says Robert Kozinets, an associate professor of Marketing at York University in Toronto, who has studied the brand and parental responses to it. For many parents, buying into American Girl can seem like shorthand for keeping their daughters protected—for buying them the kind of pristine childhood they would want for them in an ideal world.

But there is something else just as powerful and more immediately pertinent that the audience is encouraged to take from the *American Girls Revue*. The show—and more broadly, the American Girl brand—has placed the little girls in the audience in a rather weighty historical continuum, and has bequeathed the present to them. The (fictional) girls that came before them—Addy, Kaya, Samantha, and the rest—did their part to settle the West, end slavery, survive the Great Depression, support the troops, and secure equality for women. They did all of this so that the modern American Girl—addressed in all of the brand's messaging as "You"—could enjoy the freedom to express her own unique individuality. "What they sell is, first, this is your history," says Carolina Acosta-Alzuru, assistant professor of Advertising and Public Relations at the University of Georgia, who wrote a Ph.D. dissertation on the doll company. "Then they sell that 'American girls' are girls that speak out, that love their countries, that are good friends, and that take care of themselves. And of course, American Girls own American Girl dolls."

And here is where the true power of the brand lies: in using the rhetoric of self-esteem and personal power to fuel emotionally charged consumer binges. After the singing of the anthem, the small army of fashionably dressed girls clutching their fashionably dressed dolls is directed out of the theatre and back onto the retail sales floor—a department store–sized temple built explicitly to honour each and every one of them—with renewed inspiration.

Walking around American Girl Place, it quickly becomes apparent that the historical dolls have been displaced as the centrepieces of the brand by a newer line of American Girl dolls called Just Like You.™

The collection consists of roughly twenty dolls, each with a different combination of eye colour, hair colour, skin colour, and facial features—so that each girl is invited to buy a "mini-me" version of herself. In the catalogue, the collection is introduced this way: "You're the inspiration for a whole new line—a collection of simply great stuff that celebrates who you are today, and what you love to do. In fact, it's even named after you—American Girl!"

Mothers and hordes of little girls clamour around the Just Like You™ display case, musing over which doll has which girls' eyes, hair and freckles. A Just Like You™ "starter package" costs $102. If you have blue eyes and blonde hair, so can your doll! If you wear glasses, why not buy your doll a pair, too ($6)? Broken leg? No problem: the "Feel Better Kit" comes with crutches, a cast, an ice pack, and a bandage for $26. Jewish? L'Chaim! There's a menorah for your doll ($14). The fashionable Dress Like Your Doll™ line of clothing and accessories invites girls to get a matching outfit in their own size, in the bargain. In 2006, the company introduced its Truly Me™ line of cosmetics and fragrances—lip glosses, face masks, and scented body lotions that purport to "celebrate the qualities that make you original—your hopes, your dreams, your inner star that shines so brightly!"

There is seemingly no end to the number of ways in which a girl can express her unique, one-of-a-kind self through American Girl stuff. She can buy her doll miniature versions of everything she has ever dreamed of, from a pretend flat-screen TV and entertainment centre for $40, to a Vespa-type scooter and helmet for $65. Or doll-sized passports, library cards, musical instruments, spending money, and miniature versions of *American Girl* magazine. There are even *dolls* for the dolls, so that the experience comes to seem like a hall of mirrors—all reflecting an idealized version of the girl back to herself. "Your Just Like You™ doll will help you share your story with the world!" the catalogue says. "Everything we do is a celebration of You!"

Parents can take their girls to the American Girl photo studio, where they can get a portrait of themselves with their dolls, often in matching outfits. In the American Girl Library, there are dozens of self-help books to help girls be the best You possible, with titles like *Real Beauty: 101 Ways to Feel Great About YOU!* The stores also offer special learning programs for its customers—everything from cooking to hairstyling classes. One such class in the Chicago store is a workshop for girls on money management called "Making Cents," held semi-regularly in the theatre. (Lesson one: Figure out what your unique skills are and make money using them. Lesson two: Splurging is okay if you *really, really* want something.) More remarkable than any lessons imparted is the fact that parents have grown to trust this brand so implicitly, they will *pay* ($24) to have the American Girl Company teach their kids about money.

The appeal of the brand is perfectly understandable—it's a masterfully crafted amalgam of hyper-simplified traditional American ideals and modern self-esteem rhetoric. The combination results in one giant all-American "celebration of You," always comfortably couched in the vocabulary of moral and mental wellness. It's what Alcosta-Alzuru calls the brand's "righteous cloak:" "[It's] that very pure message that we are good for your daughter. We understand what growing up is. We think girls need to claim their place in society," she says. "These dolls and these accessories will make for a wholesome, educational play experience and that concept is never contradicted." What more could any engaged, progressive parent want?

The historical backdrop and the educational aspects of the sell serve to bolster and legitimize the idea that investing in American Girl dolls and accessories is an investment in the girl herself. Girls have a *right* to self-esteem, the message goes, and therefore they have a *right* to these products. In an era in which we are constantly being educated about an enormous self-esteem crisis among young people, you'd have to be a bit of a jerk not to jump at an opportunity to buy your daughter a piece of it. And so, standing near the American Girl Place cash register, it's not unusual to hear purchases being rung up for $200, $300, $500, and more. Rationally, of course, we all know that self-esteem is not so simple. But marketing is all about simple, saleable—and emotional—messages. And any parent who has ever been repulsed by the image-obsessed Barbie and Bratz dolls is fertile ground for American Girl's more subtle appeal to self-centredness. American Girl may be one of the most artful and successful uses of the You Sell in branding.

But it's certainly not the only one.

THE YOU SELL

Turn on any television set, read any magazine or newspaper, or venture online for even five minutes and you'll begin to notice that the language of entitlement is everywhere. *Everywhere.* The You Sell is a pitch that has evolved over time to become the dominant theme in consumer culture. In its simplest terms, the You Sell is the message that you are an inherent VIP. Nobody else can tell you what to think or do. You deserve the best. You're entitled to nothing less. You are unique—an original—and as such, each and every choice you make should be a reflection, an amplification, of your essential, irreplaceable self.

Everywhere we turn, it seems someone is confirming our inherent worthiness to us. The You Sell is in ads for TV services that allow you to watch your shows on-demand—"where you want, when you want." It's in commercials for retailers like Best Buy that invite you to "Get yours." It's in Nescafé ads that tell you, "It's all about you." Where marketers used to primarily sell products or brand values, they're now selling You—an idealized, self-actualized version of yourself—back to you. Whether the conduit is clothing, computers, credit cards, hotel rooms, software or furniture, when it comes to advertising, *You* are the real goods. We—or rather You—have become the only real product anyone is pushing.

Of course, advertising has always promised us a better life through stuff. But listen for it, and you'll notice the pitch has changed. The shift is subtle, but powerful.

1) The You Sell is not aspirational, but affirmational

Effective advertising has always involved strategic feats of deception. But the You Sell contains a different sort of lie, one that is significantly harder to spot since the wisdom of it seems to spring forth from your own head.

Lifestyle advertising used to be about the idea that if you buy a particular product, you will, by extension, acquire an array of desirable qualities associated with that product—glamour, intelligence, physical attractiveness, wit, personal strength. Think of beer commercials: with a pint of Labatt Blue, you too could join a log-cabin party in the Canadian Rockies populated by horny bikini-clad coeds. This is aspirational modelling—the kind you'd see in cigarette ads, where the men are manly and the women are liberated and the only thing ostensibly separating you from them is a lighter. Aspirational ads ask: "Wouldn't you like to be a Pepper, too?"

The You Sell turns this model on its head—instead of being aspirational, it is affirmational. The message is always deferential. It says: *You are already perfect, just as you are.* You know it; the advertisers know it. Now, it's just a matter of enhancing your inherent specialness and broadcasting it to the world via a kick-ass array of products. All advertising is rooted in fantasy. But with aspirational advertising, the dream world is "out there." It's a world to which you do not (yet) belong, where the people there are beautiful, skinny, wealthy, and happy. You can aspire to belong, but the fact that you never quite *do* is what keeps you buying. With affirmational messaging, on the other hand, the dream world comes to *you.* These ads tell us: *All those phonies out there? They should be so lucky as to associate with the likes of you.* In a narcissistic culture reared on self-esteem rhetoric, the implicit message that "you're not good enough" is no longer appealing. Consumers today respond better to honey.

Perhaps the quintessential example of this shift is the L'Oréal Preference beauty campaign. Since 1973, L'Oréal Preference has featured beautiful models and celebrities like Heather Locklear in its TV ads, flipping their hair, and with a wry smile declaring the brand slogan: "Because I'm worth it!" The message was always, if you aspire to be as desirable as Heather Locklear knows *she* is, you'll use this product. But in 2004, L'Oréal's advertising team got wise to the idea that women don't want to hear that Heather Locklear is "worth it." They want to be told that *they* are. In other words, the message shifts from, "hey, this is what you could be" to "hey, this is what we know you already are." Now, L'Oréal Preference ads feature the same beautiful models with the same incandescent hair. Only, instead of luxuriating in their own natural beauty, this new generation of spokesmodels looks coyly into the camera and tells you, the consumer, "Because *you're* worth it!"

2) The You Sell makes you the authority—and the star

Whereas aspirational advertising creates unattainable targets for consumers to strive for in perpetuity, affirmational advertising encourages a different sort of skewed self-perception. The You Sell places You at the heart of every narrative—as the star, the winner! The You Sell is all about reinforcing the "democratization" of luxury, the idea that things that were once seen as luxuries are now regarded as everyone's entitlement by virtue of being able to afford it. You should never feel guilty about self-indulgence, the You Sell tells us. If fact, the *worst* thing you could do is accept less than you deserve, or, God forbid, let somebody else tell you what's what. Only *You* know what's right for you. James B. Twitchell, a professor of English and advertising at the University of Florida, has written extensively on the new luxury: "Call them yuppies, yippies, bobos, nobrows, or whatever, the consumers of the new luxury have a sense of entitlement that transcends social class, a conviction that the finest things are their birthright," he writes. "Never mind that they may have been born into a family whose ancestral estate is a tract house in the suburbs."

Cell phones, designer sneakers, televisions, cars and computers—they're all the domain of the masses now. Things we used to consider *wants*—microwaves, televisions, washers and dryers—have largely become *needs*. In a 2006 Pew Research Center study, two-thirds of Americans reported they needed (rather than just wanted) a microwave oven—this compared to a decade ago, when two-thirds saw this appliance as a pure luxury. Ninety percent now say they *need* a washing machine. Seventy percent *need* air conditioning. Half say they *need* a home computer and a cell phone and almost a third *need* high-speed Internet. The You Sell tells you it's your entitlement—not just to have everything you want, but to get a free upgrade, too.

3) The You Sell invites you to buy yourself

Like aspirational advertising, the You Sell is built on the understanding that we use consumption as a crucial means for constructing the personal identities we wish to present to the world. But whereas the former is primarily used to sell us on aspirational qualities—specific traits like glamour, skinniness, sex appeal, sophistication, etc.—the virtue that is sold by the You Sell is You. Affirmational ads push one-size-fits-all notions of individuality, authenticity, and entitlement. In inviting you to selectively piece together "your" burger, "your" home computer, "your" airline, and so on, the You Sell helps us create a patchwork sense of self—the self we would be if our identities really were buildable from the outside in. In other words, the product on offer becomes a secondary, malleable aspect of Brand You.

Just about all lifestyle advertising today draws on the key themes of the You Sell—although some are more conspicuous than others. In its "Purely You" campaign, for instance, Dell Computers says: "We don't make technology for just anyone. We make it for only one. You." Burger King tells us to "Have it your way." Ford fawns, "Everything we do is driven by you." Air Canada offers you the "Freedom to fly your own way." AT&T transmits "Your true voice." YouTube advocates that you "Broadcast Yourself." Microsoft asks: "Where do you want to go today?" Verizon Wireless says "We never stop working for you." Pier 1 Imports reminds you, "It's Your Thing." Time Warner Cable promises to unleash "The Power of You." The Home Depot cheers you on with, "You can do it. We can help." And Alpo, looking out for your beloved four-legged friends, asks "Doesn't your dog deserve Alpo?" The desired response to these slogans is always a variation on the same theme: *Yes, I am. Yes, I can. Yes, I do. Yes, my dog does, too.*

The You Sell ignores the inherent contradiction that if everyone is special, no one is special. It knows that you will ignore it, too. Media theorists have suggested that the best aspirational ads—in dangling that dream world in front of our noses—can actually function to make people envious of the version of themselves they might become. Affirmational ads, on the other hand, present us with an idealized You and entice us to fall in love with our own reflections.

The beauty of the You Sell is that all of the work of it happens in the consumers' own head. Phrases like "Your burger, Your way" tell us nothing about the product itself, and in this way, marketers keep the idea of individuality infinitely customizable. (What kind of burger is it? Any kind! The you-tell-us kind!) To one consumer, "Your burger, Your way" might mean a double cheeseburger with all the fixings; to another, it means nothing but ketchup. Burger King doesn't even have to guess. Not only does the You Sell force each consumer to do the mental work of conceiving the burger they want, but it has the added bonus of making each one feel as though *they*—not Burger King—are the authority on burgers. Ultimately, consumers' choice of burger becomes that much more significant to them because it appears to convey something essential about who they are. If the sell is effective, consumers won't *understand* that they're not in control. What a great formula for a business.

Promiscuous with its praise, the You Sell embraces everyone equally because everyone's a potential sale. But one of the great paradoxes of the You Sell is that the more we all buy into it—and the more store-bought "individualism" we express—the more homogenous we become as a group. There can only be so many meaningful status signifiers in the public's consciousness at a given time—and the more status a product or brand carries, the more people choose to incorporate it into their personal-identity scrapbooks. We all wind up using the same signifiers to send the message, "There's no one else like me!"

Critics of consumer culture may be quick to decry this approach as a product of corporate psychological engineering. But in fact, consumerism is always about symbiosis, as much as the anti-consumerism movement would like to downplay the free will of the average buyer of stuff. The You Sell is enormously successful right now, but it is largely a byproduct of a generation of relative political calm, technological advances, and spectacular economic growth. It exists because people have had cash to burn. Increases in real income and decreases in family size have allowed for a major boom in discretionary spending. In 1973, American families spent, on average, 62 percent of their annual economic output on primary necessities like food, housing, and clothes, according to the U.S. Bureau of Labor Statistics. In 2005, families spent only 49.6 percent—or just less than half. With so much extra cash to burn, we now have the luxury of allowing our needs to become more specialized, and less pragmatic. Faced as we are with a deeply uncertain economic future, this is a decidedly impractical mindset to hold.

And so, as tempting as it is to pin this consumer frenzy on the "corporate machine," the You Sell is a machine we've all helped to build, and we feed it every day. "There's a lot of tsk-tsking that goes on in popular conversation about how bad consumer society is but we're on the producer side, too," says Kozinets. "There is no giant robotic presence that's doing this to us. When we talk about how it came to be, well, people must've wanted a lot of stuff and wanted to differentiate." Marketing is the art of telling us what we want to hear. Right now, one refrain has become the dominant request: *Tell Me I'm Worth It. Over and over again.* From a marketer's standpoint, what could be easier?

As for the rest of us, the real question is: why are we so desperate to hear it?

GROWING UP IN MR. ROGERS' NEIGHBOURHOOD

One could argue that the You Sell, or the affirmational model, is a progressive step in advertising messaging. For years, we've railed against advertisers telling us that we're not good enough—and that we need products and services to compensate for our innumerable shortcomings. And in a sense it is. But the You Sell is catering to a different set of human frailties. Whereas the aspirational model counted on consumers to not feel good enough about themselves, the affirmational model relies on people's need for—even addiction to—constant reassurance. It tells us that everything we do is right. This is a totally modern phenomenon.

Of course, every generation expresses the same complaints about its successor: Young people today are selfish. They have no work ethic. They have no idea how good they have it. This will probably always be the case. Martyr tales that parents tell their children about miles-long uphill walks to schools run by militant nuns are an age-old cliché. Still, it would be crazy to deny the reams of evidence that there has been a massive attitudinal shift over the past twenty to thirty years. Before the "self-esteem movement" of the seventies and eighties, teachers could use red pens without being accused of damaging students' sense of self-worth; bosses didn't feel compelled to celebrate their employees' birthdays with cake; and U.S. presidential candidates didn't ask the public to vote on their campaign songs. The move toward a culture of entitlement exists on a continuum, and stretches out over decades. But "kids today" are the most up-to-date, state-of-the-art products of this increasing environment of self-absorption. We've taught young people to invest in different assumptions—about what they should expect from the world and what the world should expect from them. And it worked.

In a delightfully ironic 2007 study conducted by VISA USA, 68 percent of Baby Boomers reported they believe that members of the young generation, ages 18 to 28, are too self-centred and focused upon themselves. This is a generation the Boomers—the original Me Generation—made in their own image. Psychology professor Jean Twenge of San Diego State University explored the mindset of young Americans in the research she conducted on a group she's labelled Generation Me—also variously dubbed the Echo Boomers or Gen Y—defined as those born in the seventies, eighties, and nineties. This was her diagnosis: "Today's young people…speak the language of the self as their native tongue. The individual has always come first, and feeling good about yourself has always been a primary virtue. Generation Me's expectations are highly optimistic: they expect to go to college, to make lots of money, and perhaps even to be famous."

Insofar as narcissism can be spelled out in numbers, the Boomers appear to be on to something with regards to their younger counterparts. With each successive generation, we are indeed becoming more full of ourselves. In her research, Twenge and her colleagues quantifiably analyzed the responses of 16,475 U.S. college students who completed the Narcissistic Personality Inventory (NPI) between 1982 and 2006. The NPI is a measure of "normal" narcissism in the culture. It asks people to respond to such statements as: "If I ruled the world, it would be a better place," "I think I am a special person," and "I like to be the center of attention." Twenge found that the average 2006 college student scored higher in narcissism than 65 percent of students did in 1987. Also, 25 percent of 2006 college students qualify as having what experts refer to as "elevated narcissism"—they display higher-than-normal levels of entitlement, vanity, authority, exploitativeness, exhibitionism, and superiority—50 percent more than there were in the early 1980s. Young people, in other words, have a different way of thinking about themselves. But these thought processes came from somewhere.

Relative to their Boomer parents, who were mostly raised by hard-working, Depression-era traditionalists—constantly reminding them of sacrifices made so that they could have opportunities their ancestors never had—today's college-age kids were raised economically secure and politically liberal. They were taught to believe that it's okay to indulge, to explore, and to express themselves—and that guilt is a total waste of energy. Boomers had fewer children, more of whom were wanted thanks to birth control and the affluence of the eighties and nineties. As parents, Boomers did not want to forgo personal fulfillment for the sake of some martyrish notion of sacrificing for their children. Boomer parents worked long hours. They wanted a lot for themselves *and* their children. They were the first to experiment en masse with two-income households, divorce, and blended families. They micromanaged their children's activities, often functioning more as friendly advisors than authorities. They wanted their kids to grow up "well adjusted," but not at the expense of their own personal growth and happiness.

With each new generation of moms and dads since World War II, parenting experts have observed more coddling, more overprotectiveness, and more concern about their kids "being heard." More than just being extensions of parents, kids have become an inextricable part of parents' sense of self. Journalist Susan Gregory Thomas identifies this new style of child-rearing as "attachment parenting." It is, she says, characterized by a "high level of closeness and connection between parents and children and erring on the side of being too involved, too loving, too reaffirming, too indulgent." Parents don't want to discipline their kids. They ask them their opinion on everything—from what they want for dinner and what time they should go to bed, to what kind of car the family should drive and where they should go on family vacations. They want their children to have a voice.

This inclination to give voice to kids' every thought, opinion, and whim is further bolstered by the media, who have a lot to gain from cultivating it. Cartoons, video games, music, and movies targeting kids push what sociologist Juliet Schor, in her book *Born To Buy,* calls the Kids Rule! Effect. Brands like the Nickelodeon Networks, she writes, create an "Anti-Adult bias" by establishing an us vs. them mentality among kids. On shows like *The Amanda Show* and in *Nickelodeon*

Magazine, she says, kids live in a colorful, fun, creative world, while the world of adults is bleak and square. Kids are presented as authorities, while adults are clueless and totally embarrassing. This dynamic, says Schor, adds to kids' "pester power" by giving them a sense of authority and empowering them to have important consumer opinions. In essence, the Kids Rule! Effect creates a divide between parents and child to the point that parents—hell-bent as they are on connecting meaningfully with their children—feel the need to try even harder to bridge that gap by appealing to kids through consumer goods.

How did we get here?

Don Chance is a Louisiana State University finance professor. In a 2007 *Wall Street Journal* article, Chance expressed shock over the increasing number of students popping by his office to request some extra grade points to boost their averages. His theory—and not a bad one—is that Mr. Rogers, the shoe-flipping, cardigan-wearing children's TV show host, is to blame. Rogers, he said, did more damage than anyone could've imagined by telling "several generations of children that they were 'special' just for being who they were."

Indeed, as Mr. Rogers' core audience has matured, we have begun to witness the "special-as-I-am attitude" that Chance was referring to trickle up into the adult world. The parent-child codependency that Gregory. Thomas and others have written about—buttressed by decades of affluence—has resulted in the creation of what developmental psychologist Jeffrey Arnett of the University of Maryland defined as "emerging adulthood"—the extended period of delayed responsibility between eighteen and twenty-nine (and older) in which young people are technically adults, but remain free from responsibility to sow their oats, and are able to try on identities, really focus on themselves, and discover what it is they *truly* want to do with their lives.

Study after study reminds us that allegiances to traditional authorities, like parents, teachers, politicians, and media, have waned. Students expect that authorities, much like their parents, are there to serve them. For their 2007 book, *Ivory Tower Blues*, University of Western Ontario sociology professors James E. Coté and Anton L. Allahar surveyed professors on their campus to determine whether they perceived student engagement to be improving or eroding. About 20 percent thought students were not as academically prepared for or engaged in their courses as students in the past; 24 percent thought students were less mature; and 22 percent thought students were less willing to accept professors' judgments on grades. Their findings echoed what other student engagement studies in Canada and the U.S. have found. "Compared to past generations," they wrote, "millennials were given higher grades in high school for less effort; as a result, fewer have been seriously challenged to develop their intellects and associated motivations to understand the world in increasingly complex ways. As a result, they are more likely to expect things to be done for them by their professors—as if professors were like high school teachers—rather than taking the initiative to do certain things themselves, like reading and thinking about course material in preparation for classes."

Similarly, the American journalist and social critic Peter Sacks tells the story of how he left his career in his late thirties to teach journalism at an unnamed college in the mid-1990s and experienced his own type of culture shock upon entering the classroom. His students, 80 percent of whom were between the ages of eighteen and twenty, sat slumped in their chairs, staring at him, he writes, "with looks of disdain and boredom, as if to say, 'Who in the hell cares where you worked, or what your experience is, or what you know? Say something to amuse me.'" Attendance was routinely shoddy, mobile devices were frequently in use, and most of his writing students, he says, simply refused to read. "To be sure," he writes, "dealing with the students' rudeness, narrow-mindedness and lame excuses was inconsistent with my idea of teaching college-aged adults, and I often reacted to what I considered juvenile behaviour with visible irritation." In one instance, a particularly inept writer named Jodi came to confront him with a paper he had marked with a grade of C, which "clearly didn't match her self-concept." "I've never gotten below a B in writing," she told Sacks, implying that it was he who needed to improve his judgment skills. When he explained to her why she deserved the C, she said, decidedly unimpressed, "It's just your opinion."

In the end, Coté and Allahar conclude, students often get the grades they demand for very little work, which has led to an epidemic of inflated grades and underqualified graduates—particularly as classrooms become too crowded for professors to keep track of each and every individual's progress. "Faculty members are but employees of what have become the large business operations we call universities," they write. "As employees of these businesses, many professors find their jobs difficult when working with undergraduate students who have been implicitly promised a product (degree) in exchange for their tuition." At universities in particular, students are increasingly treated like customers, and they've been taught the mantra "the customer is always right" very well.

As it turns out, Mr. Rogers and his fellow self-esteem champions may have unwittingly helped to produce a generation that can't see its own shortcomings clearly. For decades, Linda Sax, director of the University of California–Los Angeles Higher Education Research Institute, has watched grades go up, even as students have become less engaged—missing more classes, on average, reporting more in-class boredom, and doing fewer hours of homework. Still, in 2000, the Institute's annual freshman survey found that more than 34 percent of freshmen reported earning an A average in high school, up from 12.5 percent in 1969. Conversely, the C-student is slowly vanishing: in 2000, only 12 percent of freshmen earned C averages, compared with 32.5 percent in 1969.

Students have the self-esteem to go with their inflated grades. In 2006, the Higher Education Research Institute's survey of freshmen found that "students' self-confidence in academic ability continues to soar," with 69 percent considering themselves "above average" or in the top 10 percent of their peer group, compared with an already bloated 59 percent in 2000. Surely *somebody's* exaggerating.

I WANT MY SELF-ESTEEM

Oprah Winfrey has identified low self-esteem as "the root of all the problems in the world." In fact, very rarely does anyone question the size or the terrible repercussions of the "self-esteem crisis." Certainly not advertisers. They tell us the problem is enormous, but that it can be easily ameliorated, for a reasonable price. The solution: *more* affirmation.

Mister Rogers, obviously, is only one tiny manifestation of the larger self-esteem movement—an offshoot of the human potential movement—which assumed that in order to achieve happiness and success, and to avoid life's many pitfalls like dysfunctional relationships, substance abuse, crime, and career stasis, you have to have a very high opinion of yourself. The path to "Generation Me," or whatever you want to call it, is paved with good intentions. Beginning in the eighties, programs designed to boost children's sense of self-esteem were installed in schools and, in looser ways at home in the form of books and TV shows like *Mr. Rogers' Neighbourhood.* Throughout the seventies and eighties, according to Twenge's research, the number of studies published on the benefits of self-esteem programs doubled, and in the nineties, it doubled again. Today's under-thirty-five set are the first generation to be raised entirely in this institutionalized climate.

As a construct, self-esteem has achieved almost devotional status in North America, so much so that in the United States, there is an independent non-profit organization, the National Association for Self-Esteem, devoted to its study and promotion. The organization is premised on the belief that raising self-esteem is a crucial factor in combating the climbing rates of youth dropouts, gun violence, teen pregnancies, suicides, and eating disorders. And so, back in the 1980s, school districts across the U.S. began implementing curricula designed to boost kids' feelings about themselves. Educational programs and colouring books—with titles like *I Believe in Me: A Book of Affirmations, 1-2-3 Special Like Me!* and *Celebrate Yourself: Six Steps to Building Your Self-Esteem*—were introduced to teach young people that they were special, lovable, and capable just the way they were, independent of anything they did or said.

The assumption that a child's self-esteem should be guarded jealously at all costs has led to experimental school policies in Canada and the U.S. that, when we stop to examine them objectively, border on the absurd. But self-esteem indoctrination is a powerful force to combat—we generally figure that, best-case scenario, such initiatives are beneficial. Worst-case scenario, they're harmless. In many cases we've witnessed a drastic reduction—or an all-out ban—on competition of all sorts, which can lead to hurt feelings for those who don't take the prize. Now, it's ribbons and trophies for everyone. No failing grades. No grades at all in some cases. In 2005, the U.S. National PTA recommended the age-old game tug-of-war be recast as a "tug of peace." At some schools, "tag" is prohibited because it's too competitive and it singles out one kid as being the loathsome "it." There are stories of teachers not correcting homework in red pen anymore because the colour is too harsh and could erode self-esteem. One California elementary school principal suggested using lavender instead, "because it is a calming color." In October of 2008, a teachers' union in Britain expressed outrage at the notion of children as young as ten being invited to partake in the hiring process of new teachers in north London. Prospective hires were subjected to "speed dating" style interviews by students who then rated candidates according to their responses. Common sense, and decades of life in the real world, should tell most adults that nobody's doing anyone a favour here.

Even early on, not everyone was sold on institutionalized self-esteem. Lilian G. Katz, an international leader in early childhood education from the University of Illinois at Urbana-Champaign, and a critic of such programs, recalls in her writing visiting a first-grade class in a suburban elementary school where kids were producing booklets called "All About Me." Aside from basic age, home, and family information, the pages were filled with answers to such queries as, "What I want for a present," "What I watch on TV," and "Where I want to go on vacation."

"Instead of encouraging children to reach out and understand and investigate phenomena worthy of their attention," writes Katz, "the headings of the pages turned their attention toward themselves." After examining booklets and other materials like these, Katz was among the first to pose the questions: "Why should children's attention be turned so insistently toward themselves? Can such superficial flattery boost their self-esteem?"

WORK SHOULD WORK *FOR* ME

This attitude, call it self-esteemism—not entirely charming, but certainly not without its uses—is now beginning to surface in the workplace as "Generation Me" transitions into its professional years. Corporations, which used to be the evil machines that chewed people up and spat them out, are now in a position of having to appeal to this young generation on its own terms, faced as they are with a potential employee shortage. With the entire Boomer generation set to retire in the coming decade, companies need to attract the best of the young cohort, and they know it. In many cases, the workplace is learning to adapt to this new generation's inflated sense of self. Employers are learning to speak to would-be hires in the language of the You Sell in order to attract the best young talent out there. Some companies are using online social networking sites like Facebook or YouTube to recruit candidates and appear hip.

"Rather than speak about the needs and wants of the employer, more and more corporate recruiters are starting to speak in terms of the needs and wants of the candidate," Winnepeg-based recruiter Steven Rothberg, founder of CollegeRecruiter.com, which caters to U.S. students and graduates, said in a newspaper interview.

For example, in seeking to recruit staff, Harvey's—the popular Canadian burger chain that makes your burger "just the way you like it"—set up a website called StandardIsLame.com, where it invites young people to "Customize Your Work," the same way they would customize an Angus Burger. Why would a young person like you want to work at Harvey's, the site asks rhetorically? "We live for custom. At Harvey's guests get it how they want it—now that's unique. We understand and appreciate your individuality. It's what makes you— YOU." Job seekers, they say, can expect their job at Harvey's to mould to them. "At Harvey's, we're all about custom culture," the site says. "We have custom stations and we want custom people to fill them. No run-of-the-mill, cookie cutter, robot associates droning on by the fry station day in and day out...Enjoy custom work, custom contests, newsletters and...oh yeah...a custom site just for you."

Similarly, Merrill Lynch, dedicated to attracting the best possible employees, is always looking for new ways to sell them on the company—including inviting their parents (their *de facto* managers and agents) on their recruiting efforts. In 2006, the company introduced a "parents day," inviting the families of prospective interns to tour the trading floor. This sort of parental involvement is not uncommon, according to a Recruiting Trends survey conducted at the Collegiate Employment Research Institute at Michigan State University: these days, 41 percent of employers surveyed said that moms and dads routinely obtain informational materials for their kids. Moreover, 31 percent said parents submit résumés on behalf of the students; 26 percent said parents actively promote their son or daughter for a position, and 4 percent said that parents have actually attended the job interview with their son or daughter.

Once employers have attracted the most talented youth, they need to fight to keep them—because, research tells us, this young generation is fickle and easily turned off. A 2007 U.S. Conference Board study found that less than two out of every five workers under the age of twenty-five are satisfied with their jobs—the lowest level of job satisfaction ever reported in the twenty-year history of the Conference Board survey. These "kiddults," as they're sometimes called, don't feel that they should have to make sacrifices or put themselves in an uncomfortable position to pay their dues. The way they look at it, they have no dues to pay. Grunt work is someone else's job.They want work–life balance, high salaries, flexible schedules, ample benefits and vacation time, and plenty of autonomy and creative work right out of the gate. "A lot of managers are now saying, 'What do we do with these young people who expect praise at every moment and think they're going to be vice president of the company in five years?'" Twenge says. "What a lot of businesses have done is they have responded with *more* praise and *more* mechanisms for recognizing employees." This is because they recognize that, on the whole, today's young recruits are not as reluctant to quit an unsatisfactory situation as previous generations. Worst-case scenario, they often have the option of moving back home with mom and dad. (Indeed, in 2006, a third of Americans between eighteen and thirty-four, and 44 percent of Canadian adults aged twenty to twenty-nine, were still tucking themselves into their childhood beds at mom and dad's house.)

And so employers across North America are resorting to measures that are clearly unheard of to keep new hires feeling appreciated. According to a 2007 *Wall Street Journal* report by Jeffrey Zaslow, corporations like Lands' End and Bank of America "are hiring consultants to teach managers how to compliment employees using email, prize packages and public displays of appreciation." Universal Studios Orlando doles out "applause notes" to its 13,000 employees to mark a job well done. The Container Store Inc. "estimates that one of its 4,000 employees receives praise every twenty seconds" through such efforts as its "celebration Voice Mailboxes." According to Zaslow, one power-wheelchair manufacturer in Texas even went so far as to hire a "celebration assistant" charged with the task of handing out helium balloons and throwing confetti at employees. Employees want to be publicly recognized just for fulfilling their job description—and they want to feel that, on a personal level, they are considered an asset to the work environment. "Marking milestones is major," Jason Ryan Dorsey, a self-styled expert on his generation, told *Fortune* magazine. "No birthday should go uncelebrated, and the first day on the job should be unforgettable." Through the eyes of their Depression-era grandparents, who probably weren't feted on the first day of work at the pulp mill, these people must seem like a different species.

SELF-ESTEEM VS. NARCISSISM

In light of perceived attitudinal shifts among young people, some have taken to asking the question: Could it be that while parents, teachers, and experts in early childhood psychology have been trying to cultivate self-esteem, with the best of intentions, they have in fact been cultivating a general tendency toward anti-social behaviour? In the course of conducting an extensive research review in 2001, Nicholas Emler at the London School of Economics came to the startling conclusion that most of our commonly held beliefs about low self-esteem are myths, with no reliable data to support them. "There is absolutely no evidence that low self-esteem is particularly harmful," Emler told psychologist Lauren Slater, in an essay she wrote on the subject. "It's not at all a cause of poor academic performance; people with low self-esteem seem to do just as well in life as people with high self-esteem. In fact, they may do better, because they often try harder."

Not only that, he said, but people who have an unjustifiably high opinion of themselves can, in many cases, pose a far greater social threat than those whose sense of self-worth is very low. Although low self-esteem is a risk factor for suicide, depression, teenage pregnancy, being bullied, and having an eating disorder, Emler found that it is not a risk factor for delinquency, violence toward others, drug use, or alcohol abuse. In fact, young people with very high self-esteem are *more* likely than others to hold racist attitudes, reject social conventions, and engage in risky behaviours like drinking and driving. "Widespread belief in 'raising self-esteem' as an all-purpose cure for social problems," said Professor Emler, "has created a huge market for self-help manuals and educational programmes that is threatening to become the psychotherapeutic equivalent of snake oil."

Roy Baumeister, the Eppes Eminent Professor of Psychology and head of the social psychology graduate program at Florida State University, suggests that self-esteem proponents may have unwittingly created a generation of people for whom social connections are *more* difficult, not less. In a study he conducted in 1998 at Case Western Reserve University in Cleveland, Ohio, on narcissism and displaced aggression, Baumeister and his colleagues concluded that low self-esteem doesn't cause violence, as psychologists had previously assumed. Rather, aggressors are more likely to think very highly of themselves. In two studies, the researchers measured participants' levels of self-esteem and narcissism. Next, they were given a chance to aggress against someone who had insulted them, someone who had praised them, or an innocent third party. There appeared to be no real correlation between self-esteem and aggression. But the study found that the combination of narcissism and insult led to extremely high levels of aggression toward the source of the insult. In a separate experiment, Baumeister and his fellow researchers found that some people with higher levels of self-admiration were more willing to administer painful blasts of noise to a subject than those with a more modest sense of self. (Think of those jerks in tricked-out muscle cars who rev their engines threateningly and blast bad gangsta rap.)

In 2003, Baumeister and a team of North American psychologists conducted a review of every major study conducted on self-esteem over the preceding two decades and concluded that there is no evidence that boosting self-esteem through school programs or therapeutic means leads to positive outcomes. People with high self-esteem claim they are more likable, attractive, and have better relationships than others, the researchers found, but these advantages might only exist in their own minds. Objective data, including what their peers thought of them, did nothing to confirm their high opinions of themselves; in some cases, people with quantifiable high self-esteem turn out to be the least-liked people in the group. "Raising self-esteem will not by itself make young people perform better in school, obey the law, stay out of trouble, get along better with their fellows or respect the rights of others," Baumeister concluded. "…Using self-esteem as a reward rather than an entitlement seems most appropriate to us."

Part of what makes the true scope of the "self-esteem crisis" so hard to determine is that there is a great deal of confusion surrounding the definition of the term "self-esteem"—and how it differs from narcissism. The National Association for Self-Esteem characterizes those with a lot of it as having "tolerance and respect for others." They are people who "accept responsibility for their actions, have integrity, take pride in their accomplishments, are self-motivated, willing to take risks, capable of handling criticism, loving and lovable, seek the challenge and stimulation of worthwhile and demanding goals, and take command and control of their lives." When an individual works hard and accomplishes things, he learns to see himself as capable and competent, which leads to more accomplishments. It's a cycle of positive reinforcement. In this sense, it's truly not only *who you are* that counts, it's *what you do*. "In sum, healthy self-esteem refers to realistic and accurate positive appraisals of the self on significant criteria across a variety of interpersonal situations," NASE says. "It also includes ability to cope with the inevitability of some negative feedback." In other words, self-esteem is realistic and resilient.

Narcissism, on the other hand, makes people insecure and needy. The DSM-IV, the bible of psychiatric diagnosis, defines people with narcissistic personality disorder as exhibiting an exaggerated sense of self-importance and "uniqueness," an unreasonable sense of entitlement, a preoccupation with fantasies of unlimited success and power, a tendency to exploit others, a shortage of empathy, and an excessive need for admiration. Narcissists expect special treatment, although they don't feel the need to extend the favour to anyone else.

"They tend to exploit others, to be seekers of sensation, experiences, and thrills, and to be highly susceptible to boredom," writes

Lilian Katz. "Many of these characteristics seem to apply to our culture in general and our youth in particular."

The National Association for Self-Esteem tells us that much of the confusion over the term "self-esteem" does indeed stem from early unproven programs and strategies that lavished children with unmerited praise. "Most feel that it is critical that any efforts to build self-esteem be grounded in reality," writes Robert Reasoner, former president of NASE. "It cannot be attained by merely reciting boosters or affirmations, and one cannot give others authentic self-esteem. To do so is likely to result in an inflated sense of self-worth."

The difference between self-esteem and narcissism is that, while the former is based on the ability to form solid relationships with others, narcissism is really just about thinking that your space in the world should take priority over everyone else's.

"It manifests in a number of ways," Twenge told us. "People who score high tend to have less empathy for others. They have a harder time taking someone else's perspective. When they're faced with common resources they take more for themselves and leave less for other people. They have problems in relationships and they tend to cheat in game play. In general, their viewpoint of relationships is, 'what can you do for me?'"

For decades, social scientists have been using the Marlowe-Crowne Social Desirability Scale to measure an individual's need for social approval. The numbers, Twenge found in the course of her research, have plummeted since the fifties and sixties, particularly among children. The scale asks young people to respond to such statements as "I never forget to say 'please' and 'thank you'," "I am always careful in my manner of dress," and, on the other hand, "I am sometimes irritated by people who ask favors of me." In 1958, half of kids age nine to twelve agreed that social conventions weren't very important to them. Which sounds like a lot until you hear that after kids the same age took the test in 1999, more than three-quarters of them reported they just didn't care what anyone else thinks.

And so, while it may seem on the surface that young people as a whole feel great about themselves, they're not necessarily operating from a place of "healthy" self-esteem. Superficially, there appear to be certain benefits to narcissism—someone with high scores in this area, for instance, probably comes across as a great candidate for a job opening or to be the next American Idol. In the long term, however, narcissism presents certain struggles, not only for the larger society, but for individuals themselves. According to Twenge, for example, data show that narcissists are more likely to end up with anxiety and depression. "It seems that that happens because they drive people away," she says. "And yet, narcissistic or not, all of us need good, close relationships and good relationships with co-workers to be successful in both personal and professional life. Narcissists screw that up and so they end up with bad outcomes."

The You Sell is right there to provide the constant reinforcement that those of us with socially conditioned narcissistic tendencies so desperately need.

THE LONE HERO

It's not as though we collectively woke up one morning, tripped into a puddle, and fell in love with our own reflections. The You Sell didn't create this generation—it just knows how to reach it. The whole notion of self-esteem and its importance have deep roots in the American tradition of individualism. Crack open the history books and you'll find it's a front-and-centre part of an ideological continuum of western liberal thought. Reverence for the individual—the lone hero with his or her innate, unwavering moral compass—permeates our art and literature, and it underpins all the seminal philosophies upon which our democratic society is premised.

In his book *Bowling Alone*, the Harvard political scientist Robert Putnam points out that individualism and community have consistently worked at odds in the American psyche.

"Liberation from ossified community bonds is a recurrent and honoured theme in our culture," he writes, "from the Pilgrims' storied escape from religious convention in the seventeenth century to the lyric nineteenth-century paeans to individualism by Emerson ("Self-Reliance"), Thoreau ("Civil Disobedience"), and Whitman ("Song of Myself") to Sherwood Anderson's twentieth-century celebration of the struggle against conformism by ordinary citizens in Winesburg, Ohio to the latest Clint Eastwood movie." The rebel's personal journey toward self-actualization—from Huck Finn to Tony Soprano—is one of the bedrocks of the American story.

Over the years, business has grown increasingly wise to the broad appeal of the "individual" theme. In fact, Emerson's "Self-Reliance" was explicitly invoked in Reebok's pseudo-radical (but disastrously executed) UBU campaign, in which the company prompted its audience to buck convention and be themselves at any cost. The campaign was designed in response to Nike's wildly successful "Just Do It" campaign, which told audiences they have infinite resources inside of them. In Reebok's ads, photographs of fringe-type characters are juxtaposed against quotations taken from Emerson's 1832 text: "Whoso would be a man, must be a non-conformist" the voiceover says as two elderly couples do an odd square dance in sneakers. "A foolish consistency is the hobgoblin of little minds," it says as a middle-aged man in business dress hits a paddleball on a string.

Doing it Your Way is almost a patriotic act in America—and in countries heavily influenced by it the search for self-fulfillment is a phenomenon that transcends socio-economic groups. In fact, it may be the only truly universal belief we share. But, the American search for self-fulfillment is based on a very narrow conception of the term "self," one that is confined to the thoughts, feelings, and perspectives that course through one's own head and body. In a paper published in 1991, psychologists Hazel Rose Markus of the University of Michigan and Shinobu Kitayama of the University of Oregon theorized that our concept of "self"—as individual consciousness divorced from anything external—is, to a large extent, culturally constructed. To prove their point, they examined how American children and Japanese children differ in how they are taught to understand the concept of self. The Western understanding of the concept, they concluded, is "independent," that is, it has given rise to a culture of self-actualization and a focus on developing one's unique potential. When it comes to other people, they write, the Westerner often uses social interaction for strategic purposes—that is, how can this person help me to best express and experience myself.

In contrast, in Japan at that time—and in many other non-Western nations—people traditionally assumed an "interdependent" construct of the self that involves seeing oneself in terms of one's placement in, and contribution to, the larger group. (This is presumably changing as a global culture emerges.) In Japan, this "ethos of social relativism" translates into "a constant concern for belongingness, reliance, dependency, empathy, occupying one's proper place, and reciprocity." Within this model, the worst-case scenario is exclusion from the group. "This is in sharp contrast to the American nightmare," the authors write, "which is to fail at separating from others, as can occur when one is unduly influenced by others, or does not stand up for what one believes, or when one goes unnoticed or undistinguished."

This nightmare has arguably come to shape how we define a life well lived—and a life wasted. In a 1985 paper they wrote for the *Journal of Consumer Research*, marketing professors Russell W. Belk and Richard W. Pollay described how our very definition of what it means to live "the good life" changed over the course of the twentieth century. There are two lexicographic meanings for this term. The first is "a life lived according to the moral and religious laws of one's culture." In this definition, life functions as a means to a "spiritual end" and therefore requires that a good person renounce, or at least de-emphasize, material pleasures in order to cultivate spiritual rewards. In the West, however, we have increasingly come to prefer the second definition of the good life, that is, "a life abounding in material comforts and luxuries." This is a definition that America has successfully marketed around the world, including modern Japan.

"At the same time that increases in discretionary income may have enabled pursuit of the good life through consumption," the authors write, "a parallel change in the social values sanctioning such increased hedonism seems to have taken place." Responsibility for the group has become increasingly incompatible with our preferred interpretation of "the good life"—that is, to be distinguished, to be indulged, to be heard—which could pose a challenge given the tough economic times ahead.

It's an evolution that seems to have happened gradually, but in hindsight it has changed the way we function as a collective shockingly fast. Many of these changes in values really began to manifest in the period between the end of the Second World War and the late sixties, when the wartime manufacturing industry shifted to peacetime needs and opportunities. The U.S. economy experienced one of its longest-running growth periods, and young people, motivated by the ethics of the war to think independently and question authority, were restless for all manner of change—an energy that manifested in the form of Vietnam war protests on campuses, and experimentation with drugs and sexuality, among other things.

"For the Boomers, who grew up in the 1950s and 1960s," writes Twenge, "self-focus was a new concept, individualism an uncharted territory." They witnessed their mothers and fathers often languishing in unhappy marriages, forced to abide by what the Boomers viewed as an outmoded vision of domestic life. They saw that traditional institutions like family, church, and state often functioned to choke off the individual spirit, and they wanted change.

The seventies witnessed the advent of the "Me" generation—the era of *Free To Be You and Me* and the human potential movement, marked by economic turbulence and more political disillusionment in the wake of the Watergate scandal and President Richard Nixon's subsequent resignation in 1974. Post-Watergate, the thinking among young people, social observers noted, was that one person may not be able to improve the world, but they can improve themselves. "By the late seventies," wrote marketing and public-opinion guru Daniel Yankelovich, in 1981, "my firm's studies showed more than seven out of ten Americans (72 percent) spending a great deal of time thinking about themselves and their inner lives—this in a nation once notorious for its impatience for inwardness." There is a reason this cohort popularized the mood ring.

Periodically, we predict that this relentless inward focus is all ending, that it has served its purpose—liberating us from systems that kept us personally confined. Yankelovich was optimistic when he wrote at the dawn of the eighties that seekers of self-fulfillment were beginning to realize that they had pursued a "self-defeating strategy." He wrote that, after years of preoccupation with the self, evidence showed Americans becoming less self-absorbed as the seventies drew to a close. "There is less talk than in earlier decades of status symbols (big homes, diamond rings, fur coats) and less comparing one's self to the neighbors." In hindsight, this seems comical. As we now know, the eighties ushered in a high-water mark for self-absorption—and that was *before* iPhones, $200 designer jeans, and MySpace were even invented.

A far more prescient reading was that of the American social critic Christopher Lasch, whose landmark book *The Culture of Narcissism,* was written around the same time (1979). This was just the beginning, he prophesied, of a culture increasingly steeped in its own myopia. According to Lasch: "After the political turmoil of the sixties, Americans retreated to purely personal concerns. No hope of improving life in ways that matter, people turned their focus inwards: to seek psychic self-improvement. Learning how to relate, eat healthy, overcome the 'fear of pleasure.'"

All of the things outside one's self are too big, too cumbersome, too impossible to affect, and any attempt inevitably becomes too disruptive to our own personal pursuit of happiness. So the focus was increasingly placed on grabbing your moment in the sun.

"To live for the moment is the prevailing passion—to live for yourself, not for predecessors or for posterity," Lasch wrote.

If Lasch—who died of cancer in 1994 at age 61—was pessimistic then, he'd be despondent today. Self-exploration as defined by the boomer generation at least served an undeniable political purpose, and involved collective action—for instance, in the form of marches against war, segregation, and women's oppression. Today's You-centred culture is largely apolitical (only in rare cases is You Sell able to harness political energy, which we will explore later on). By comparison, the You Sell form of self-discovery is empty and circular. It serves no purpose except to keep itself active in perpetuity, creating a downward spiral of consumption. *You're the best,* it says, *and here's what the best have.* Not even 9/11 and the so-called "end of irony" that it ushered in were enough to change this long-term trajectory.

Is it any wonder that a generation raised in such a climate would be particularly receptive to the You Sell: the message that You are entitled to the best, and that *this* is what the best have? Smart brands have gladly hopped on the self-esteem bandwagon, recognizing a great opportunity to boost sales, and to rack up bonus public relations points at the same time. Take Dove, the soap brand. In late 2008, the Unilever-owned "No. 1 personal wash brand" released a U.S. report declaring a "national self-esteem crisis" affecting the majority of American girls—a "crisis" that some of Unilever's other brands (including Axe and Slim-Fast) arguably benefit from. Among Dove's remedies was its continues sponsorship of the Girl Scouts of America's Uniquely ME! Campaign "to address the problem of low self-esteem among eight- to fourteen-year-old girls." In the program, girls are asked to contemplate their own "amazing" specialness, and they're invited to make collages celebrating themselves and to play a "getting-to-know-me game" called a "Me-O-Meter." In addition to Dove's wildly successful "Real Beauty" ad campaign—featuring regular sized, and shaped, women who are beautiful "just as they are"—the Uniquely

ME! program has helped to position Dove as one of the leading self-esteem brands. In a similar vein, Nike launched its 2008 "Here I am" campaign in Europe to promote the self-esteem aspect of sports and athletics to women.

The beauty of the You Sell is that it is not elitist. It flatters indiscriminately. It's endlessly tolerant and inclusive because—black, white, gay, straight, tween, or senior—everyone's a possible customer. In this sense, the You Sell also has served as an important social leveller. To have stuff *just for you* is empowerment in this society. The You Sell tells us: as long as you buy, you count. And so, the more disposable income minority groups have, the more marketers will cater to them in their messaging, thereby legitimizing and normalizing their place in society. Which is why in recent history, we've come to see things in advertising we wouldn't have dreamed of four decades ago: Home Depot commercials for women, and Air Canada ads pitching relaxing vacations for gay couples, featuring "his" and "his" slippers. The You Sell is incidentally progressive.

THE AGE OF OPTICS

One of the curious aspects of a culture dominated by narcissism is a blurring of the distinction between perception and reality. In much of the self-esteem curricula we've seen in schools, perception is the only reality that matters. The message is that regardless of who you are or what you do—what grades you get, what you look like, or how fast you can run—you are a special person, people like you, and you have unique qualities. Narcissism relies on these psychic buffers. The You Sell operates in the same manner. In order for the You Sell to be successful, it is important to cultivate and bolster a lack of true self-awareness among consumers. It doesn't matter if you're actually rich, cool, glamorous, or discerning, as long as you *think* you are projecting these qualities in public. And there are endless products that can help with that. This is what the age of optics is about—it's an exercise in willful delusion on a mass scale.

According to the late American psychiatrist Alexander Lowen, who focused a great deal on narcissism in his work, narcissism is a condition that leads individuals to place undue importance on their own image—to spend more time and concern managing how they're *perceived*, than how they actually feel. We've become conditioned to believe that others will respond to us and value us for the image we present to the world, and through the products we consume and display. In this sense, neither form nor function is really what's important: optics is the key.

The problem is that, as we've already seen, real self-esteem—that is, the kind we intended to cultivate in ourselves and our children—works in the opposite manner. It only grows out of real effort and meaningful challenges, not out of empty flattery. If individuals are not taught to cope with frustration, setbacks, and negative feedback, they often wind up devoting a significant amount of energy to what psychologists call "impression management," playing at being things that they are not, to win and maintain the admiration of others. If individuals respond to negative feedback by striving to manage the impressions they make on others to gain their approval, said Lilian Katz in her assessment of ill-conceived self-esteem programs, they also learn that much of the praise they receive is similarly unreliable and unwarranted because they know it came only as a product of their constructed behaviour.

That we are utterly preoccupied with "impression management" is easily witnessed in political discourse—where what one *says* is more important than what one clearly meant to say, a concept that public intellectual Michael Ignatieff, a Canadian member of Parliament and former Harvard professor, refers to as politics' "lunatic literalism."

"Nothing is personal in politics, because politics is theater. It is part of the job to pretend to have emotions that you do not actually feel," he wrote in a 2007 opinion piece for the *New York Times Magazine*.

"In public life, language is a weapon of war and is deployed in conditions of radical distrust. All that matters is what you said, not what you meant."

Take for example a seemingly encouraging study that came out of UCLA's Higher Education Research Institute survey, which has examined the attitudes of U.S. college freshmen for over forty years. In their 2006 study, researchers were pleased to report that the percentage of freshmen who predicted they would participate in community service had increased significantly; also, freshmen rated "being a community leader" as more important than ever (about a third considered it "very important" or "essential"). But as psychology professor David G. Myers of Hope College in Holland, Michigan, points out, one of the hallmarks of the inflated self is overestimating how admirably one would act in a given situation. And so it is important to reiterate that while it's wonderful that all of these students are making altruistic proclamations, the survey is not a measure of their actions but of their intent. In a separate study, social psychologist Steven Sherman of Indiana University called residents in Bloomington, Indiana, and asked them to predict how they would respond, hypothetically, were they asked to volunteer three hours of their time to an American Cancer Society drive. Almost half predicted they would rise to the occasion. But when a second random batch of residents was called and asked in earnest to pitch in, a paltry 4 percent agreed to do so.

Optics are so closely tied to narcissism, in fact, that studies have shown that people who score high on the Narcissistic Personality Index behave entirely differently when they're under scrutiny—when, researchers discovered, there is a perceived opportunity for glory. In a 2002 study they conducted at Case Western University, Baumeister and Harry M. Wallace asked subjects to participate in a range of activities to rate their levels of engagement under different circumstances. In one such experiment, they asked subjects with elevated narcissism to play a modified version of the game *Operation.* When the subjects were told in advance that a particular task was widely thought to be difficult to achieve, the subjects' performance levels would rise—that is, they recognized the exercise as an opportunity to impress. When they were told a task was considered to be quite simple, the subjects exerted themselves very little.

In another experiment, Baumeister and Wallace tested their subjects' creativity by asking them to list potential uses for a particular object. The subjects were split into three groups. The first group was told there would be no evaluation, and that their answers would be anonymous. The second group was asked to engage only in self-evaluation. In the third, subjects were told their answers would be publicly evaluated. Baumeister and Wallace found that subjects with high narcissism performed best when they knew their creativity test would be evaluated by others.

"Narcissists crave opportunities for self-enhancement," they concluded, "and some tasks offer more self-enhancement value than others. Narcissists should perform well when task success will be taken as an impressive sign of personal superiority. However, when task success will be unimpressive, narcissists should perform relatively poorly." Conversely, they wrote, those with low levels of narcissism will perform steadily regardless of who is paying attention. "Just as the mythical Narcissus was obsessed with observing his own reflected beauty, modern-day narcissists crave chances to observe their reflected greatness."

YOU'RE NOBODY UNLESS YOU'RE TALKED ABOUT

Fame, a modern obsession, perhaps best illustrates the ultimate distinction between aspirational and affirmational modelling. Celebrities are generally not concerned about what their fans think. They don't want individual peoples' approval, they want mass affirmation. In other words, if you care what somebody thinks or feels, you *aspire* to win their approval. But fame is about mass adulation. It's about everybody knowing your name. Period. A "Big Brother" cast member might say,

"I don't care what you think of me" or "I'm not here to make friends." Britney Spears may choose to record a cover of Bobby Brown's "My Prerogative" ("Everybody's talkin' all this stuff about me/Why don't they just let me live?") And yet, they betray a need to keep themselves in the public eye in a manner that seems almost pathological.

In 2006, Drew "Dr. Drew" Pinsky, a University of Southern California assistant clinical professor of psychiatry, and his research partner, S. Mark Young, a USC professor of sports, entertainment, accounting, and communications, released the findings of the first academically extensive study of celebrity personalities. Pinsky and Young were the first academics to manage to get sufficient unfiltered access to a range of celebrities to study them, via Pinsky's radio call-in show, "Loveline," which featured a different celebrity guest every night. They collected data from 200 actors, comedians, musicians, and reality TV stars—and measured them using the Narcissism Personality Inventory, the same standard psychological tool Jean Twenge used to test U.S. college students.

Not surprisingly, Pinsky and Young found that celebrities scored significantly higher on the Narcissistic Personality Inventory than the average American. But their results produced two unexpected findings. First, they concluded that narcissism is not a result of celebrity, but that people seek out fame *because* they have elevated narcissism. The prospect of fame and its attendant adulation, they concluded, is what attracts narcissists to seek out celebrity in the first place. Second, to bolster their point, they found a negative correlation between the actual skill level of celebrities and the degree of narcissism they betray: Musicians, who had the highest skill level among those surveyed, scored the lowest on the NPI, while female reality TV contestants—a role that demands little in the way of technique—scored the highest.

Other experts seem to go a step further, implying that narcissism is basically contagious, and that increased exposure to shows like MTV's "The Hills" is putting us all at risk. W. Keith Campbell, a social psychologist and an expert in the study of narcissism, told the *Los Angeles Times* that reality TV in particular is pushing the culture to be more self-absorbed. "By definition," he says, "it's supposed to be reality, and you have a sample of people who are more self-absorbed, more entitled, more vain than the normal population and that is going to pull the population in the direction of narcissism. If the level of self-absorption you see on "Laguna Beach" or "The Real World" is viewed as normal, the culture will be pushed in that direction."

Fame is the ultimate form of vain flattery, which probably explains our increasingly wild obsession with celebrity culture, in which every little thing a person does—from picking up dry cleaning to picking her nose—is worthy of documentation and CNN coverage. The celebrities we herald are representative of our era—the Paris Hiltons, Lindsay Lohans, and Britney Spearses—with their multiple addictions, coarse self-indulgence, and recklessness with their own lives and the lives of others. Lasch's assessment of the symbiotic relationship between media and self-absorption is truer than ever: "The media gives substance to and thus intensifies narcissistic dreams of fame and glory, encourage the common man to identify himself with the stars and to hate the 'herd' and make it more difficult for him to accept the banality of everyday existence."

Stunningly, Jean Twenge's studies on narcissism and young people found that the average college student in 2006 scored about as high on the Narcissistic Personality Inventory as the average celebrity from the sample collected by Pinsky. Which would probably explain why one national U.S. survey found that "more college freshmen said they wanted to be an actor or entertainer than wanted to be a veterinarian, a dentist, a member of the clergy, a social worker, an architect or work in the sales department of a business." Given the choice between fame and contentment, 29 percent of today's young people picked fame, compared with 17 percent of boomers who were surveyed when they were the same age.

Young people are not just willing but eager to give up their privacy in exchange for a mirrored existence. As the slogan for the CW's popular primetime drama *Gossip Girl* says: "You're nobody unless you're talked about." In fact, increasingly, life events have no value unless they are publicly validated—and luckily, the Internet has been the most useful tool all the time in terms of providing average people with (at least the potential of) an instant audience. The Internet is a bottomless well for venting, spewing, and proclaiming one's most personal and private feelings. Anyone with computer access and an Internet connection can do it. In the world of Facebook and MySpace, friendship has taken on a new definition. Friends are things you collect and display. You can also rank them in such a way that it paints a desirable picture of you—who you know, who likes you, who you endorse, etc.—so that everyone knows your place in the hierarchy. The actual relationship that exists between "friends" is irrelevant.

The look-at-me phenomenon is perhaps most evident in the proliferation of blogs, or online diaries, of which there are now roughly 65 million and growing. Underlying the current practice of archiving one's life is the belief that everything a person does is worthy of documentation. Bloggers, vloggers, and MySpace and Facebook users often dish on everything from their sex lives, divorces, breakups, career foibles, insecurities, to their fears about love and parenting, to their brash outright ambition for fame and adulation. "I've always thought of myself as being in a movie, that my world is larger than life," Eric Schaeffer, creator of "I Can't Believe I'm Still Single: The Eric Schaeffer Blog," told *Psychology Today*. A 2006 U.S. study found that 61 percent of thirteen- to seventeen-year-olds have a profile—and half of them have photos—and that percentage is quickly rising. A strong Web presence can have a way of making the most mundane aspects of people's lives seem important. As the journalist Lakshmi Chaudhry wrote in *The Nation*, "When it is more important to be seen than to be talented, it is hardly surprising that the less gifted among us are willing to fart our way into the spotlight. Without any meaningful standard by which to measure our worth, we turn to the public eye for affirmation."

With each passing day, it seems, the boundary of appropriate public and private expression continues to erode. *Radar* magazine, in its

June/July 2007 issue, took an in-depth look at the burgeoning world of homemade online pornography—user-generated sites like Xtube.com and pornotube.com, which allow anybody to upload their favourite home movies. "The ability to point-and-click one's way to Guccione-ville is an innovation of Web 2.0, which has fostered a profane perfect storm of interactivity, convenience, anonymity, and global reach," the author, Peter Hyman, writes. Within its first year, PornoTube already contained more than 80,000 videos on its system, and was attracting roughly 12 million viewers a day. "These new porno hubs are essentially X-rated versions of Flickr and YouTube, with unambiguous clip titles like "3 Friends Fucking Greek Student" and "My GF Jerking Me in a Train Station." And they are quickly creating a new genre of porn that is, of, by, and for the people. Abe Lincoln would be proud."

But whether we're talking about American Girl or pay-per-use porno for the masses, once we strip away the ubiquitous surface message of "Celebrating You!," we quickly find that the brand of individualism being sold to us isn't about being a radical free thinker, or even someone with a unique perspective. Rather, the You Sell is a type of affirmation that only perpetuates a need for more affirmation. There is far more to be gained by being the guy who invented Xtube than by being a conventional pornography producer. The owners of Xtube.com are betting that consumers are willing to do all the work (by assuming the expenses and logistical requirements involved in producing homemade sex videos), and then pay the site for nothing more than hosting their content, all to feed consumers' addiction to expressing their unique individuality. When you compare the two business models, it seems like they've placed a good bet.

THE CHICKEN AND THE EGG

Are we becoming more narcissistic because of the You Sell or is the You Sell a corporate response to the fact that we've become more narcissistic? The answer is probably both. Social messaging and consumer culture are profoundly symbiotic in the cultivation of narcissism. In a sense, it's like a feedback loop—institutionalized self-esteem has made us open to the You Sell, which then reinforces cultural narcissism with more You-centred messaging.

The extent to which advertising really does have the power to shape our understanding of the world and ourselves has been a fundamental concern of media theorists for decades. We know by now that media not only reflect a society's values, but they also amplify and create new, altered realities. (Back in the sixties, communications theorist George Gerbner's famous "mean world" study showed that bad-news stories and ubiquitous crime dramas, for example, had the effect of convincing viewers that the world outside their window is a far more dangerous place than it really is.) "Far from being a passive mirror of society," writes cultural critic Jean Kilbourne, "…advertising performs much the same function in industrial society as myth performed in ancient and primitive societies. It is both a creator and perpetrator of the dominant attitudes, values and ideology of the culture, the social norms and myths by which most people govern their behavior. At the very least, advertising helps to create a climate in which certain attitudes and values flourish and others are not reflected at all."

Your little girl, American Girl tells you, is a star who shines so brightly. The company logo even features a single shining star. But it's worth asking: What will the future look like when we've got fifty million American Girls, all of whose stars are shining so brightly that each one is blinded by reflected light?

CHAPTER TWO

THE EGO BOOM:
Rise of the Cat People

I n the mid-seventies, Burger King launched a series of television ads featuring young restaurant employees clad in brown, orange, and yellow polyester, singing a catchy little tune, telling customers that they could have their burgers any way they wanted. "Hold the pickles, hold the lettuce. Special orders don't upset us. All we ask is that you let us have it your way!" The ad was an obvious shot at the nation's dominant burger joint, McDonald's, where a Big Mac meant getting "Two all-beef patties, special sauce, lettuce, cheese, pickles, onions on a sesame seed bun," whether you like pickles or not. And while the "Have it your way" campaign didn't change the course of the fast food business, it was unquestionably ahead of its time. The slogan was dropped after a couple of years in the seventies, but was revived in 2004.

In 1975, customers may not have been particularly jazzed by the idea of getting their burger "their way," but in 2007 priorities have changed and so have the rules of branding. Alan Hallberg, the head of worldwide advertising for multinational technology firm Cisco Systems, explained the shifting landscape to *Marketing* magazine last year. "Consumers have gone from being dogs, who are responsive, eager, needy and when you whistle they come running, to being cats who have a life of their own, not nearly as needy and come to you when they feel like it." The single biggest challenge for big business today is to adjust to a world in which "the audience is on stage and you're in the audience."

To most of us who grew up in the age of self-esteem, all of this sounds wonderfully democratic and empowering. But business doesn't have much experience with democracy, and traditional advertising has never worked on the principles of conversational give-and-take. For generations, marketing has operated on the power of persuasion, not accommodation. Brands worked like beacons: projecting a desired image, and a closely guarded set of values, that attracted consumers. As Hallberg says, all the brand had to do was whistle, and if it hit the right frequency, the dogs would come running. McDonald's didn't have to offer a lot of choices because it wasn't shy about telling you that the Big Mac was the best burger in the world, and it was just perfect as it was. Millions were spent to build up the public goodwill and respect that marketers call "brand equity." Cadillac meant luxury, Pontiac excitement, and Chevy was synonymous with rugged dependability. Seiko watches emphasized style, while Timex famously "took a licking and kept on ticking."

But over the past decade or so, marketers have come to realize that those kinds of messages just don't resonate with a new generation of savvy and cynical consumers, who don't much like being told what they should buy or how they should think. Today's consumers expect brands to bend to their desires, and conform to their expectations, not the other way around. For the most successful brands, that means fashioning a line of products around flexibility and self-expression. Bob Kauffman, a spokesman for Dell Computer, explains it this way: "People are looking to make a statement with the technology they buy." And what kind of statement is that? Well, who's to say? "We're trying to be perceived as the blank canvas, for each individual customer to fill the way they want to."

Dell wove this "blank canvas" approach into the very heart of the company from the beginning. For other companies, the transition has been more of a struggle. And those who cannot customize (or are afraid to give customers that much control over the brand) compensate with dizzying variety. Back in the 1970s, while BK was heralding flexibility, McDonald's was content to offer about five major menu items, each flanked by those famous fries and a Coke. The menu at a typical McDonald's today would be unrecognizable to those early burger pioneers: deli sandwiches, chicken wraps, even salads and apple slices for the kids (not to mention an ill-fated effort to add pizza to the menu in the 1990s). And as McDonald's has gone global, it has adjusted its international menu to match local tastes, all in a multi-billion-dollar effort to adjust to a world in which the customer expects brands to meet them on their own terms, and to offer choice and flexibility at all costs. A Big Mac is still two all-beef patties, special sauce, lettuce, cheese, pickles, onions on a sesame seed bun. But if you'd like them to hold the pickles and add some bacon—no problem.

Nothing illustrates the change in brand mentality better than the radical shift in philosophy at Coca-Cola since the early eighties. In 1980, one of the company's central challenges was how to deal with the rapidly growing market for diet soft drinks. Coke's diet product was Tab, which was sweetened with saccharine and was losing market share to archrival Diet Pepsi. After much discussion, reps from an outside ad agency suggested that the company needed to launch Diet Coke to capitalize on its powerful brand name. According to industry lore, senior executives rejected the idea out of hand, coolly explaining that the singular Coca-Cola brand was sacrosanct. This was a time when the company regarded Coke as "The Real Thing." And it was more than just a slogan. The company would not add any modifier before or after the words Coca-Cola. Coke was "It." End of story.

Except, of course, it wasn't the end at all.

In 1982, faced with losing control of the fastest-growing segment of the soft drink business, the company introduced Diet Coke. It took ninety-six years for Coke to introduce its first spinoff product and in the twenty-five years since, it has unveiled more than two dozen varieties, from Cherry Coke to coffee-flavoured Coke Blak. There are more than a dozen versions of Diet Coke, the latest being Diet Coke Plus, fortified with vitamins and minerals, and they just keep coming. Coke is still "It," whatever "it" happens to mean to you.

This explosion in so-called brand extensions represents an attempt by less flexible manufacturers to adapt to a world in which consumer choice is valued above all else. The fact that store shelves now stock a dozen different types of Tide detergent, and Mr. Christie has marketed twice that many varieties of Oreo cookie is all a manifestation of the Ego Boom in action.

Still, the prophets of the customized economy think these established brands aren't going nearly far enough. Brand extensions like Cherry Coke Zero, with no sugar and no caffeine, may appeal to today's choice-obsessed "me-centred" consumers, but variety is a tepid substitute for real customization, according to Joe Pine, perhaps America's most prominent guru on the subject. He imagines a day when a consumer at a vending machine will be able to order a soft drink, and customize the mix. "I'd like 80 percent regular soda because I like the taste and 20 percent diet because I feel a little guilty about the calories," he says. And why not add various flavour options—a splash of cherry and a drop of vanilla? Feel like a jolt? Let the buyer set the level of caffeine—not just with caffeine or without, but everything from zero to 200 percent of the regular dose. Then you'll have truly customized soda for the masses, he says. "Really the only thing standing in the way is the mindset of the companies."

That shift in mindset is already well underway. The You Sell is a hugely powerful tool in the hands of marketers, but its power to drive the way we consume is limited by the ability of big business to produce products that feel individualized. To make that happen, corporations have had to change the way they think about production as well as sales; they had to be convinced that mass marketing and mass production can happen on an individual basis. They had to start building brands one customer at a time.

Once that mindset began to change, it gathered ferocious momentum.

When high-tech manufacturing was combined with the seductive power of the You Sell, and our own deep-seated desire to express ourselves through the things we consume, we had the makings of an economic awakening whose true reach and potential is just now coming into focus. It was the spark that ignited the Ego Boom.

PURELY YOU

The northern countryside of North Carolina is tobacco country. In the Piedmont Triad, named for the three bordering cities of Winston-Salem, Greensboro, and High Point, the farmland is interrupted only by the occasional prefab housing development here and there, with names like Hickory Creek and Weatherstone. In field after wide-open field, red soil still sprouts the broad leaves of the cigarette trade— a living tribute to the region's economic heritage. But right in the heart of the Triad, on 100 acres in the middle of the nicotine crop, stands a gleaming 750,000-square-foot monument to a whole new economic future.

Dell Computer's North Carolina operation is not so much nestled among the farm fields as carved from them—a two-storey, ultramodern complex of glass and steel, built in 2005 for about $115 million, plus about a quarter billion in tax credits and incentives kicked in by local and state governments. Dell already had plants in Austin, Texas, and Nashville, Tennessee, to go along with factories in China, Malaysia, Brazil, and Ireland. But here, the company envisioned something on a different scale: the world's biggest and most advanced facility dedicated to producing fully customized products built on demand.

The official goal here is to churn out a custom-built desktop computer roughly every three seconds. In reality, they do better than that on most days, and the aim is for 12 to 20 percent improvement in efficiency and speed every year. The factory shipped its first unit in September 2005—less than nine months after breaking ground.

It shipped its one millionth computer eight months later, and its five millionth a little more than a year after that.

Inside, there's no deafening roar of machinery—just a small army of casually dressed workers checking monitors and making adjustments to the black boxes quietly rolling by on the three and a half miles of conveyor belts that twist through the facility. Natural light spills from huge windows and skylights onto a sprawling and spotless shop floor. There's nothing especially remarkable about the operation, unless you know everything that's behind it—and then the word "remarkable" doesn't begin to cover it. To those who've spent the past two decades imagining individualized sales and service on a massive scale, this is the future come to life.

The Dell facility represents the cutting edge of an emerging economic model based on the notion that mass production can be turned on its head. Dell is among the most advanced companies in terms of technology and marketing sophistication, but it is certainly not the only company that has dedicated itself to building a custom economy, in which consumer goods can be targeted toward the individual wants and needs of millions, or even billions, of buyers. Gone are the days in which big companies worshipped at the altar of standardization. Today, manufacturers across an ever-expanding swath of the consumer market are telling the world that they can have products designed "just for you, by you." And that promise has proven deeply appealing to generations increasingly enamoured with their own uniqueness.

As more and more of us stand up and demand to be the designer of every last corner of our lives, Dell and others have found extraordinary profits in a marriage of digital technology and the Internet, with ultra-flexible manufacturing techniques. That marriage is the basis of the emerging custom economy, and it's being consummated in places like this, amid the rural tobacco fields of North Carolina.

Mehran Ravanpay is the friendly and unassuming engineer who oversees the whole operation. "With flexibility comes customization," he says simply. His matter-of-fact delivery belies just how revolutionary that sentiment is in the world of manufacturing. In most factories the trick is to eliminate variables that lead to mistakes and slowdowns. Dell takes the opposite approach. By the time orders arrive here, customers have already specified the size, speed, colour, and capabilities of the computer they want. The vast floor is divided into several dozen "build pods"—miniature production lines where most of the plant's 1,100 workers spend their days, working in teams of four or five, adding various components to plastic computer shells. Each person in a pod is responsible for about seven different components. When a computer shell rolls along a conveyor belt and arrives at a "build pod," a screen lays out the order and identifies which components should be installed. When one assembler's job is complete, the shell slides on to the next person, responsible for installing another set of components. Eventually it goes to a tester, who makes sure all the "custom" parts have been installed as requested, and are connected properly. Finally, software is loaded and the system is electronically tested to confirm that everything works.

The whole process is monitored electronically through a central operations cell, a dim room where about a dozen managers "watch the wall" upon which various diagnostics are constantly flashed. This room is Dell's air traffic control: directing work, anticipating bottlenecks, and diagnosing problems as soon as they arise. Want to know how many processors are in stock? The wall knows. Want to know the location of the Inspiron desktop destined for the home of Martha Smith in Buffalo, New York, and how long it has been waiting in Pod 12 to have a disc drive installed? The wall knows that too.

There are twenty-five different computer platforms built here, from the XPS, a super-powerful PC gaming system, to the company's most popular Inspiron line of conventional desktops. And every system has roughly twenty interchangeable hardware components to be loaded and tested, depending on the customer's specifications. Amazingly, the factory holds virtually no inventory. Dell orders replenishment parts every two hours and takes delivery twice each shift. It's all designed to ensure that a company that pulled in $56 billion in revenue last year can turn on a dime and deliver a customized computer to a customer's front door less then a week after the initial order, no matter what. Not even the forces of nature are permitted to disrupt delivery. Last winter, when Austin was hit by a freak ice storm, production was simply shifted automatically to Nashville and North Carolina, and every unit got out on time.

This is what has come to be known, among business geeks and management consultants, as "mass customization." This is the spectacular profit potential awaiting companies that manage to drill into their customers' desire to feel special, to get involved, and to be treated like individuals.

Joe Pine wrote the book on the phenomenon back in 1993. At the time, his ideas seemed a lot more like business fantasy than emerging reality. He described a new industrial model in which flexible manufacturing technology could satisfy the public's growing fascination with exclusivity, and the building realization that the primary means by which Western consumers express ourselves is through the products we buy. Today, he calls Dell a "shining example" of what mass customization can do.

The power of the You Sell is such that even someone who doesn't know the first thing about computers will get very interested in "building a PC to fit your life" in all its glorious singularity. And Dell has gotten very good at pulling those strings. In 2006, it began blanketing websites and newspapers around the world with an ad campaign built around the tag line "Purely You." Flyers and banner ads exhorted the masses to take charge: "You're unique. Your Dell desktop can relate." "Pack your PC with your own personality." "Your Dell PC: It's what you make of it."

Dell doesn't just sell computers. It promises a fully networked, high-speed reflection of your very soul—and it can be had for as little as $16 a month on approved credit. As Dell spokesman Bob Kauffman explains, "We've been customizing for years, but that was largely focused on technology—what kind of processor do you want? How much memory? More recently, we found out from talking to our customers that they were looking for more personalization."

Dell was the first and most conspicuous player in the computer industry to embrace the potential of this new model, but perhaps the greatest endorsement of its success is the way that its major competitors—Hewlett-Packard, Sony, and Apple to name a few—have shifted their own strategies to mimic Dell's powerful appeal to individualism. From custom-etched designs, to software and services that will adapt to your every want and need, computers are no longer sold as appliances but as life accessories. By doing so, HP and Apple, in particular, have emerged as formidable rivals, even beating Dell at its own game lately. In 2008, Sony unveiled a series of ads built around the tag line "This laptop is *Me*."

That is the essence of the Ego Boom—an outright appeal to the creativity, but also the narcissism, of the modern consumer—the notion that no computer could ever really live up to your expectations unless you were guiding its very creation. Of course, there's a significant gap between the appeal of the You Sell and the reality of what you're getting. The customer isn't really building a "custom computer" so much as he is ticking off a handful of boxes on a multiple-choice order form. But that doesn't seem to dilute Dell's seductive pitch.

It's about mindset. And that mindset is what took the company from zero to $50 billion in sales in less than twenty years, and made Michael Dell "the Henry Ford of Mass Customization." That pitch, and the hundreds of others just like it, has turned the traditional rules of branding and production on their head.

OUT WITH "WE," IN WITH "ME"

Mass production of everything from clothes to food was already well underway by the early 1900s when Henry Ford started building his Model-Ts in Michigan. But the changes introduced by the Ford Motor

Company would soon earn the company iconic status in Western industry. The defining moment came in 1913, after a Ford engineer visited a slaughterhouse and watched as cow carcasses were moved around and various workers removed different cuts of meat. He imagined a similar process, only in reverse, with workers staying in one spot, performing the same task over and over, as a moving assembly line brought unfinished cars around the factory on conveyors. The process was safer, faster, less expensive, and resulted in better-quality products. The innovation spread throughout the fledgling auto industry and beyond, ushering in a new era of standardization and quality for all sorts of industrial products. As efficiency rose, prices fell and demand flourished. But no sooner had industrialists perfected the art of serving huge groups at low cost than they began looking for ways to serve smaller groups even more profitably.

The lessons of mass production soon gave way to segmented markets. The auto industry, for example, discovered that, thanks to the efficiency of assembly lines, the customer didn't have to limit himself to a single model of car; you could make some flashier and more luxurious, while others were more basic and inexpensive. Throughout the twentieth century, market segmentation became more and more specialized, leading to the growth of niche markets and the explosion in brands targeting smaller and smaller slices of the Western world's ascendant consumer culture.

In 1987, Stan Davis wrote *Future Perfect*, in which he coined the term "mass customization." Davis described a future in which manufacturing technologies would become so flexible that people could have almost anything made according to their exact specifications, at an affordable price. Every purchase and every product would be individually tailored, and thus a perfect expression of the personality and taste of the buyer. As Davis explained, the natural progression was from mass markets to market segments to niche markets, and eventually to a world in which every person is "a market of one."

Pine made this notion the subject of his MIT master's thesis in

1991, which later formed the basis of two best-selling books and a thriving consulting career. By the early 1990s, flexible manufacturing was already ramping up, but the magic catalyst to usher in the customization era was still a few years away. It finally arrived with the mass adoption of the World Wide Web.

For Frank Piller, the beginning of the e-commerce age coincided with his own epiphany about the power of the nascent You Sell. A business professor at Germany's Technical University of Munich and visiting scholar at MIT, Piller has dedicated his academic life to following the emergence of mass customization ever since 1994, when he visited New York and saw Levi Strauss's flagship store offering made-to-measure custom jeans. Bespoke tailoring had always been a luxury offering for high-end suits and dresses. Here was a major company offering the service for the ultimate casual, mass-market fashion item: the humble blue jean. He wondered if that kind of personal service could be the next great wave in consumer marketing, and within a couple of years, he'd found his answer. "The Internet really made consumer customization possible," Piller says. "By the late 1990s, business had essentially mastered flexible manufacturing. But only with the Internet was it now possible to make that connection between vast numbers of consumers across large areas and to connect them to flexible manufacturing."

This is no gimmick, it's an emerging economic model that resonates deeply in our increasingly self-centred culture, Pine says. And its self-feeding cycle of growth is not unlike the one that drove the industrial revolution. "The mass production cycle of the last century was driven mainly by price," he explains. Companies got better at producing high-quality goods in huge volumes, which allowed them to cut prices and draw in more business. Consumers suddenly had access to better-quality things, at lower prices than ever before, at the same time as incomes were rising. As demand increased, so did volume, which allowed prices to keep falling—until there was a car in every driveway, a refrigerator in every kitchen and a radio in every living room.

"Now we're seeing that cycle work in the other direction—toward customization," he says. The spread of flexible manufacturing technology, combined with the mass communication tools of the Internet, open up a world of opportunities for people who want to feel that their buying decisions make them unique. The more we spend on personalized goods, the more companies invest in the Ego Boom. And the more that companies invest in the Ego Boom, the more widespread and affordable personalization becomes.

THE DESIGNER EFFECT

In 2004, Frank Piller and an associate, Nikolaus Franke at the University of Vienna, set out to test the economic forces behind customization. By then it was pretty clear that, despite growing up with the mass market, today's consumers seemed especially focused on exclusivity and personal designs. But the researchers also knew that there had been a couple of high-profile failures in the customization business. Mattel had introduced a "my design" Barbie that went nowhere, and Levi's, one of the original mass customizers, had recently shut down their "Original Spin" website. The professors wanted to get a better handle on the financial limits of the urge to "co-design."

Such things tend to be pretty hard to measure. You can ask people why they buy the things they do, but the answers aren't of much use. Most of us don't really think too deeply about that stuff—we buy because we want. And often the stuff we say we value is very different from what we spend our money on once we hit the mall. Piller and Franke already had plenty of evidence that consumers were interested in playing a role in the design of products they buy. Businesses promising various forms of customization were popping up and thriving everywhere. But is this a measurable economic phenomenon or a novelty that quickly wears off? And perhaps more importantly, is it worth the trouble and cost? Are our tastes really as unique as we like to think? Or, given the chance to design something just for ourselves, will our mass-market training win out, driving most of us toward predictable "mainstream" designs?

The researchers decided to focus their study on wristwatches, using a make-your-own toolkit provided by a Hong Kong company called Idtown, which let customers configure their own mid-market Swatch-type timepiece. The study involved 165 university students, who were told that if they agreed to participate and answer a few questions, they'd get a free watch out of it. The researchers gave each student a broad selection of design alternatives to pick from: 80 different bands, 60 different cases, 150 unique faces, 30 styles of hour/minute hands, and 30 different second hands. The range of possible designs ran into the hundreds of millions, and the students were asked to use this toolbox to design their ideal watch. The point, the researchers explained, wasn't necessarily to stretch their creativity or to make something intentionally outlandish, but rather to come up with a design they would really like to wear. The creations were tracked, and at the end the researchers asked what the subjects would be willing to pay for their creation if they found it in a store.

The first important lesson gleaned from the study was enough to chill the hearts of traditional retailers: personal taste is wildly divergent. The 165 participants came up with 159 different designs for their ideal watch. That suggests that stores would have to stock an almost infinite variety of models in order to be assured that they had the perfect watch for every customer who walks through the door. Most of us, however, have learned to compromise a bit when looking for a new watch. We look around and try to find something that satisfies most of our criteria, within our desired price range. We are, generally, relatively happy with something that meets 80 percent of what we're looking for. But even at that, the study suggests the need for huge varieties in order to capture a sizable chunk of the market.

The researchers examined their results and found that if you wanted to satisfy 80 percent of the 169 people in the study 80 percent of the time, you'd still need to offer 101 models. If you wanted to limit your stock to a more manageable 31 models you'd only be satisfying about 40 percent of those 165 students in the study. What's more, the researchers weren't able to identify any usable patterns from the designs. There was no "mainstream" design element that shone above others. So it's not like you could put on just any strap, as long as you had a particularly popular combination of face and hands. Once you turn customers loose with a broad range of options to choose from, the collection of design choices is chaotic.

Lesson number two was even more important, and not terribly surprising to those familiar with the narcissism of today's consumer: we love the stuff we make, and we think the products of our creativity are worth big money. When asked how much they'd be willing to pay for their watch, the designers came up with an average value of 48.5 Euros. That compared with a value of 21.5 Euros when they were asked to value similar, mass-produced watches, and 23.1 Euros when asked to value the creations of others in the study. Even controlling for the fact that study participants often exaggerate their willingness to pay for goods, the results still pointed to a huge price premium for the self-designed watches. "The active role of designing the product oneself is likely to constitute a psychological benefit to users," the study concluded. "An analogous effect can be found in people who hang up 5,000-piece jigsaw puzzles they have completed themselves instead of hanging up pictures, although objectively jigsaw puzzles look less attractive than simple (and much cheaper) posters."

Aside from this insight into the decorating habits of jigsaw lovers, the study put its finger on a key economic force behind customization. The designer effect is twofold: people have wildly varying tastes (something that becomes more evident when there are abundant choices) and they place a substantial premium value on things they created themselves. Quantifying the financial edge of the designer effect remains an inexact science, however. In 2006, the global consulting firm KPMG released a report focused on the clothing industry which cited polling data showing that about 20 percent of North American adults want customized apparel, and are willing to pay, on average, 30 percent more for it. Several other studies have suggested a willingness to pay at least an extra 25 percent for the chance to "co-design" and ensure a perfect fit.

Just as important to the businesses looking to cash in on the custom economy, those most interested tend to be the most desirable customers. Last year, Forrester Research issued a report showing that consumers who search out and buy customized products tend to be significantly younger, better educated, and wealthier than the average shopper. And a 2007 study by J.C. Williams Group found that younger consumers, who've grown up immersed in MySpace, iTunes, blogs, and chat rooms, are far more likely to favour shopping in the world of infinite choice promised by e-commerce.

The result of that marriage made in cyberspace is an accelerated kind of commercial Darwinism. Out of the triumph of individualism and the near-universal embrace of the You Sell has evolved a breed of super-consumers, whose spending habits are driven by the desire to express themselves. In this world, consumption becomes a kind of performance, limited, not by talent or creativity, but by the availability of credit—a fact reflected in the soaring loads of consumer debt racked up over the past decade. In 2005 and 2006, the U.S. personal savings rate fell into negative territory for the first time since the Great Depression, meaning that for the first time since the Dirty Thirties, American consumers spent more money than they made.

On the other side of this evolutionary breakthrough in consumer culture are the thousands of businesses who are getting more and more efficient at enabling and stoking the appetites of the masses—on an individual basis, one uber-shopper at a time.

MY i-ndustrial REVOLUTION

At some point in the past decade or so, the words "mass produced"—once synonymous with reliable quality—became anathema. Generic now means dull, and anything "standard" is really sub-standard. One prevailing question is gradually changing the landscape of the consumer culture: Why should I settle for something that was built for everybody, when I am so very special?

"I hate to use the word narcissism, but there is certainly some of that at work here," Joe Pine says from his home office in Minnesota. "And there is a risk at a global level that we are, in fact, creating a society of narcissists—people who don't know the meaning of sacrifice or compromise, who are accustomed to having their every whim satisfied. And the 'Net generation has grown up in an environment where they can get so much, exactly as they want it, exactly when they want it. I don't think we're there yet, I don't think we've reached the point where that danger is being realized, but it's certainly an effect that could flow from all this."

Whatever the risks, from the perspective of big business they remain dwarfed by the enormous opportunities, as demonstrated by the staggering explosion in the customization economy over the past five years. There are the obvious champions, like Dell, and Apple Computer's phenomenally successful line of "i" products—iPod, iMac, iPhone. And practically every major online retailer now tracks purchasing and search history to assemble user profiles and to generate automatic recommendations and suggestions geared to each customer's individual tastes. But the true cutting edge of the custom economy is advancing the art of the You Sell, and those efforts extend all the way from headline-grabbing multinationals to the tiniest start-ups.

Piller now maintains a blog and an academic journal dedicated to tracking the growth and spread of mass customization, and helps organize an annual conference where hundreds of business academics gather and present papers on the phenomenon, with names like

Applications of Kansei Engineering to Personalization (a contribution from the Biomechanics Institute of Valencia, Spain) or *Modeling Consumer Behaviour in the Customization Process* (from researchers at the Hong Kong University of Science and Technology).

Joe Pine has long since given up trying to monitor every new vein of the custom economy. "I used to be able to follow all the new applications," he says. "But the proof of the explosion is that I just can't keep up with it anymore." As with any emerging phenomenon, the many faces of customization run from the ridiculous to the sublime, with tentacles running into virtually every corner of the retail landscape.

Clothing may have been the first major manifestation of the custom economy, with Levi's among the companies that offered personal fittings and embellishments, even in the pre-Internet era. But the Web has opened up this territory to the entire apparel industry. Lands' End, Target, and Tommy Hilfiger are just a few of the major labels willing to send made-to-order pants and shirts to your front door. Converse offers an interactive website where users can design their very own Chuck Taylor shoes, choosing from dozens of colour combinations and personal touches. MiAdidas has been offering customized athletic shoes for several years, and Nike ID has extended the model to include swoosh-emblazoned sportswear, all designed by you, the customer. In the custom apparel world, more new entrants arrive on the scene practically every week.

For most consumers, though, the music business was likely their first brush with customization. Aside from Apple's wildly successful iPods, there are now dozens of online services promising to deliver a personalized listening experience, not just to entertain but to broaden your musical horizons. The best-known is Pandora. Based on the so-called "music genome project," the service uses computer analysis to break down the musical DNA of thousands of artists and songs. Close to 400 attributes are mapped for every song, and as you use the service, telling Pandora what you do and don't like, the program looks for the patterns in instrumentation, lyric, and structure that tie together your eclectic tastes, continually refining its picture of your preferences and generating song lists and recommendations especially for you. The Web is a virtual playground for music lovers sick of the Top-40 radio format. Last year, British pop group Erasure put their song "Don't Say You Love Me" on the Web and invited fans to create their own mix. Changing seven variables from vocals to rhythm, there were about 40,000 different possible mixes. Once you created a mix you liked, you could buy it (for about $4), and no other user is able to download exactly the same mix—meaning your creation was yours alone.

That same air of exclusivity has provided the matchmaking industry with a quantum leap in popularity ever since the Web came along. Mega-dating sites like eHarmony, Match.com, and Lavalife promise personalized dating help and introductions screened to meet each client's unique personality profile. The industry continues the ever-more-sophisticated quest to turn matchmaking into a science. The days of ticking off boxes and filling in your favourite hobbies are over. For example, Chemistry.com was launched in 2005 by the same company behind Match.com. Using a profile quiz developed by Dr. Helen Fisher, "world renowned biological anthropologist and an expert in the science of human attraction," the site aims to identify those ineffable qualities that make certain personality types mesh, while others clash. Fisher hopes to use data and case studies gleaned from the site to study the brain function behind love, mapping the physical and emotional elements of attraction. Once again, the appeal of the services relies on the principles of the You Sell: your match is a selection that has been made based on a quasi-scientific analysis of the essential You, not some wild guess about who you might like.

The fastest growth market in the customized world, however, may exist in the burgeoning market around personalized health care. After all, if everybody is unique right down to their genetic code, how can the same treatments and generic medicines work for all of us? This basic question is behind hundreds of studies and products aimed at putting an end to the era of standardized medicine. Nutrigenomics is one such field of study, dealing with the ways that genetic differences affect each individual's health and reaction to various treatments. There are already several companies that promise to design a health regimen especially for your body chemistry and genetic profile. Ideal Health, for example, asks users to buy a urine sampling test kit ($100) which the company uses to produce "an accurate, scientific window into your personal biochemistry." Then they'll ship you your Custom Essentials multi-vitamins, formulated based on your own personal test results for $70 a month, with urine testing repeated at six-month intervals.

The list goes on and on, and grows every day. If the bobblehead dolls of athletes and famous actors make you feel a little inadequate, there are several services on the Web willing to take a few pictures of you and, for $50 and up, transform them into seven inches of plastic glory. For more traditional toys, there's American Girl or the Build-a-Bear workshop, which lets kids and parents make their very own teddy bear. The company had sales of $437 million last year. For those who have always imagined their life story as a romance novel, a handful of companies will now insert your name and specific details into a bodice ripper. Some even offer "wild" or "mild" versions of the stories, depending on how steamy you like your romances. Or if you want something even more personalized: for $100,000 they will write your own personal history into romance novel form. Several companies have sprung up willing to turn a map of your DNA into an art piece to hang on your wall.

Even if it's disposable or perishable, it can be customized. If store-bought wrapping paper just doesn't make the statement you're looking for, namemaker.com will print personalized gift wrap and ribbons with any message you choose—for about four to five times the cost of the regular stuff. For those who simply can't face the indignity of picking the almonds out of their cereal anymore, a German company called MyMuesli will let you pick and choose from a wide variety of grains, flakes, and dried fruit, and will ship your custom cereal to your front door.

The rate of growth in the custom economy is dizzying. Dell's sales have grown at an annual rate of more than 16 percent over the past three years—an increase of more than $14 billion between 2004 and 2006. Apple's sales rose by 46 percent over the same period, driven overwhelmingly by the popularity of the iPod. Results at smaller companies are harder to track, but a survey last year by software maker Cincom Systems found huge optimism among companies involved in customization—more than a quarter expect demand to increase between 25 and 50 percent annually over the next few years.

It's not that the customized economy is going to replace mass production or put an end to the mass market—Piller estimates that even in the most successful industries, custom products are unlikely ever to make up more than about 25 percent of the market. What's more important, he says, is the change in mindset and philosophy that accompanies the spread of personalization. That's a shift with the potential to change even the way traditional mass marketers sell. "Today's consumers want an experience that goes beyond the simple purchase of a product," Piller says over the phone from his office in Germany. To illustrate, he points to one of his country's longest-running experiments in mass customization: MiAdidas.

The world's second-largest athletic-shoe maker, Adidas began offering customers the chance to design their own athletic shoes in 2001. Since then, they've expanded the program, taken it online, and have seen interest surge. MiAdidas represents a tiny fraction of the company's overall sales. But it is profitable, and provides both a fresh way to attract new customers and a valuable means to gather customer information about what sorts of products and designs customers are looking for. "Adidas calls it the best marketing campaign they've ever had," Piller says. "It pays for itself, and if people are engaged by the idea of customization it means they're already buying." It wasn't long before Nike followed with its own take on custom shoes and apparel—Nike ID. Early last year, the company announced that its newest merchandizing maxim is "the consumer decides."

"Clearly the power has shifted to consumers," CEO Mark Parker told assembled analysts and investors. President Charlie Denson added, "Another thing that is very, very important to us as we look to the future is the value that the consumer is placing on customization." The emerging consensus amongst business executives and academics is this: the value that Denson refers to is enormous, it's growing, and it's still not clear just how much potential it holds. "For business," Pine says, "there is almost no logical end point for this."

PIMP MY RIDE

Even the most hidebound of heavy industries are gradually waking up to this reality. For generations, the car business has understood, perhaps better than any other business, the power of aspirational marketing. Ever since General Motors began aiming different brands at different demographic groups, the industry has known that a car is a reflection of the personality of its owner. Go to any car lot and the sell is all about who you are.

Still, Pine says the personalization on offer at the car lot for the past fifty years falls far short of what today's customers have come to expect. "They talk about getting a car just for you, but once you get through all the marketing they still really want you to pick something off the lot that's already been built," he says. "If you really dig in your heels, you can get something built for you, but even then they are really just looking for something that was already being built that closely matches the things you're looking for." Furthermore, if you go with a factory order, you'll generally have to wait months for it to arrive. And today's me-centred consumer isn't really into waiting.

That helps explain why the aftermarket car customization business has soared in the past decade. In 2006, American car owners spent a record $36.7 billion on parts and accessories to transform their cars, adding wild colours, exhaust pipes, and suspension systems, not only to increase performance, but to turn millions of off-the-lot Dodge Neons, Chevy Cavaliers, and Honda Civics into rolling works of art. MTV seized on the phenomenon, creating the popular TV show "Pimp My Ride" dedicated to showcasing the creativity of the car subculture.

There's big money to be made if major manufacturers can harness the impulse of car owners to have a ride unlike any other. In 2003, Toyota launched Scion, a new brand aimed directly at young car buyers looking to customize. The company rolled out three models, all with base prices of less than $20,000 but with a list of about forty accessories, aesthetic enhancements, and options like spoilers, wings, and neon lighting systems inside and out. The brand is marketed heavily through the Web, especially social networking websites like MySpace and SecondLife, and it drilled directly into young and well-to-do consumers' most interested buying exclusivity and individuality. Click into Scion's website and you're invited to play a video game, *Rise of the Deviants*, in which the player (a "deviant" who drives around in a shiny red Scion) attacks "Sheeple" who run around the city painting things grey. Once you've trounced enough Sheeple, you get to go to a Scion factory and customize your own deviant machine. The marketing message behind the game is none too subtle: don't follow the boring grey sheep. Be deviant. Drive your very own, unique, customized Scion.

This is none too flattering to Toyota's traditional core market, people who like their reliable grey Camry, but being boldly, unapologetically different is exactly the image Scion and its customers are trying to project. That requires breaking some of the defining conventions of the industry. The Scion's typical buyer is younger than the buyer of any other major car brand, and spends $1,000 to trick out their car with custom enhancements. In its first year, Scion sold just over 90,000 vehicles in the U.S. Two years later, sales hit 173,000, with the company reaping more than $170 million selling dealer-installed accessories. Toyota realized early on that exclusivity is critical to the appeal of youth-oriented brands like Scion. And so, in 2007, the company decided to intentionally slow growth—restricting supply to about 150,000 cars—further enhancing the brand's "cool factor."

For now, the Scion remains the exception in the auto industry. But that may be changing too. In 2007, BMW announced that it was developing a "fully flexible" production line capable of producing made-to-order cars in five days. Place the order on Monday, and see the car roll off the assembly line Friday—it's the first true attempt at replicating the Dell manufacturing model in the auto industry. BMW expects to have the system in place within a decade, and if it has anything close to the same level of success as in the computer business, it will just be the beginning.

THE DOLLAR VALUE OF "FUN"

James Surowiecki, *The New Yorker*'s revered business columnist, coined the phrase "the wisdom of crowds" in his 2004 book of the same name. And, on the surface, it would seem that the changing nature of branding is really about accepting the logic behind his theory; specifically, that your customer base can make better decisions, projections, and innovations than any of the best experts in your marketing department. Hundreds of businesses small and large are now tapping into what they believe to be the power of that mob intelligence—tossing aside focus groups, taste tests, psychological profiles and sales projections, and simply throwing open their doors to the cacophony of feedback that the public is dying to share. The buzzwords echoing through the marketing departments of the Fortune 500 are no longer "brand equity" but "crowd sourcing."

Simply put, crowd sourcing means entrusting the masses with an ever-escalating set of decisions that were previously the sole domain of the experts. Last year, for example, a website called Mediapredict.com joined forces with publisher Touchstone Books to let the public read about fifty book proposals posted on the Web, and to predict which ones were most likely to win a publishing contract. The public buys and sells the titles like stock futures, based on their own predictions about which would be most successful. At the end of the process, Touchstone picked one winning proposal. And while they didn't make any promises about following the judgment of the crowd, the point was to tap into a random sample of observers and learn what the great faceless, nameless public had to say about various book ideas.

Other companies have gone much further, making a community of more or less anonymous amateurs the driving force behind their corporate identity. One such operation, Threadless.com, is a Chicago-based T-shirt maker. Graphic designers Jake Nickell and Jacob DeHart started the company in 2000, simply asking anybody who wanted to contribute a T-shirt design to send it to their website, which then posted the image and asked users to rate it on a scale from 1 to 5. The designs that scored best were then printed onto T-shirts and sold through the site for around $15 to $20. The winning designer got an honorarium of $1,000. In the seven years since start-up, the community contributing designs and ratings has exploded. At last count, the site boasted more than 300,000 members. It receives about 125 new design submissions a day and chooses four to six new designs to print each week. And the honorarium for winning designers has gone up to $2,500 ($2,000 in cash and a $500 Threadless gift certificate).

A typical run would be about 1,500 shirts and the winning designs almost always sell out. The most popular designs are periodically reprinted, netting the designer an additional $500 bonus. Karim Lakhani is an associate professor of business at Harvard University and has been studying the amazing success of Threadless as part of his ongoing examination of the crowd sourcing phenomenon. He has found an astonishing commitment to the brand, and legions of people who see Threadless as a perfect union between fashion and hobby. The fact that more than 99 percent of designs are never produced, and that even winning designs don't earn much, doesn't seem to matter.

"Rational economic models have trouble dealing with enjoyment,"

Lakhani explains. "We think of work as activity requiring payment. But if the workers are enjoying their work, the payment component of the economic model gets messed up. But that's what we hear—people enjoy being involved in the creative process, and also the social aspect of the community."

That's an impulse not to be underestimated. From the outside, Threadless cultivates an outsider image: a social club for artistic kids for whom a walk into The Gap is like a harrowing trip into the heart of corporate mediocrity. But from the inside, Threadless is a multi-million-dollar business thriving by simply providing its customer base with a blank canvas on which to create, and letting the group vote on whose creations are best. There are dozens of others finding ways to use the same model for everything from writing software (as in the case of Calgary, Alberta–based Cambrian House) to scientific problem solving (as in the case of Innocentive, a project of Proctor & Gamble's).

"This means the community becomes the curator, the manager, and the brand. The meaning of the brand arises from the community," Lakhani says. "The company still has legal ownership, but very little control. They are co-creating the brand identity with the community. The initial reaction to all this from most entrenched established companies is 'oh no.' But I think the most enlightened ones figure out how to manage this and how to turn it into an advantage. We don't teach this stuff in business schools yet. But I think that'll change. What we're seeing is that community-based co-creation gets amazing results."

And those results are ultimately what matter. Steve Rubel is a senior marketing strategist with the global PR firm Edelman, and heads the company's "me2revolution" project—an effort to help clients integrate the Web into their marketing and PR efforts. Rubel has become something of a digital generation guru through his blog Micropersuasion, and he believes the days of major brands serving as mass market beacons are over, a development he sees as potentially great news for business.

"The most powerful brands have always struck a nerve with cultural undertones that were ready to be unleashed. The difference now is that it's much easier to identify these themes by scanning the Internet or using it to engage with consumers directly in a conversation on the topic," he says. "Existing brands may need to reposition themselves to 'surf with the wind' rather than guess its direction."

But here's the central paradox of the You Sell: "In the long run this will make brands even more powerful."

By giving up the position of authority figure and arbiter of what ideas are market-ready, and giving consumers the sense that they are in control, companies massively increase their profit potential and the loyalty of consumers who truly see themselves reflected in the brand, rather than the other way around. Dell never runs the risk of having too many parts on hand, and never needs to worry that it'll be stuck with stockpiles of unwanted machines that have to be sold at a loss. Threadless knows its products will be a hit long before it prints a single T-shirt, because its customers have said so. And Toyota never has to wonder whether Scion drivers would prefer blue or amber neon lighting to spruce up the passenger cabin of their cars. They simply offer both and profit either way.

The question for the rest of us is this: How is it that major companies are making billions of dollars by providing us with an endless array of tiny questions to answer and variables to select from? And why are we so eager to pay for that privilege?

LITTLE THINGS THAT MEAN A LOT

In 2001, the Finnish cell phone giant Nokia was already well into the world of customization. Nokia's most popular phone models all had a common shape, and a spinoff industry had sprouted up selling colourful plastic faceplates for Nokia phones in shopping malls around the world. Teenagers especially seemed to love the idea of replacing the plain grey faceplate with something quirky or funny, or maybe just something that went with their outfit. Nokia had caught on to an emerging reality that has since become conventional wisdom: cell phones weren't just technology and their appeal went far beyond their function. They were both status symbol and fashion accessory, especially among young buyers.

With that in mind, when Nokia began to introduce phones capable of connecting to the Web and downloading from it, they began to offer an array of new ringtones for a couple of dollars each, giving kids yet another way to make their phones unique. It took a little while to catch on, but soon it was an industry unto itself.

The first downloadable ringtones were barely recognizable mono versions of old hits. Part of the fun and the novelty was playing "name that tune" with your friends as your phone droned the notes of "Funky Cold Medina" in your pocket. As phone technology improved, so did sound quality. Within a few years, you were getting pristine digital music clips alerting you to incoming calls and text messages, and demand skyrocketed. Even as conventional music sales plummeted, thanks largely to the plague of Internet music piracy, record labels made millions licensing artists young and old to be converted into cell phone-ready clips.

In 2004, only about 5 percent of U.S. cell phone users had downloaded a ringtone. A year later, that number was up to 23 percent, and more than half of all users aged twelve to twenty-four had personalized their ring paying up to $3.50 each time they did. For the music business this was a double bonus. Not only did they make money on each song, but every download was like a little commercial for the artists, as their song clips played in school hallways, shopping malls, and fast-food joints around the world.

In 2006, the worldwide ringtone business hit $4.4 billion, up from $3.7 billion the year before. There were many who predicted that the ringtone business would prove to be a fad, but Michael Nash, the head of digital strategy for Warner Music Group, knew better. "The ringtone is not just a thirty-second snippet," he told CNN. "It's like a digital T-shirt." Young consumers see their phones as part of their identity, and having just the right ringtone is an essential expression of their personality, to differentiate from their friends. Almost overnight, having the coolest, most shocking, most ironic ring was just as important as having the right labels in their clothes. Music and phone companies had stumbled onto a little gold mine by feeding that deep desire to be different…but not *too* different.

In many parts of the world, the ringtone market is lucrative enough to create its own stars. Last year, for example, the song "This Is Why I'm Hot" by rap artist MIMS sold more than 2 million times as a ringtone clip, according to Nielsen SoundScan. But the song was purchased in its entirety just 1.4 million times, and MIMS' full CD, "Music Is My Savior," sold just 257,637 copies, roughly one-tenth of his ringtone figure. Likewise, the singer Huey had a ringtone hit with his song "Pop, Lock and Drop," downloaded to 1.2 million phones. But the full album, *Notebook Paper*, sold just over 50,000 copies.

The question that few ever stop to ask, of course, is whether a downloaded ringtone is really ever an authentic statement of one's character. How is it that smaller and smaller things have come to mean so much more? Why do we really care about the colour of our phone faceplate, much less whether your phone plays "This is Why I'm Hot" and not "Sweet Home Alabama"? It's still just a cell phone, in form and function almost indistinguishable from everybody else's. And yet it's so much more than that, and we're willing to pay substantial sums for the thrill of imbuing eight ounces of plastic and metal with the essence of our true identity—as expressed through thirty seconds of pop music.

THE POWER OF SMALL DIFFERENCES

You don't have to look very hard before you begin to suspect that this golden age of individualism is a marketing angle much like all those that have gone before. These multi-billion-dollar industries, celebrating you in all your glorious uniqueness, are being built more on an illusion of self-expression than anything authentic. Whether it's custom vitamins, custom T-shirts, or your much-loved customized car, you're dealing in minuscule aesthetic variations—distinctions without real differences.

Even at Dell, once you strip away all the exciting talk about "building a computer to fit your life," it becomes apparent that the average customer is neither capable nor interested in actually "building" a computer. Dell provides a simple list of options and add-ons to choose from, much the same way a car company lets you choose whether to buy air conditioning, or upgrade to a nine-disc CD changer. It's true that Dell builds most of its computers on demand, but they do this to minimize risk and to keep costs down—not because you're special. In fact, today you can walk into Wal-Mart and buy a Dell right off the shelf. Once you keep that in mind, it's not surprising that last year's major product innovation from Dell, one tied to the launch of a whole new marketing campaign built around the slogan "Yours is here," came down to the fact that the company is now offering its computers in eight bright new colours. Sometimes, "customization" comes down to the fact that your laptop is pink and your husband's is green.

This hardly qualifies as cutting-edge innovation. For one thing, Apple had introduced colour to its line of computers almost a decade earlier. Bob Garfield, *AdAge* magazine's resident curmudgeon, was just one of many observers who thought the whole campaign was ripe for parody. "Dell belatedly has discovered you have cone cells in your retinas," he wrote. "But it'd better have another insight up its sleeve, because this one will be hard to keep proprietary."

But it was hard to argue with the logic of the move, and Garfield acknowledged as much. In a world where consumers are so obviously smitten with the notion that they are in charge and that everything they buy ought to somehow reflect their character, slapping plastic colour panels on the sides of a computer is enough to bolster the illusion that your computer is really an extension of your personality. Never mind that Dell computers are, more or less, exactly the same as other PCs. Dell's appeal to individualism became the model for all other computer companies to follow. It's no coincidence that Apple, a company that always marketed itself based on quality and ease of use, made individual expression and style the centerpiece of its post-2000 resurgence. Hewlett-Packard actually overtook Dell as the world's biggest computer maker in 2007, powered by the marketing slogan "Finally the computer is personal again." And Sony took personalization to new heights with its Sony Style campaign and website, which allowed buyers to create their own customer designs. All these multiple-choice sales processes and the marketing messages create the feeling of exclusivity and control, in a product that is virtually indistinguishable once you strip away the wrapping. And it's that feeling that matters.

"From the consumer's point of view, I get a product that really fits my needs. Even if it's the exact same computer as thousands of other people's, I don't really care," Piller says. "It feels like it was just for me. It's very much about getting that psychological reward: 'I configured my own computer.'"

Does it matter what colour your laptop is? It does if it matters to you. And that is the real commercial power at the root of the designer effect and the You Sell—we attach a premium value to anything we feel arose from our creative impulse, even if that thing is the very definition of a bland mass-market commodity or an intangible digital bauble. Of course, when it comes to consumer goods, there's no harm in any of this. Why not enliven the boring process of buying electronics with a little more selection and flexibility? There's no harm in configuring our gadgets or buying a pair of pants that really makes us look the way we want to. And if people want to while away the hours online, living a virtual life as the tattooed punk rocker they always yearned to be, then so be it. If big business has found a more profitable way for people to feel better about what they buy and experience, everybody wins.

The bigger questions surround the mindset that makes this such a powerful proposition, and the economic imperative that drives the evolution of the You Sell deeper and deeper into our lives. In practice, it has meant imbuing ever-more inconsequential transactions with the importance of identity. It's no longer just cars, or a home, or jewellery or even clothes that make the man. A cell phone ringtone can do that too.

In 1967, the French socialist philosopher Guy Debord predicted that the logical extension of consumer culture was one in which everything is treated as inherently meaningful, and blurs the distinction between needs and desires. To remain healthy, economies must grow. And once society develops to the point where practically all people have satisfied their basic necessities of life, then the need to maintain "boundless economic development can only mean replacing the satisfaction of primary human needs ... with an incessant fabrication of pseudo needs."

To be sure, Debord was hardly the kind of intellectual most would want fashioning the social order of a free society. He was heavily influenced by Marx, blamed capitalism for much of life's ills, eventually descended into alcoholism, and ended up committing suicide in 1994. But you don't have to share his doomed politics and grim worldview to recognize that his central prediction has come true. An ever-increasing share of the West's standard of living is now based on creating and satisfying pseudo-needs: multi-vitamins based on our personal body chemistry; an iPod song list that reflects not just our tastes but our personal history; a T-shirt with deeper meaning.

Perhaps the most fundamental pseudo-need propelling the Ego Boom is the need for control over life's tiniest details. Perhaps we shouldn't be greatly surprised that fake needs like that are most often satisfied through illusion and myth. Dell doesn't really let you "build your own computer," but it creates the *sensation* that you have. For the vast majority of iPod users, their playlists aren't so much a reflection of their personality as of the programming choices of top-40 radio executives. And those multi-vitamins might be customized to fit your body chemistry, but you'd be hard pressed to learn much about a person by dissecting their daily tablets.

We've taken great comfort in these illusions that surround us, chiefly that our individualism has tamed the forces that shape our culture: Hollywood, Wall Street, and Madison Avenue. We hear it every day—the advertisers, movie studios, record labels, and media giants that used to tell us what to buy, how to look, even what to think, have surrendered *en masse* to the power of the individual. From now on, you will decide on everything. Freed from the mediocrity of the "mainstream," the world will be a better, fairer, more progressive, and diverse place.

As myths go, this one may have been the most seductive of all. Like the kids on the Autopia ride at Disneyland, we can speed up and slow down, even steer a little bit, and go through all the motions of driving. But the track is set and everybody ends up in the same place. It's not control, but it feels like it. And once big business had mastered the techniques of creating that illusion of control, all they needed to ignite the Ego Boom was to start celebrating You, and your singular brilliance. Sure, it's an illusion, but it's a very profitable one.

CHAPTER THREE

THAT'S SHOW-ME BUSINESS

L ike any significant social transformation, the Ego Boom creates losers as well as winners. And on first blush, it would appear that the most conspicuous victims of the custom economy (and the explosion of niche markets unleashed by the digital age) are those mega-conglomerates who made their billions by creating mainstream pop culture over the past century or so. The record labels, movie studios, television networks, and book publishers that defined mainstream taste for generations suddenly find themselves like the clueless partygoers in *The Poseidon Adventure* just after the wave hit. The world has turned upside down, and only a clever few are going to survive.

Robert Thompson is a professor of popular culture at Syracuse University, and one of the country's best-known analysts of media trends. He has spent almost a decade observing what might just be the biggest upheaval in the creation of mass culture since the invention of the telegraph. "We spent the first eight decades of the twentieth-century building the biggest mass audience in human history…bigger than the Romans, the Greeks; even the Catholic Church never commanded mass attention like American popular culture up until the 1980s," he says. "Until then, we had everybody across all demographics spending at least a few hours a week, if not a day, all eating from the same cultural trough." But those days are gone forever. "Fragmentation is the story of the early twenty-first century."

Up to now, the main debate surrounding this age of fragmentation is whether it ought to be celebrated or lamented. There are those who will tell you this fragmentation is the best thing to happen to our culture since the invention of the printing press—a sort of cultural emancipation of the masses. There are others who'll tell you it's nothing short of a disaster—the first perilous step toward the dissolution of a society that no longer shares the same cultural touchstones. Interesting though that debate is, the evidence suggests that both camps are wrong, that the much-discussed shattering of the mainstream is actually just another manifestation of the Ego Boom. As such, fragmentation should be viewed not as a revolution, but an evolution of the very same dominant "big media" industry.

Like all forms of evolution, it has produced a new breed of even stronger mass media brands dominating and redefining mainstream mass culture. And, naturally, that process of evolution has resulted in the extinction of other once-dominant brands, ill suited to the new rules of the Ego Boom.

Consider the fate of one such brand: "Monday Night Football on ABC." It may be difficult to remember now, but there was a time when it qualified as a genuine American cultural icon, a dominant media brand worth tens of millions of dollars annually. The story of its decline and fall illustrates the enormous power of the Ego Boom to reshape the landscape of entire industries. It also sheds some light on why the reports of the death of mainstream media have been greatly exaggerated.

A CHILLY NIGHT IN CLEVELAND

On September 21, 1970, nearly 86,000 fans crammed into Cleveland's cavernous old Municipal Stadium to watch what was, in the end, a largely forgettable football game between two teams that wouldn't even make the playoffs that year. The hometown Browns defeated the

Jets by a score of 31–21. The game lives on in history, not because of anything that happened on the field that night, but because it marked the birth of a new era in televised sports: the first broadcast of "Monday Night Football on ABC."

The show was an audacious gamble from day one. It broke the mould of the American football tradition, in which high school games are played on Friday nights, college games on Saturdays, and the pros take the field on Sunday afternoons. For millions of football-mad Americans, this weekly ritual defined the natural rhythm of the weekend from fall through early winter. It was an almost-sacred custom that big-idea TV executives trifled with at their peril. But Roone Arledge, the ABC exec who conceived MNF along with long-time NFL commissioner Pete Rozelle, had far more profound changes in mind to win them over.

The Monday night broadcast was meant to be more than a football game. For example, there would be nine cameras to cover the action instead of the traditional five. This would allow greater use of hand-helds, to get closer to the action, and take dramatic close-up shots of players and coaches between the plays. Arledge would also pioneer the extensive use of instant replays and on-screen graphics to heighten the drama and make it easier for neophytes to follow the game's twists and turns. But, more than anything, he wanted MNF to pioneer a new sort of sports storytelling, one that would focus on plotlines and characters within the game. His announcers, Howard Cosell and "Dandy" Don Meredith, would be relied upon to provide colourful commentary, playing up the momentous and the humorous in the narrative unfolding before them.

So, on that first Monday night, late in the game, when New York's brash quarterback "Broadway" Joe Namath threw an interception that sealed his team's loss, the cameras lingered on him on the sideline, shoulders slouched in defeat, letting that image tell a story somehow bigger, more profound than one bad play in a game that probably wouldn't mean much in the long run. As Frank Gifford, himself an ex-football star who went on to become one of the sport's most recognizable broadcasters, once observed, "Roone Arledge turned a football game into live theatre." And North America quickly took notice. That first season, "Monday Night Football" became one of North America's top shows. The show garnered an average rating of 18.5 in its debut season, meaning more than 18 percent of the televisions in the United States tuned in for the weekly gridiron clash—even when it wasn't much of a game.

Don Ohlmeyer served as producer of MNF from 1972 to 1977. The secret of the show's success, he says, was that it reflected the industry's somewhat cynical focus on creating the "least objectionable" option for the widest possible swath of the viewing public. The thinking was simple: since most homes got only a handful of channels, the big networks could win the biggest audience by providing a program that most people could agree was at least okay, even if few really loved what they were watching. From there, it became an exercise in melding the storylines of prime-time drama with the athletic spectacle of pro football.

"What made it so wildly successful in the seventies, was, we said: 'Screw the football fan, he's gonna watch anyway.' But there's not enough of them to make a successful series in prime time. So we were trying to appeal to the casual football fan—the guy who doesn't sit in front of the TV on Sundays. He's out raking the leaves, doing something with his kids, or going for a drive with his wife. We wanted to get him. We also wanted his wife—you know, they're sitting in bed at nine o'clock, we're the least objectionable programming for both people. 'I'll sit and watch a football game with him.' And as we managed to make people feel like this was a real event, it became that kind of shared experience that went beyond hardcore fans."

Sure, there were plenty of people who hated football and would never watch. But for almost two decades, a lack of choice, an abundance of hype, and some old-school Hollywood storytelling meant "The Game" on ABC could count on a weekly audience well above twenty-five million.

THE EGO BOOM

And then, suddenly, the wind changed direction. It's hard to say precisely when, but some time in the late 1980s, just as cable television was gaining mainstream acceptance across America, and viewers suddenly found themselves with dozens of new viewing options, "Monday Night Football" began to slip from the forefront of North American consciousness. In 1980, the average American home received nine channels. In 1990, thanks to the arrival of cable, the number was up to 33. In 1995, there were 41 channels reaching the typical household, and the proliferation continues. According to Nielsen Media Research, in 2005 the average American household could choose from 96 different channels.

Presented with a new world of unfettered choice, bombarded by marketing messages urging viewers to embrace their individuality, break free of social conventions, and go their own way, they did ... by the millions. The thin edge of the You Sell had arrived in the world of big-budget entertainment. And with that, the traditional network model of producing the "least objectionable programming" which had spawned a generation of bland-but-popular prime-time pablum, began to sputter. It was no longer enough to be a decent compromise, and the most expensive productions, like "Monday Night Football," were the first to feel the squeeze.

First ratings stagnated even as the licensing fees to the NFL kept rising. Then, beginning in 1995, MNF went through seven straight seasons of declining viewership. ABC tried changing announcers, introducing more rock 'n' roll highlight montages, more shots of nubile cheerleaders, and attractive young women to report from the sidelines, but nothing worked. By 1998, television analysts were already wondering, in disbelief, if cancellation was inevitable.

In 2000, Don Ohlmeyer—who had gone on to an illustrious career leading NBC's West Coast division, launching such hit shows as "Friends," "ER," and "Will and Grace"—returned to MNF in hopes of reigniting it with new announcers and yet more tinkering. Ratings continued to slide and Ohlmeyer left the show. Finally, in April 2005, the network announced that "Monday Night Football's" 36th season would be its last on ABC. Audiences and ad revenue had been falling for the better part of a decade, and in that last season, the network had lost an estimated $150 million producing MNF. No amount of glitz and glamour could bring the magic back.

In a world where every person represents a niche market unto themselves, MNF now only appealed exclusively to hardcore football fans. The weekly game was shifted to the all-sports network ESPN beginning in 2006, where advertisers would pay a premium for access to a well-defined audience of male sports fanatics, and subscription revenues would help underwrite the show's hefty production costs. It's not that "Monday Night Football" was ever really an indispensible part of American culture, but it was a powerful mass market brand. And with its shift onto cable it came to reflect the new economics of entertainment in the age of the Ego Boom.

A MILLION LITTLE PIECES (OR MORE)

In fact, it's not so much that fragmentation is a revolutionary development, it's just that the fragments keep getting smaller. When Henry Ford brought new technology into the auto business, niche marketing in cars soon followed. Over the past century, one sector after another, from clothes and computers to furniture and finance, has relied on technology and marketing to subdivide the mass market more and more—unleashing greater profit potential with every slice. The culture industry is a relative latecomer to this game.

If popular culture cracked with the arrival of cable, it broke into pieces once the VCR made it possible to watch Hollywood movies at home, on your own schedule, and to tape your favourite TV shows. With the spread of the Internet and other digital technologies over the past decade, the fissures have widened and multiplied. The arrival of digital video recorders, home theatres, podcasts, streaming video over the Internet, satellite radio, and video iPods, means that the viewer is no longer a passive spectator. Just like all titans of the custom economy, Big Media has invited its customers to take control of what we get and how we get it. It's the difference between sitting at the kitchen table, eating whatever your mom puts in front of you, versus stepping up to an endless 24-hour entertainment buffet. At least, that's the sales pitch.

Chris Anderson is perhaps the best-known cultural critic charting the rise of digital culture and the simultaneous demise of traditional media. In his acclaimed book *The Long Tail*, Anderson argues that the proliferation of choice—in TV, movies, music, books, you name it— has caused "the shattering of the mainstream into a zillion cultural shards" and as a result "the mass market is turning into a mass of niches." Hits, he says, are an endangered species, and he has spent the past few years documenting dozens of case studies in which businesses have blossomed by appealing to narrowed interests and audiences that would previously have been considered too small to justify investment. At the same time, he points to stagnant or declining sales of pop music albums, movie tickets, and of course the slide in network ratings that has killed expensive exercises in prime-time mass popularity, like "Monday Night Football." In the world he describes, 10 million Internet blogs are killing major newspapers; obscure, low-budget film- makers are sapping the audience from cinemas offering familiar Hollywood fare; and armies of amateur producers are finding micro- audiences for their own unique brand of arts and entertainment. And all of that is happening in large part because a new generation of con- sumers, enamoured of their own individuality and intoxicated by the limitless cultural diversions on the Internet, are turning their back on everything that once constituted the mainstream.

In 2006, just as Anderson's *The Long Tail* was capturing the imag- ination of millions of executives and digital tech junkies around the world, his thesis received a major boost from the phenomenal overnight success of YouTube, the Internet start-up that beckoned the world to "Broadcast yourself." Based on relatively simple technology,

YouTube allowed users to upload video files to the World Wide Web, to be viewed by anyone, for free. Thousands of people used the site initially as a convenient means of posting home videos on the Web, sharing them with an audience that was never expected to branch out much beyond family and friends. But soon, some of the funnier videos started to find a larger audience. Others began posting highlights from their favourite TV shows, like "The Daily Show with Jon Stewart," "South Park," and "Saturday Night Live," plus sports highlights from around the world. In a few celebrated cases, You Tube videos racked up phenomenal viewing totals—rivalling those of major network shows. One clip called "The Evolution of Dance" was viewed more than 35 million times as it was emailed from person to person around the world. Another regular poster, known as LonelyGirl15, developed a dedicated audience in the hundreds of thousands, who would return week after week to view her confessional video diary entries. Even after it was revealed that LonelyGirl15 was a California actress playing a role, her serial continued to attract sizable audiences and landed its star, Jessica Rose, on the cover of *Wired* magazine (edited by Chris Anderson) in December 2006.

Two months earlier, Internet goliath Google had bought YouTube for $1.65 billion. It was, by far, the most lucrative and audacious deal to date in the burgeoning custom economy, and was a bold statement on what Google clearly saw as the future of the media business. YouTube had minuscule revenue, a tiny staff, and no profits, and yet, in the eyes of the market, it was already worth half as much as the *New York Times*.

Google's billion-dollar bet could be boiled down to this: popular culture just wasn't so popular anymore. At least, not in the same way it was ten years ago. And Anderson, along with dozens of other prophets of the digital age, predicted that future success would depend on how effectively one appealed to the billions of niche markets, narrow tastes, and micro audiences. Or, as the subtitle of Anderson's book explained: "the future of business is selling less of more." The only thing still up for debate was whether this was a cultural emancipation or an apocalypse, and that depended very much on which side of the old media/new media divide you cashed your cheques.

Ohlmeyer left the television business just as the digital wave was crashing down on the networks and went on to teach television communications at California's Pepperdine University. He looks at the precipitous drop in ratings among the top American television shows and he despairs. He sees families with four televisions, all in different rooms, each member watching their own show or logged on to the Internet, and wonders what will become of a society that doesn't share the same stories. "Nobody's really focused in on the dangers all this poses to society, as we become a more profoundly isolated group of people," he says, sitting in his home near Los Angeles. "Culture is shared experiences. Shared institutional memory. Shared history. Shared language. And that is changing dramatically throughout the United States ... We've lost that. We've lost that element of shared cultural experience, that was important to conversation, and the way we related to each other."

But to Anderson, these are just the plaintive moans of dinosaurs, slowly succumbing to their inevitable fate. To him, the mainstream was always an artificial construct based on scarcity. Few could afford to record music, film a show, or make a movie. And even if you could, there was no way to break into the expensive and tightly controlled world of mass marketing and worldwide distribution. So, big companies made ungodly profits by herding the clueless masses toward mediocre movies, albums, and TV shows, which were successful primarily because there was nothing else available. But now, thanks to digital technology and the World Wide Web, production is cheap and distribution to a global audience is practically free. He argues, in essence, that the proletariat has seized the means of cultural production, and the result is a more dynamic, democratic, responsive culture. No matter how obscure your tastes and interests, you can find something that's right for you. The era of the fat, lumbering, big-budget, inoffensive,

uninspiring, homogenized blockbuster with the maddeningly predictable "Hollywood ending" is o-v-e-r. The very smartest will adapt.
The rest will die unmourned.

NOT DEAD YET—REDEFINING THE BLOCKBUSTER

What if both Ohlmeyer and Anderson are wrong? What if this is
neither apocalypse nor emancipation, and the era of audience-
controlled entertainment is only as individualistic as that Dell laptop
designed "just for you"? What if, in the end, not very much has
changed at all? What if media fragmentation is really just a more
profitable way to sell what amounts to the same products through a
multitude of new channels? What if, by turning us loose at the cultural
buffet, they made compulsive eaters of us all? Well, then the "me
media" revolution would be much like everything else fuelling the Ego
Boom. It would mean that by selling us on our own individuality,
putting a feeling of control in our hands, big business has engineered
a new golden age based on the same old star system.

In fact, that is exactly what has happened. There is a fundamental disconnect between what we say we want from our mass media and entertainment (more control and a more diverse, dynamic pop culture) and
what we continue to consume (mega-selling blockbusters). The major
corporations that make up so-called "big media"—companies like Time
Warner, Viacom, NBC Universal, Disney, and News Corp.—have per-
petuated and expanded their dominance over the entertainment industries by relying on a form of You Sell that appeals explicitly to our ego. By
giving us options that *feel like* control, and by seeming to respond to
audience demands and desires, they have created entertainment brands
that are both durable and wildly profitable. But once you scratch beneath
the surface, mass entertainment hasn't changed much at all.

Let's consider some numbers. At the end of 2005, there was no
shortage of evidence to suggest Big Media was in Big Trouble, just as

Anderson said. American box office receipts had just gone through their worst one-year downturn in modern history, slipping from more than $9.5 billion in 2004, to just under $9 billion in '05 due to a fourth consecutive year of falling ticket sales. Worldwide, box office revenue declined by roughly $2 billion. Perhaps even more terrifying: DVD sales slipped in 2005 for the first time ever. In the face of competition from broadband Internet, digital file sharing, and immersive video games, Hollywood was losing its touch. It wasn't just that people had finally grown tired of loud theatres, sticky floors, extortive concession stands, and steadily climbing ticket prices—it seemed they were losing interest in the product itself, just as the prophets of a new media paradigm predicted.

If 2005 was the year of Hollywood's Armageddon, however, 2006 was the year Hollywood got smart, and maybe a little bit lucky. The industry's comeback started with a handful of films released at the very end of 2005—*The Chronicles of Narnia* started with a $65.5 million opening weekend and remained strong, pulling in more than $10 million for six consecutive weekends. *King Kong*, released a week later, was deemed a commercial disappointment because it underperformed the lofty expectations created by its $205 million budget, but it too reached the major hit category, pulling in $218 million at the box office domestically and $549 million worldwide. March brought the sequel to animated children's hit *Ice Age*. Then *X-Men: The Last Stand*, *Cars*, and *The Da Vinci Code*.

Finally, in July came the biggest blockbuster of all—*Pirates of the Caribbean: Dead Man's Chest*, which logged the biggest opening weekend ever, $135 million, and became the first movie in Hollywood history to pull in more than $100 million in just two days. Even better news for the producers at Disney's Buena Vista studios, the Pirates sequel was no flash in the pan. That opening weekend was the first step toward a worldwide box office bonanza that would eventually top $1 billion, only the third movie ever to crack that barrier, along with *Lord of the Rings: Return of the King* (2003) and *Titanic* (1997).

When all the receipts were tallied, American box offices raked in $9.28 billion, up more than $400 million from the swoon of 2005, and ticket sales rose by 40 million—arresting the industry's four-year slide. Just as noteworthy, a strong crop of late-2005 releases helped reignite home video sales as well—with sales of DVDs rising 3 percent and rentals spiking by 12 percent. From almost any perspective, Hollywood's performance in 2006 qualifies as a major resurgence, and 2007 proved to be just as strong. The total number of tickets sold in the U.S. came in at more than 1.4 billion and total revenues again topped $9.2 billion, on the strength of major hit sequels in the *Spider-Man, Shrek,* and *Pirates of the Caribbean* franchises. In December of last year, the latest Harry Potter sequel, *Order of the Phoenix,* was poised to break the $1 billion barrier in worldwide ticket revenues, when the DVD was released in North America and racked up more than $100 million in sales in its first weekend. So, what was behind Hollywood's dramatic two-year comeback—staged just as those disruptive digital technologies were gaining mainstream acceptance in North America and Asia?

Kevin Yoder may know as much as anyone in Hollywood about the marketing of movies for a popular audience. He is co–chief operating officer of NRG, the biggest audience-testing and market analysis firm in California, where he works for major studios, screening rough cuts of movies to gather feedback and project how well the films are likely to do in the marketplace. He is a man who loves his work. When he talks about movies he gets excited, effortlessly pulling examples from across decades of filmmaking to illustrate his points about the evolution of the worldwide audience. Yoder agrees with Anderson on one critical point: the explosion of entertainment options means, the public can no longer be counted on to automatically stampede toward whatever big-budget extravaganza Hollywood rolls out. That's a fundamental change in the way that popular entertainment must be marketed, and it's an extension of the same reversal affecting all consumer brands in the era of the Ego Boom. Alan Hallberg talked about consumers shifting from a "dog" mentality (responsive, eager, needy) to a "cat" mentality (fickle, hard to impress, independent). That same dynamic is playing itself out in the mass media business.

"The ability to control when one receives content, and where and in what format you wish to consume it is going to be a huge factor in how content is created and distributed from now on," he explains over the phone from his office in Los Angeles. "That's not a trend or a theory, it's reality. And it's at the forefront of everybody's thinking in the industry. Entertainment used to be based on a very linear model, a push economy—you consumed what was fed to you. Now people have the option to decide what they want to consume in an immersive environment. Do you want to concentrate and get carried away, or do you want to multi-task, or just veg? The key for the film industry, if you want to receive the box office revenue, it has to be an experience worthy of the big screen." But that doesn't mean the industry is necessarily in dire trouble. In fact, it is already opening huge new opportunities for profit—a fact to which studio executives awoke only after watching the movie business's dramatic swoon between 2001 and 2005.

If you're going to sink big production dollars into moviemaking, you have to ensure that the movies lend themselves to multiple viewing platforms. They must reward the immersive theatre experience, but also have the potential to create buzz online, lend themselves to various merchandising spinoffs, and drive demand for the extras available on DVD. The potential for multiple sequels is also essential. This means the science of making a major movie has gotten more complicated. But while the risks have increased, so have the rewards.

It's still possible that Anderson and others are right—that 2006 and 2007 were just anomalies, and that the Internet and the fragmentation of audiences has triggered the long-term cascade of dominoes that will shatter the dominance of major studios selling to a rapidly disappearing mainstream that nobody wanted to belong to in the first place. This point of view, widely espoused in the technology media and by a handful of influential, Web-savvy journalists like Patrick Goldstein of the *L.A. Times*, suggests we'll all ultimately be better off, happier, smarter, and more sophisticated once we reject the culture industry's artificial renderings of the world, and refuse the gruel on offer in the common cultural trough described by Thompson. As Goldstein wrote in early 2007, "celebrity has been rudely down-marketed and democratized." Why else would low-budget, Internet productions distributed virally through email and on free sites like YouTube, have become so suddenly, wildly successful? Why else would the ratings for network programs be in such a steep long-term decline?

This was nothing short of a "tectonic shift in the worldwide media economy," wrote National Public Radio media critic Bob Garfield in *Wired* magazine, and it was being driven by "the hitherto futile aspirations of the everyman to break out of his lonely anonymous life of quiet desperation, to step in front of the whole world and *be somebody*, dude." That shift had already decimated the cozy, lucrative world of big-label music recording—liberating the masses to listen to exactly the music they most like, without having to conform to the big-business revenue model. And soon it would do the same to the mega-media conglomerates that bring us our movies, our television, and our news.

The trouble with that assumption is that actual consumption patterns aren't changing nearly as much, or as quickly, as you'd expect. By and large, blockbusters still rule. Rumours of their death have arisen from a misinterpretation of the data coming out of the embattled music industry.

R-O-C-K IN THE U-S-A

The music industry's struggles in the digital age do indeed provide a terrifying example of what happens when a business fails to adapt to shifting technology and fails to understand the expectations and desires of its audience. The rise of Napster and other digital file-sharing services in the late 1990s led to a massive wave of piracy, which immediately sapped demand for legally recorded music among the industry's most lucrative consumers. Hardcore music lovers were the first to wake up to the possibilities of trading relatively small music files over the Internet. The music industry was caught completely flat-footed, and most labels offered no alternative means to buy digital music legally until several years later when Apple Computer unveiled the iPod and the iTunes music store. The digital music wave quickly expanded into a multi-billion-dollar business, but by then millions of music fans had gotten used to pilfering music rather than buying it. Widespread piracy continues practically unabated today—massively distorting the economics of the business.

One of the most critical changes was that digital music forever changed the basic unit of transaction. For decades, music was purchased as LP albums, featuring ten to twelve songs each. When cassettes came along, they had been engineered to hold about the same amount of music. When CD technology hit the marketplace, it offered greater storage capacity. The industry, however, decided for the most part to stick with the same offering: ten to twelve songs, roughly an hour of music, for around $15. But with the digital revolution, albums were cracked apart and songs could be traded individually. Now, you could just buy the best song on any album and pay only $1 for it, or nothing at all. And with that single change, music became a business denominated by singles and millions of $1 transactions. Singles now outsell albums by a margin of roughly 17-to-1. This shift in the industry's revenue model coincided with a continentwide decline in listenership for commercial radio stations, traditionally one of the industry's most powerful marketing platforms.

So, the market for pop music had been obliterated by digital technology, unlimited choice, and falling prices. Score another one for the discerning masses over the purveyors of insipid "radio-friendly" bands created by marketing departments. But did people initially flock into digital music downloads because they hate pop music? Or was it because it was more convenient, offered wider selection, and allowed users to customize their playlists, after a lifetime of paying $15 for an album that featured three hits and seven duds? Like the movie business, 2006 proved to be something of a comeback year for the music industry. Sales of albums on CD declined again, by 5 percent. But, for the first time, that lost revenue was more than replaced by a rise in digital sales—legally downloaded singles jumped 65 percent to 582 million, and sales of full-length digital albums more than doubled to 33 million, good for more than $300 million in revenue. The trend continued in 2007, with yet another substantial rise in digital music downloading, and even more erosion in the market for compact discs.

On his blog, Chris Anderson argued that the industry's recovery still reflected a wholesale rejection of big-label blockbusters. He pointed to the fact there were only 406 gold, platinum, and multi-platinum albums in 2006, the worst year for "blockbuster albums" since 1990. But the rise of digital music—now representing 10 percent of all sales and increasing rapidly—means that comparing sales of physical albums to past years is no longer a particularly instructive exercise. What we do know is that there were several blockbuster songs in 2006. In the final week of the year, for example, Beyoncé sold 269,000 digital copies of her song "Irreplaceable." Daniel Powter's "Bad Day" was the top seller of the year, being legally downloaded more than two million times (according to Nielsen SoundScan), the first track ever to break the two-million mark.

Perhaps even more surprising, live music concerts in North America had a record year in 2006. Total ticket revenue hit $3.6 billion—up 16 percent from a year earlier. The top 100 tours pulled in almost two-thirds of that total, selling 1.6 million more tickets than a year earlier. And the gain wasn't the result of price inflation—the average ticket price actually dropped by 7 percent. Yes, even in the moribund music business, it seems, the blockbuster is still very much alive. The same can be said for the publishing industry—rarely even mentioned among the major cultural industries anymore, the past few years have, nevertheless, produced two of the biggest publishing phenomena in the history of bookselling: *Harry Potter* and *The Da Vinci Code*, not to mention a host of smaller blockbusters like *The Secret* and *A Million Little Pieces*, both spawned by the one-woman blockbuster factory Oprah Winfrey.

Look across every major medium: there was strong demand for big-name artists, blockbuster franchises, and no shortage of hits. A quick survey of profit reports for the major conglomerates that control most of the world's movie, music, and television studios showed a fairly robust recovery and an unabashed embrace of the digital revolution. For guys whose very survival was supposed to be threatened by the Internet, executives from Viacom, Time Warner, Disney, and News Corp. were sounding like avowed Web-lovers. Les Moonves, the chairman of the CBS network, even made a keynote address to the 2007 Consumer Electronics Show in Las Vegas, the annual gathering of the world's most enthusiastic digital geeks, talking about all the opportunities presented by the new media age.

"The bottom line is, there is no such thing anymore as old and new media," he said. "We're just media."

Say hello to the new boss, same as the old boss.

CHICO VS. SIMON COWELL

So, has the "mass culture" broken down, or has the traditional means of distributing and selling it merely fragmented? Clearly, in a world of personal video recorders, MP3s, iPods, and video-on-demand, the whole notion of a broadcast schedule has been thrown out the window. But if it is just the sales and distribution models that have changed, is that really cultural emancipation, as the digital utopians argue? Is it the ruination of Big Media conglomerates? Or is it the greatest commercial opportunity to come along since the printing press?

It may be that nobody in the world has spent as much time confronting these questions over the past few years as Jack Oken. A thirty-seven-year veteran of the TV advertising business, Oken is now a top executive with Nielsen Media. For almost a century, Nielsen has been the gold standard for reporting to advertisers about who is watching what, where, and in what numbers. What began primarily as a written survey evolved over time into a sophisticated technological operation with boxes that record the viewing patterns of various members of almost 100,000 "Nielsen Households" across the U.S. Writers, directors, actors, advertisers, and TV executives live and die by the numbers that Nielsen produces, but in an era in which fewer and fewer people are obediently sitting on their couch watching what the networks serve up, the traditional way of measuring the cultural and commercial impact of a given show seems to be quickly breaking down, and no one is more aware of that fact than Oken. His job is to figure out what to do about it.

"We're going through a period of the most significant upheaval in consumer technology that we've ever seen, and there's no reason to think it's going to do anything but accelerate as we go forward," Oken says. "We have to move from measuring what has been essentially a static medium, to developing the ability to follow that video wherever it goes, no matter what platform it gets played on."

The challenge that Oken faces, and the enormous efforts that Nielsen is undertaking to overcome it, suggest that all those cultural critics who've written off the power of traditional media on the basis of declining Nielsen ratings may have gotten trapped in an obvious error—measuring today's cultural icons using yesterday's metrics. To illustrate the point, consider two shows: "American Idol" and "Chico and the Man."

In September 1974, NBC rolled out a new half-hour comedy centred on a young Hispanic labourer named Chico, played by Freddie Prinze, and his unlikely friendship with an old, cantankerous mechanic played by Jack Albertson. The show perfectly reflected the prime-time politics of the day, and was an immediate hit. At the time, CBS's "All in the Family" was America's number one program. "Sanford and Son" was number two. "Chico and the Man" made it to number three in its debut season just ahead of a new "All in the Family" spinoff called "The

Jeffersons." All four of the U.S.'s top-rated shows were weekly half-hour situation comedies that explored themes of racial politics and bigotry. All four were considered breakthrough programs in a nation that was just coming to terms with the implications of the civil rights movement of the late 1960s.

That first season, "Chico and the Man" garnered an average rating of 28.5, which translates into an estimated weekly audience of 19.5 million viewers. The show made Freddie Prinze a star, and gave NBC another desperately needed franchise to compete with CBS, which was utterly dominating the prime-time ratings. To put the show's success in perspective, its 28.5 rating was only good for third place that season, but ratings that high are unheard of today. It has been more than twenty years since any show on television garnered a similar score.

In 2006, the top-rated show was "American Idol," the Fox Network's nationwide talent contest in which a pool of twelve finalists, selected from thousands of auditions, sing for a panel of celebrity judges. Viewers at home are asked to call phone lines to vote for their favourite. Each week, host Ryan Seacrest asks viewers to "get ready to take control" and the contestant with the fewest votes gets dumped on live television, until just one singer is standing. Since its debut in 2002, "American Idol" has become a bona fide cultural phenomenon and a multi-billion-dollar enterprise. The show's initial performance was reasonably good, breaking into the top twenty-five shows of 2002, but every subsequent season has seen a gain in its average audience. In the fifth season, aired in 2006, 63 million votes were cast for the show's finale. Last year, the finale's vote total climbed to 74 million. As the show never fails to trumpet, this is substantially more than voted in the most recent U.S. congressional election.

Still, if one were to look strictly at Nielsen ratings, the show's average score of 17.7, while better than any other show on television in 2006, wouldn't have been good enough to crack the top twenty in 1975, the year "Chico and the Man" hit it big. This is the sort of statistic routinely cited by critics who believe that the old concept of a cultural main-stream is disappearing. But if this discussion of ratings seems misleading, and you can't quite believe that "Chico and the Man" was as powerful a cultural force in 1975 as "American Idol" is today, that's because it is, and it wasn't.

First, consider the fact that Nielsen ratings are meant to convey a share of the total U.S. television households that were tuned in to a particular show at its allotted time slot. In 1974, there were about 68.5 million U.S. households with TVs, and last year there were 111.4 million. As a result, "American Idol's" 17.7 rating translates into about 19.7 million households (on average) tuning in to the show on an average Tuesday night last year. That's a fraction more than the 19.5 million households watching Chico educate Jack about the changing nature of east L.A. back in 1974. Some might still argue 19.5 million households in 1974 represented a far greater percentage of the U.S. television-watching public than it does today. And that's true, but it misses out on several crucial factors in "American Idol's" power as a cultural brand.

For one thing, "American Idol" airs twice (and sometimes three) times a week. In fact, the show was both the number one and number two–rated prime-time series in 2006, and it has taken two of the top three slots for three years running. So, on consecutive nights, AI can count on attracting more than 19 million households to its live broadcasts. For an advertiser, that makes it a doubly powerful brand with which to be associated. Even more important, "AI" is commanding that audience in an environment where the average American household has twelve times more channels to choose from than they did when Chico ruled his time slot. And because "American Idol" is a competition, its ratings tend to boom at the première, and at the show's conclusion. The final episode of "AI's" fifth season, which aired in May 2006, attracted an audience of 36.4 million. The next season's premiere, in January 2007, pulled an audience of 37.7 million, as the "AI" juggernaut continued to gain momentum. But even all this fails to capture even a fraction of the true cultural reach of "American Idol." The Nielsen ratings do not include the millions of fans who download clips from the Internet; or who flock to "Idol" chat rooms to discuss and debate the results; or who turn out by the thousands for "American Idol Live" concerts featuring contestants from previous seasons, and who buy "American Idol" compilation CDs, featuring performances by the finalists.

To put that in perspective, consider this: CKX is an entertainment company that co-owns the Idol franchise along with FremantleMedia. CKX's take of "Idol" revenues rose 42 percent, to $28.8 million, between 2006 and 2007. Conservative estimates suggest the 56-stop *Idol Live* concert tour grossed more than $30 million by itself.

A discussion of ratings also doesn't begin to take into account the spinoff revenues that have been created by the show's unparalleled marketing platform. Up to the end of season five, in just four years the show had produced six artists whose albums had cracked the million-sales mark—this in an era of declining album sales overall. Kelly Clarkson, winner of that very first (and lowest-rated) "AI" season has produced two albums with more than 9 million copies sold worldwide. Carrie Underwood went from "Idol" to a career as a Grammy Award–winning country star with sales of more than 8.7 million.

Robert Thompson, the professor of pop culture at Syracuse University, says "American Idol" illustrates something important about the power of mainstream media in an era of fragmentation in which fewer and fewer people are sitting passively in front of the TV. It is a show that reaches out to the viewer and asks them to get involved, to offer an opinion, and to help shape the progress of the story as it goes along. When millions of people are willing to spend $1.50 per call to vote for their favourite contestant, you know you've made a connection to the viewer. "The show is just so brilliantly put together," Thompson says. "The funny thing is, it's not even my idea of great music, but that doesn't matter. I went to an 'American Idol' concert here in Syracuse once just to get an idea of the demographics of the show, and I tell you, it was all over the board. I had a sixty-year-old couple on one side of me, and on the other side I had two mothers with nine screaming seven-year-olds, and I saw some of my university students there."

"Chico and the Man" might not rank among the great shows in television history, but back in 1974 it was a perfect example of a winning formula—it was a funny, heartwarming story that could lure a big audience back to the couch week after week, for about twenty weeks out of the year, to watch eight minutes of commercials for every twenty-two minutes of comedy. "American Idol," on the other hand, engages a viewership that has come to believe it should have some influence over the course of events unfolding before them, and in the age of PVRs, it can do so on its own schedule. If a viewer really engages with the show, they will get the CD, chat about the show online with other fans, see the live concert, play the video game, and download video clips not seen during the live broadcast. At every step, not only are producers raking in more revenue, advertisers and sponsors get yet another opportunity to make a connection with the audience.

The show is far more than just a singing competition. It is one of the most powerful media brands in the world. It is also the quintessential example of what the people at Nielsen Media have come to think of as the age of the "aggregated blockbuster." Audiences may splinter in how they choose to experience a pop phenomenon—over the Web, on big-screen TV, downloaded to a handheld device and watched on the bus ride to work—but Hollywood still retains its ability to produce highly profitable cultural brands. If anything, the advent of the You Sell has increased that power. It means that clever marketing, with product placements, downloadable episodes, behind-the-scenes documentaries, and magazine articles can make a blockbuster out of shows like "Lost" and "Dexter," even though their actual audiences are relatively small by network-TV standards. Hollywood has found multiple avenues to monetize the essential currency of mass culture: fame.

"Fame as a concept has taken off, not only in the United States, but globally," explains Mark Green, senior vice-president at Nielsen, and a member of Oken's team. "It strikes at something very deep in the core of human beings, and the only way fame survives is by having a thematic interest in common things. That is what makes something famous, and the platforms to facilitate that fame culture are only expanding. I don't think the whole culture of fame is ever going away."

There is an obvious irony in the fact that millions of consumers will pay for the privilege of voting in a prime-time singing contest, even as participation in general elections falters. The very same people who complain that the political system doesn't offer enough for them are nonetheless enthralled by the prospect of helping anoint the next great American singing star. But we'll talk more about the challenges that the Ego Boom presents for politics later. For now, let's just say that the success of "American Idol" and its many imitators is based largely on their appeal to an audience that wants to feel like they are participants—not just witnesses, but co-creators.

THE DIRECTOR EFFECT

For a brief moment, when YouTube exploded onto the scene in 2006, it suddenly seemed as if Big Media was losing its grip on the fame culture. It seemed viewers were just as interested in spending time wading through thousands of short video clips of anonymous amateurs as they were in spending time with the prime-time characters Hollywood spent millions developing. When Google bought YouTube in late 2006, it really seemed as though the nature of the industry had changed overnight. To some, as millions of people retreated into their own me-centred existence, it was proof that there was less and less desire to be part of any larger shared culture, particularly not one driven by Hollywood marketing departments and their big-budget extravaganzas. Who needs professionals when the public is just as likely to see themselves in the goofy exploits of amateurs? But the appeal of that new model began to weaken almost as quickly as it appeared. "The thing about YouTube is, when you first discover it, it sucks away about four hours a day," explains Thompson. "By the second week of watching videos of dogs doing tricks, you're less enchanted by it. By the fourth week you realize you're wading through an unbelievable morass of just idiotic stuff. Once you get beyond the very top, most-viewed clips, it gets pretty lame pretty quickly."

However, YouTube and similar user-generated video sites aren't going away, he says. Instead, they've created a new medium unto themselves. The real lesson of these sites is this: the Designer Effect works just as well in film and video production as it does in making watches. And so, there will likely always be people eager to create their own short films, and there will always be people interested in watching. Call it the Director Effect. These sites may well create their very own star system, which could overlap and intertwine with Hollywood's, and they will almost surely create their own market system which will create profit opportunities for those who play the game best. LonelyGirl15 seems to have been at the forefront of a new movement that will create content specifically designed for that medium: short, serialized clips, with low production values, meant to be played on a small screen.

"There's no question all this user-generated content and broadband distribution is a challenge for traditional media, but it was a challenge when cable came along too," Oken says, sitting in Nielsen's futuristic technology room surrounded by a dozen video monitors of differing shapes and sizes. In time, Oken points out, the threat from cable became yet another spectacular profit opportunity, for big (and small) studios. The point, he says, is that the best producers find ways to exploit technological innovation to extend their reach and dominance. "They just have too much experience, and creativity and understanding of what it takes to produce things that people want to watch," he says. "You know, it's *hard* to produce a really good TV show. It's *really* hard. You don't just set up the cameras and start rolling." From his perspective, YouTube is evolving, not into a competitive medium likely to sap the dominance of big-studio productions, but as an essential marketing vehicle for people to share and comment on their favourite shows of the past and present. Far from being a mortal threat, Internet video sites have proven to be a phenomenal means of extending the reach of those mainstream brands, in part because people are more likely to come back several times a week to watch different clips from "The Daily Show with Jon Stewart," than to watch grainy video camera footage of "The Evolution of Dance."

A 2007 study by i2 Partners, a New York–based management consultancy, reached the same conclusion: YouTube and Internet video distribution will not replace conventional TV and movies because the big studios control all the best content, and have the money to monopolize all the most talented and recognizable producers, directors, writers, and actors. "A shift toward broadband media will come largely on Hollywood's terms and at an incremental pace," the report concluded. And the dominant players in that new medium will, more than likely, be the same as those who dominated "old" media.

It didn't take long for Big Media to crack the code of how to corral this new finicky and fickle mass audience by grafting the principles of the You Sell onto a business based on mass communication. The key was flexibility and depth. If you make it easy for the audience to consume your product in a variety of forms, and on its own schedule; if you provide the audience with a deep treasure trove of extras and tie-ins; if you create the impression that they are playing a part in something rather than just watching it unfold—then people will take "American Idol," or "Lost," or "24" and make them part of their world. Of course, the reality is, these shows are not really "interactive." The action is still controlled by the screenwriters and directors, and the story arc unfolds over the course of months with little genuine "input" from the audience. But it's the impression of give-and-take that creates audience loyalty. And therein lies the holy grail of commercialized culture. John Ruffolo is a senior technology, media, and telecommunications consultant with Deloitte and Touche, and co-author of a 2007 report entitled

"Power to the People," which explained many of the opportunities and challenges presented by the evolving media model. "A year ago, when it first began to be clear that the consumer is in power, companies were scared like I've never seen them," Ruffolo says. "But the smart ones are already seeing how this can work to their benefit. They're saying 'I can resist this and get blown away by it. Or I can take advantage of it and make *a lot* of money.'"

Ruffolo points to NBC's "The Office" as a prime example of a show that continually points the TV audience to the Web, where the studio has posted Web-only episodes, deleted scenes, provided a message board, opinion polls, and links to fan-created videos stitching together footage from the show into unofficial trailers and odes to favourite characters. Another NBC show, 'Heroes,' launched an online, interactive graphic novel inviting fans to "pick up where the show leaves off, and delve deeper into the "Heroes" universe." That, in addition to online episodes with cast commentary and a huge store of other information, was all packaged around the seductive tag line "Are you on the list?" For many fans of the show "Lost," the website became an essential tool in unravelling an incredibly complex plot puzzle. It allowed fans to explore different aspects and locations seen on the show, and to trade theories about what exactly was happening to the characters, as it became increasingly clear that the show's original premise about a group of plane crash survivors stuck on a desert island was only the beginning.

Even if these audiences are, in some cases, smaller than the blockbuster viewer numbers of thirty years ago, they are often far more involved—visiting the website, leaving a comment, voting in a poll, buying the complete season on DVD to get access to cast interviews, documentaries, and deleted scenes. Compare the half-hour spent with "Chico and the Man" thirty years ago to the impact that "Lost" has on its audience today—it's not even close. The same is true of successful movie franchises like *Lord of the Rings, Harry Potter, Pirates of the Caribbean,* and the most successful recording artists like Kelly

Clarkson, Fergie, and Kanye West. Today's blockbusters pull fans and revenues from dozens of sources, and while each individual slice of that pie may not seem overwhelming, when taken in combination the mainstream media brands of the Internet age are more powerful than ever before.

COUNTING GRASSHOPPERS

Still, all this fragmentation creates its share of problems. Mass audiences today are more difficult to harness, their expectations are higher, their choices are greater, and their tastes seem to be constantly shifting. In the old days you came up with good stories. If people liked them, they watched. Big companies paid big money to slap in a few commercials. And if the idea was successful, like "All in the Family," you came up with a bunch of similar offerings. When people stopped watching, you came up with a new idea.

Today, shows can run out of steam incredibly quickly, going from aggregated blockbuster to cultural has-been in the space of a single season. In a world where people expect "what they want, when they want" and are bombarded with media almost from the moment they wake up until the moment they go to sleep, the rules of engagement change profoundly. Making a lasting impression is the greatest challenge, one that requires a nuanced conversation between producers and audience members, and a whole new way of measuring who is paying attention to what.

For years, Nielsen has measured audiences by putting a box on the back of a TV and electronically tracking which channels get watched, when, and by how many people. But the digital world demands far more sophisticated tracking to take into account all the various ways that people experience and interact with media today. Nielsen is in the process of testing tags about the size of a cell phone that members of Nielsen families would wear on their clothes. The so-called Go-Meter is capable of "listening" to detect which shows you're watching. The audio from each program would be translated into a distinct audio fingerprint, unique to the show you're watching. That fingerprint would then be transmitted along with time and location data to Nielsen's state-of-the-art technology hub in Oldsmar, Florida, which would tabulate which shows that person had encountered, when, and where. Already, sound codes, imperceptible to the human ear, are embedded in the audio of many major network shows, making the process of tracking by sound even easier.

So, if you're standing in an airport lounge watching CNN, then you decide to watch an episode of "The Office" on the flight from Houston to Los Angeles, then check into a hotel and catch forty-five minutes of "Grey's Anatomy," then head out to a sports bar for dinner to watch the hockey game, the listening device knows all and sends that information on to Nielsen. Those data are crunched into audience numbers for all of the shows. But mobile audience measurement is only one of several evolving approaches, all aimed at taking a more detailed picture of the complex culture in this atomized world. Nielsen also owns NetRatings, the biggest tracking service measuring traffic and activity on the Internet, and holds a stake in Buzz Metrics, a company that combs millions of Web pages to analyze what kind of "buzz" a product, brand, or service is getting on the Web. The company doesn't just count mentions: it is also able to analyze what people are saying—positive and negative—about the shows, to get a better sense of the popular online conversation.

Eventually, your television will be operated entirely over a broadband Internet connection. Then Big Media will truly be able to tailor your viewing experience based on past habits, expressed preferences, and a running record of purchases. Your cable operator, noticing that you watch the football game every Sunday afternoon, will be able to offer you a discounted fan package with access to all the games. If you see an outfit you like on a favourite character, or a particular cell phone model in the hands of "24"'s Jack Bauer, you'll be able to buy it by pressing a few buttons on your remote control, without ever leaving the comfort of your home or having to deal with the crowds at the mall. This isn't some pipe dream, it's a technology already in advanced development.

"The more we measure, the more we understand people, not just statistically—what they watch, what they buy—but *who they are*," Oken says. "The more we know about that, the more we can provide to them that is of value. The initial reaction of the traditional media to the Internet was very very negative. But now, they are seeing the phenomenal synergies that exist." In other words, even as the audience "fragments," the big studios are using digital technology to stitch people back together into fan groups, and in that process they've unleashed massive new profit opportunities.

The open question is whether all this leads to a more dynamic culture, and a better world. That, in turn, has spawned what Thompson considers a second golden age of television, in which complex, challenging shows like "The Wire," "Lost," "Deadwood," and others flourish despite what would have once been considered paltry audiences. "Even look at a mediocre prime-time soap opera like 'Grey's Anatomy,' and compare it to 'Marcus Welby' from thirty years ago and it's just far, far better," he says. On the other hand, the current state of movie releases from major studios, especially those garnering the largest audiences, is less encouraging, he says. "There are exceptions, but now it feels a lot like you're watching the equivalent of a laboratory manufacturing experiment, all done according to some sort of marketing-driven pseudo-scientific formula rather than any sort of artistic vision." If it seems that the movies hold less sway over the popular imagination of young people than in past generations, that may be a reason why. But don't expect Hollywood to break its neck rushing to change its approach.

If there is one thing that has become absolutely clear in the Internet age, it's that the so-called power shift toward the individual audience member may be an appealing sales pitch, but there's little substance to it. And it has certainly not eroded the power and influence of Hollywood's culture factory. On the contrary, it represents a phenomenal economic bonanza for the conglomerates and power-brokers that shape, package, and sell the fame culture of the West. It is, in short, among the most powerful and profitable elements of the Ego Boom. The fragmentation of distribution, the proliferation of screens on every desk and in every room, along with the development of technology to allow users to download, upload, share, and trans-port songs, shows, movies, clips, photos, and stories at will, is driving the big business of fame and celebrity even more deeply into every corner of our lives. If these trends persist (and there is every indica-tion they will), the fine line between culture and commerce—that which separates entertainment from information from advertising and image—will disappear entirely (if it hasn't already). This is not a nefarious plot. Big Media is supplying what we have demanded.

Through our purchasing decisions we demanded bigger, more spectacular movies that we could watch either on the big screen or in our home theatres. We demanded smarter, grittier, more engaging television dramas, and prime-time event shows that got us involved. We asked for music that didn't require us to sit through two bad songs waiting for the one we liked. More than anything, we wanted the sensation that something was made for each of us, not all of us. The easier they made it, the more personal it felt, and the more we opened our cloistered bubbles to the big brands of today. Now it sometimes seems we maintain our connections to the larger world increasingly through those brands.

By adopting the rhetoric of the atomized world and the You Sell, as well as the same sorts of flexible mass production that have revolu-tionized so many industries, Hollywood has extended its reach, its influence, and its earning potential enormously. It has sold the idea that you are in control, when, in fact, you've really just taken over the schedule and the size of the screen. It has sold the notion that anyone and everyone can be famous, and in the process has focused even more attention on that central, ephemeral currency that makes the culture business work. Because fame is the glue piecing the fragmented culture back together again, we get aggregated blockbusters, even more powerful than their older models.

Hollywood, as much as any industry, has awakened to the reality that commercial success in our atomized, fragmented world requires reaching into people's isolated existence, telling them that they are important, that they are famous (or could be), that they are part of the action. Rather than "democratizing" culture, it has reinforced the existing power structure, with a handful of huge media conglomerates sitting at the top, telling us that we're in control.

It's a message that sells and is selling. Do that and we'll trade entertainment for engagement. Do that and we'll trade interaction for virtual interactivity. Do that and we'll take Meredith Grey with us on our morning commute, we'll get emotionally involved in her life and her problems, and make her catharsis our own. Even if we haven't spoken to our parents in weeks.

CHAPTER FOUR

MY OWN PRIVATE
SESAME STREET

"The secret point of money and power in America is neither the things that money can buy nor power for power's sake . . . but absolute personal freedom, mobility, privacy. It is the instinct which drove America to the Pacific, all through the nineteenth century, the desire to be able to find a restaurant open in case you want a sandwich, to be a free agent, live by one's own rules."

—Joan Didion, *Slouching Towards Bethlehem*

In 1961, the urban theorist Jane Jacobs published her seminal work, *The Death and Life of Great American Cities*, a love letter to Greenwich Village at mid-century, in which she characterized the ideal urban environment. Although she puts it in far more grown-up terms, according to Jacobs' model city neighbourhoods should function a lot like Sesame Street. For starters, there should be a diversity of residents—black people, white people, brown and pink and blue people, old people and young people, and people who aren't people but birds, frogs, two-headed monsters, and pink and orange yip-yips. Living spaces are smaller in the city—consider Big Bird's nest or the cramped quarters shared by Bert and Ernie. So an urban neighbourhood should draw people out into the streets by offering well-conceived, vital common spaces—the courtyard, the library, the extra-wide front stoop at 123 Sesame Street, for example—where neighbours can intermingle casually and cultivate a sense of shared fate. There should be amenities where locals, who have interdependent and mutually beneficial needs, can conduct business, like Hooper's store, Charlie's Restaurant, or the Fix-it Shop. And there should be "public characters," people who serve as social hubs, binding all of these loose personal connections together—like, say, a grouch who lives in a sidewalk garbage can and sees and hears everything. These are the elements that bring a city block to life.

"City areas with flourishing diversity sprout strange and unpredictable uses and peculiar scenes," Jacobs wrote. "But this is not a drawback of diversity. This is the point of it."

At the moment, city living is undergoing a major overhaul in North America. New urban neighbourhoods are springing up across Canada and the United States where industrial parks and empty lots used to be. A hundred years ago, only 10 percent of the world's population lived in urban environments, while everyone else was either tilling the soil or raising the next-generation familial workforce in rural areas. But in 2007, for the first time in history, the United Nations projected that more than half the world's population would be waking up to concrete and glass. Which means, for billions of people, the burnt-mocha smell of a Starbucks outlet may soon be a more resonant point of reference than the sight of a wild animal, a field, or a naturally occurring tree.

In a sense, this explosion of interest in urban living can be understood as a renaissance of sorts. After all, the greater the population density downtown, the more restaurants, boutiques, bars, and attractions set up shop to cater to it. Food and entertainment choices become more diverse, services more specialized, and meeting spots more numerous. In turn, one would presume, the more consumer choices a gentrifying neighbourhood provides, the more young, creative, successful people will be drawn to it—producing a modernized, networked, hipster version of Jacobs' vision: Sesame Street with Wi-Fi and fewer bell-bottoms.

Not surprisingly, this spike in urban density has brought along with it a great deal of wide-eyed optimism. William Mitchell, a professor of architecture and media arts and sciences at the Massachusetts Institute of Technology, predicts the next urban age will bring about "e-topias" where "people live and work in the same building, lead busy local lives in pedestrian-scale neighbourhoods and strong communities, but also gather virtually in electronic meeting places and link themselves up to enable decentralized production." And yet, evidence suggests that the community aspect of such prophecies is not materializing. If anything, it seems that as we move physically closer together, psychologically we're moving farther apart. New models of urban living are far more about the spaces we carve out for ourselves and the walls we build than the things we share. The biggest phenomenon currently underway in urban residential architecture is a widespread condominium boom, which makes sense: the condominium model is a physical manifestation of our changing attitudes toward home, family, and community. It is the housing model of the individual—designed to be unique, self-contained, and fully customized to your lifestyle needs. And it is perhaps the most overt evidence of the You Sell at home.

THE CONDO BOOM

Brad J. Lamb is Toronto's self-proclaimed and undisputed condo king, and the fired-up star of "Big City Broker," a half-hour TV series about the fast-paced, high-stakes world of urban residential property development and how it shapes a city's landscape. At six-foot-five, Lamb cuts a towering figure. He wears a signature pinstripe suit. He's got sharp facial features and he speaks in a clipped style laced with profanity, like a character out of *Glengarry Glen Ross*. Over the span of his twenty-plus-year career in real estate, Lamb has cultivated a reputation as a mover and shaker, and talking to him you get the unmistakable sense that he sees himself as shaping this city while everyone else is sleeping. Condos are the future, he says. Actually, he's been saying it for twenty years, and if you don't believe him, try arguing with his company's $3 billion in sales revenues ($800 million in 2007 alone).

The industrial-chic offices of Brad J. Lamb Realty are located downtown along Toronto's busy King Street West corridor where, after a spotty gentrification process, the city's most exclusive restaurants, art galleries, and interior design boutiques have established a strong foothold. Over the past several years, Lamb's firm has become ground zero for Toronto's booming condominium market, and chances are, if you've ever visited the city, you've seen the man himself: hard-to-miss ads featuring his shiny, bald pate superimposed onto the body of a lamb have been splashed across billboards, benches, and municipal garbage cans all over town. Subtlety, it seems, is not a requisite tool in the marketing and sale of condos.

"Back in the eighties, condos were *not* cool," he says, leaning back in his oversized chair. His desk is buried under precarious-looking stacks of papers, file folders and, most tellingly, a pencil sharpener in the form of a Willy Loman–type character lying prostrate with his pants around his ankles (you can imagine where the pencil goes). "They were shitty boxes in the sky. They had crappy finishes and crappy carpets and bad kitchens." Indeed, when condos were invented in the sixties, it was not as a lifestyle option, but as an economic and legal model for parsing up real estate in the sky. It was not until a new generation of visionaries came along—architects, interior designers, developers and realtors like Lamb, with a real understanding of contemporary style and demographics, that the market began to see the true potential of the residential condo model. Condos are not just four walls and a storage locker, believers like Lamb will tell you, they're an *idea*.

Though it's tempting to dismiss this kind of talk as just the self-promoting bluster of a born salesman, in cities across North America condo units are mushrooming faster than anyone can count.

Condominiums now make up nearly one-third of all new urban residential construction in Canada. In Toronto, this massive influx of downtown residences—priced high and low, built of glass, concrete, and brick, high-rise and low-rise, ultramodern and "authentic loft conversions"—is setting per-capita records. In September of 2007, 60 percent of new homes sold in the Greater Toronto Area were shelved in high-rise condos. Downtown, it seems every available square inch is being annexed by one developer or another to build one more vertical hive. Construction is happening so fast that the city is actually in competition for cranes with Las Vegas, San Diego, Seattle, Vancouver, Miami, New York, Atlanta, Houston, and others—all of which are experiencing the very same type of urban residential explosion. In the United States over the past two decades, the percentage of new-home sales accounted for by condos has more than doubled. In Canada, it's estimated that roughly 3 million people—and counting—wake up in a condominium every morning.

Much to the despair of certain architecture critics, for this style of housing the stars have aligned. But condo-mania is about much more than an exceptional number of real estate opportunities for developers in the downtown core. Rather, it's the result of a dramatic reshuffling of how people live—and don't live—together. The same impulse that drove suburbanism in the eighties and nineties—the need to create a fenced-off, affordable, and controllable space for you and yours—is driving the condo boom today, only it's been extended to new demographic groups: empty-nesters looking to downsize, young couples who can't yet afford a single-family home, and in some cases, families with young children. And so urban residential sprawl has become an ever-more vertical phenomenon. But, as much as sprawl of any sort is maligned for environmental and aesthetic reasons, it also serves an important purpose. As Robert Bruegmann wrote in his book *Sprawl: A Compact History*, "it has given millions and millions of people the kind of privacy, mobility, and choice that was once the privilege of a very small number of people."

THE EGO BOOM

More than anything, though, this explosion is about one stunning fact: that North Americans are living alone in greater numbers than ever before. For the first time in history, according to a 2005 U.S. Census Bureau report, the single largest chunk of American households now consists of one person who lives alone—no spouse, no children, no roommate or extended family.

IN THE HEART OF THE ACTION, ALONE

The way we insulate ourselves from each other has become one of the defining characteristics of modern life. The number of middle-aged, never-married persons living alone in the U.S. has climbed over 250 percent since the mid-eighties, to 3.6 million households, according to Harvard University's Joint Center for Housing Studies. Single Americans now make up 42 percent of the workforce and 40 percent of homebuyers, according to U.S. Census Bureau numbers.

Part of the appeal of the condominium form, of course, is purely pragmatic. Developers know that the more one-bedroom spaces they can carve out of a single building, the more profits they reap. And for buyers, especially first-time ones, if you've only got a single income to play with, condos are, in many cases, the only affordable option for city living. House prices have became inflated to the point where buying any sort of home in the city is a pipe dream for your average middle-class single person. Condominiums emerged as a smart alternative, particularly for these buyers, who are more inclined to care about proximity to restaurants and theatres than big yards, good schools, and nearby playgrounds. Add to that a new era of low interest rates and minimal down payments, and suddenly a whole new breed of homebuyer is pulled out of the rental market and into the world of mortgages and home equity. Two-thirds of first-time homebuyers now finance more than 95 percent of the purchasing price, according to the National Association of Realtors, which has sparked an epidemic of home foreclosures in the U.S. Not only are people taking on more household debt than they ever have, they're often doing it alone.

How does the Ego Boom factor in? With the single-person demographic garnering more economic clout than ever, condo design is now being shaped by players who have a much more sophisticated understanding of the psychological needs of this new target market. They're realizing that, as spaces get smaller and more specialized, and as people's jobs take them out of the home for longer stretches of time, spaces have to serve more functions, and contain more specialness-per-square-foot. They can't just be functional boxes in the sky. To stand out from the competition, developers have to appeal to buyers on an emotional, almost a sexual, level.

"Basically what it comes down to," says Lamb, "is we imagine the way a thirty-year-old male or female would like to live in their fantasy life. Now, everyone would like to have a bigger space, but knowing that it's all about money and affordability, we try to pack these apartments with as many seductive things as possible."

Welcome to the You Sell at home.

THE XX FACTOR

Perhaps more than anyone, women have found themselves amenable to condo life. Since 1994, households headed by unmarried women (with or without children) have accounted for nearly a third of the growth in homeowners. Condos generally provide a safe and secure way of living close to the action. There are security systems and guards. There's usually a concierge ready to sign for packages. It's low-hassle: no worrying about fixing a leaky roof or cleaning out the eaves. In fact, a whole new demographic is emerging across North American cities: the Single Professional Woman with Condo. According to a study by the Joint Center for Housing Studies at Harvard University, almost one in five homebuyers last year was an unmarried woman. That's double the rate of buying among single women only fifteen years ago.

Among other things, the condo boom reflects a massive shift in economic power—the cumulative effect of years of social evolution. Women are choosing to live alone primarily because, for the first time, they can afford to. In large part, they're the twenty- and thirty-somethings who have found themselves, either by choice or circumstances, delaying the prospect of marriage. They're financially self-sufficient and, if the numbers are any indication, they're eager to experience the freedom of a lifestyle that was considered inappropriate for them up until very recently. As Lisa de Rocha, vice-president of marketing for Royal LePage Real Estate Services in Canada, put it: "There has been a shift in mindset whereby women have distanced themselves from the traditional notion that you must first find Mr. Right and then together you buy a home. Our findings reveal that 66 percent of women who intend to purchase would not find the process of buying a home on their own intimidating."

In this sense, twentieth-century feminism—and the advent of coed universities, universal suffrage, birth control, microwave dinners, quickie divorces, and speed dating—not only revolutionized the division of labour in the home and the workplace, but, as an unexpected by-product, it is helping to reshape the entire urban landscape. Because of the feminist movement, which was rooted in a deep-seated human need for choice and personal control, women have greater economic and career opportunities. Both sexes are waiting until later in their lives to get married and have children. (The average first-time bride and groom in Canada are 28.5 and 30.6, respectively, up from 25.9 and 28.5 twenty years ago. The average age for first-time mothers in the U.S. is at an all time high of 25.2.) In many cases, women are opting out of marriage and motherhood altogether. A *New York Times* analysis of U.S. census results published in January 2007 found that, for the first time, more American women (51 percent) are living without a spouse than with one—and many of them are living in condos.

LIVING IN AN AGE OF COMMITMENTPHOBIA

In 1987, the best-selling author and relationship expert Steven A. Carter co-wrote a popular psychology book called *Men Who Can't Love* in which he coined the term "commitmentphobia." The book diagnosed an emerging breed of men who fear committed relationships with a pathological intensity. It struck such a chord that it was translated into twenty-two languages, sold more than three million copies worldwide, and inspired Carter to write half a dozen more books on the subject of narcissism and fear of commitment.

"The fact that the majority of people are now living alone doesn't mean it's a reason for celebration. It doesn't mean that we've done a good job," says Carter now, some twenty years later. The problem, which seemed significant then, he says, has exploded, among men *and* women. "I think it's a reflection of how much the culture is fragmented. How much it's fractured. Do I think it's a healthy thing? No. But I do think the underlying drive of it is that people have less and less ability to make and maintain connection."

The Ego Boom, in all of its incarnations, thrives on individualism. This proliferation of young singles and the housing to cater to them is largely symptomatic of a pandemic state of mind—an ideology of hyper-individualism that is making it harder for people to wrap their heads around commitments of any kind. Its power lies in encouraging you to keep the focus on you—a mindset that makes relationships more difficult to maintain as it becomes more difficult to deal with the inevitable compromises they involve. We all know, for instance, that the proportion of married couples in North America has been on a long, steady decline. For the first time in 2005, the Census Bureau found that married couples became a minority of all American households. Late-life divorce has become a widespread phenomenon. In the United States, the divorce rate among those over the age of sixty-five doubled between 1980 and 2004, according to U.S. census findings. All across the Western world, the number of people getting married has been plummeting. According to the National Marriage Project at Rutgers University, between the early to mid 1990s and the early 2000s, the marriage rate dropped by 12 percent in Italy, 14 percent in Spain, 22 percent in Canada, and 24 percent in the United States.

Meanwhile, other couples are choosing non-traditional living arrangements, like non-marital cohabitation or LAT (living apart together), a phenomenon explored in depth by Swedish professor Jan Trost and Irene Levin, a professor of social work at Oslo University College in Norway. These are couples who live in separate single-person residences, are unmarried, and maintain a committed intimate relationship. When the researchers began studying the phenomenon in 1993, there were 65,000 LAT couples in Sweden. By 1998, that number had doubled. In 2001, Statistics Canada found that 8 percent of the Canadian population aged twenty and over were in similar relationships. A British study published in 2000 found that one-third of never-married, childless women under thirty-five are in LAT relationships, and about 30 percent of those women do not plan to live with or get married to their present partner. As a model, living alone together has evolved as a way for people to maintain control over their time, space, and relationships, while still sharing parts of their life with someone else, albeit on their own terms.

"On average," writes David Popenoe, a professor of sociology and the founder and co-director of the Rutgers National Marriage Project, "America has been moving in the direction of secular individualism, as can be seen in the general drift of our family trends." Although he identifies certain regional and demographic exceptions, the traditional concept of "family" in America is generally being dismantled, he says, due to "the gradual abandonment of religious attendance and beliefs, a strong leaning toward 'expressive' values that are preoccupied with personal autonomy and self-fulfillment."

As a result, life for both men and women has become much more fluid. Couples couple up, they move in, they move out, they marry, they divorce, and they reunite. A 2004 University of Chicago survey

found that typical urbanites spend more of their adult live
ried—single and dating—than married. Notions of identity
ships, and family have never been more amorphous. And
culture critic Jean Kilbourne writes, takes place in a cultural
which advertising "constantly exhorts us to be in a never-ending state
of excitement, never to tolerate boredom or disappointment, to focus
on ourselves, never to delay gratification, to believe that passionate sex
is more important than anything else in life, and always to trade in old
things for new. These messages are a kind of blueprint for how to
destroy an intimate relationship." The urban condominium market
caters to this fluidity. People today keep their options open. There's an
impermanence and a flexibility to modern family structures that never
existed before. And it's this freedom of movement that makes a
person's decision to purchase real estate far less daunting than it's ever
been before.

This is particularly true of women. The idea of committing to purchasing a place by oneself is no longer tantamount to committing to
being single forever. And even if it were, that fact alone is no longer the
emotional death sentence it once was. Rather, a 2006 Pew Research
study found that most young singles in the U.S. (55 percent) don't
describe themselves as actively looking for a relationship. Quite the
opposite. Single life has become, in many cases, something to envy:
freedom, glamour, control, self-actualization. A solo investment in real
estate has become an effort in striking out rather than a retreat.

To be clear, we're not suggesting that we should all go back to the
fifties where families were "happy"—the men often in stifling jobs, the
women popping Valium between homemaking chores, and people
everywhere sweeping their troubles under the rug. The choices we have
now are hard-won. But the downside of how we've managed all of this
freedom is often overlooked. Collectively, we've swapped one limiting
approach to relationships for another: the "suffer for the greater good"
mentality has been replaced with one of "use it and lose it."

"Things have grown more disposable and it's sort of given the nod to disposability," says Carter. "A whole generation of young people was raised in broken families. Now it's like, 'Well all my friends' parents are divorced.' That's what kids say to each other, so we're giving all this tacit approval to all of these things that really eat at the core of our ability to connect and stay connected as human beings. I think it's a mess." But it does serve a purpose, he adds, by creating a generation of people with plenty of emotional holes to fill: "In rushes all the consumer angles to pacify the agony of the masses."

In other words, constant self-focus creates a feeling of disconnectedness that requires tending to, leaving us wide open to the seduction of the You Sell.

YOU'RE NOT BUYING HOME, YOU'RE BUYING A LIFE

Toronto's Queen Street West district has always been one of the city's most popular and colourful destinations—packed with bars, cafés, and trendy fashion boutiques. But travel far enough west, and the action stops dead, supplanted by rows of dollar stores and grimy booze cans. Over the past decades, entrepreneurs have sought, with some success, to revitalize the area and turn it into a sort of artists' haven. The Drake and the Gladstone Hotels, both refurbished as slick but quirky boutique hotels, have become hipster central. Artisans and small galleries began moving into the community, drawing tastemakers high and low. West Queen West, as it's often called, became another neighbourhood in transition—part-Starbucks, part-Dip 'N Sip, all potential. It didn't take long for condominium developers to recognize an opportunity.

Rene DeSantis of Montana Steele runs a marketing firm in Toronto that specializes in branding real estate projects. One of his projects is a condominium development located in the heart of West Queen West. "These condos, they're like rock stars right now," says DeSantis. "Marketing some of these high-rises is almost like launching a movie."

If you don't build anticipation among your target audience before the show starts, people will get the message that this is a bad movie, so to speak, and the builders won't get their financing. About a year and a half ago, Rene and his brother, Andy DeSantis, the firm's creative director, set out to give the building a personality—a name, a style, an overall brand—that would appeal to their target market: young professionals and lovers of urban life, mostly singles, who dig the area's gritty feel. For a name, they settled on Bohemian Embassy Lofts. They were inspired to go with "Bohemian" because of a local newspaper article that described the area that way. The "Embassy" part, says Rene, provides the weight of it. "So you get Bohemia which is free and loose," he says, "and you get embassy which is the structure and the substance to the building. It gives it almost a clubby feel. When you put those two words together, it's almost like putting black and white together."

An elaborate sales centre and ad campaign—all done up in red and black with design elements that looked vaguely embassy-like—played on the name's initials "BE" by inviting prospective buyers to "BE Here," "BE Seen," and "BE Yourself." Classic affirmational messaging. Then it addressed its target demographic by its would-be name. In an appeal to buyers, the marketing materials said: "Calling all Urbanites: Bohemian Embassy is looking for freethinking, art-loving, unconventional urbanites to take up digs in its chic, unique and oh so Bohemian residential suites." (As though an actual art-loving, unconventional urbanite would heed such a call.)

Right away, Bohemian Embassy attracted attention, but not exactly the kind the DeSantises were anticipating. First of all, says Rene, "there was a controversy with some of the artists that felt that a high-rise in that area was going to change the neighbourhood. Because you haven't seen anything like that in that kind of area." They're the same kinds of objections to non-organic transformation you'll find in Brooklyn, Williamsburg, and gentrifying communities across North America. But also, artists and residents of the community objected to the woman featured in enormous billboard ads for the building—a sort of

Goth-y-looking, vaguely dominatrix-like woman in shiny clothes. "With her, we were trying to capture a little bit of the urban bohemian type of person: that is, she doesn't really follow trends, she's a free-thinker and we felt that that model had the whole look and feel we wanted," says Andy. But locals said they got the area all wrong.

"They didn't feel that woman best represented the area," says Rene. "There were comments that she was a Russian mail-order bride. There was a lot of controversy around it. But that woman, that model, is about $20,000 or $25,000 a day."

Still, despite the cheesy approach, buyers came. Anything you can do to distinguish your building from the next one is worthwhile, since it's all about creating the perception of one-of-a-kind-ness. "There's always a bit of a risk but you have to go for it," says Andy. "We were really happy because controversy is the best PR you can have. There was a lot of talk, lots of discussion. It was the talk of the town!"

The condominium model has emerged as an extremely seductive and lucrative manifestation of the You Sell: home as a symbol of your hip, young, unencumbered self. From the architecture to the interior design, the amenities, the designer-sanctioned choices of layouts and materials, tarted-up sales centres, websites, and model suites—every facet of urban condos is marketed to meet a set of precise emotional needs: to project a fantasy life onto concrete and glass. What this urban fantasy looks like is remarkably consistent: a luxurious re-imagining of the "authentic" artists' lofts first made popular in Manhattan in the sixties, with wide-open spaces that promote creativity and fluidity and deliver a quintessential bohemian bourgeois sensibility. To add an element of urban-luxe, developers started bringing in the hardwood floors, the high ceilings, the concrete walls, and exposed brick, Philippe Starck–type bathroom, European kitchens, and stainless-steel appliances. In Toronto, buildings were given New York–themed names like Soho and Gotham and Radio City.

But far more important than the design of the building itself is the marketing campaign used to sell it. Current averages of development costs show a division of about 5 percent toward design and a whopping 15 percent toward marketing, says Mason White, a Toronto architect and a lecturer at the University of Toronto's Faculty of Architecture, Landscape, and Design.

"Marketing efforts promote condominiums as an amalgam of lifestyle and tourism," he says. "That 15 percent is people sitting in a room debating endlessly, what should we call it? How are we going to sell it? Who's our target audience? Let's do a photo shoot. What should the brochures look like? Then finally, what does the building look like? 'Oh, I don't know. Just make a space, 65 square feet, kitchen, done.'" The reason the pre-construction marketing push is so crucial, he says, is because condominiums are infinitely more "brandable" before they exist. The buildings themselves—whether they are ten storeys or twenty storeys, mostly glass or mostly brick—tend not to differ that much from one to the next. Condos, says White, "are the only building type that typically has another temporary building, the sales centre, built in anticipation of its coming."

These sales centres, staffed by attractive, stylish young people the market wants to identify with, are like sets designed to give prospective buyers the impression that they might step out of their former unsatisfying lives and into a more fabulous one just by purchasing a unit in this building. Laid out are glamorous mock-ups of the amenities you will have access to: rooftop bars, tanning cabanas, swimming pools, a gym with yoga room, a karaoke party room, a private screening room, or maybe an on-site spa. "We want to make people feel like they *are* that [fantasy] person," says Brad Lamb, "that they're living a hip, cool downtown lifestyle by being in that space—even if they're not. They can feel better about themselves. It's intentional that we've delivered the buildings and the marketing materials to make you feel that way." These are what White calls "atmosphere amenities," the less tangible things—like luxury, social acceptance, access to the in-crowd—that carry a more powerful emotional wallop than any workout or party room ever could. It's about creating an environment that tells people that, by buying this tiny piece of property in the sky, you are investing, not in a couple of rooms, but in a fully realized, designer-sanctioned, fully catered lifestyle. You are buying a more flattering, self-aggrandizing portrait of You.

Which makes perfect sense. In a customized society—where a certain degree of wealth, or the ability to borrow it, is enjoyed by a majority, and the individual is prized above all—the marketing of the condo lifestyle is designed to conform and cater to you. Or rather, an idealized You. There is a huge trade-off involved: space. However, once you've accepted that, the argument goes, condo developers will make your life so easy, and cater to your needs so explicitly, that you won't know what you're missing. The whole sell is based on a no-hassle approach for a time-crunched demographic: you pay a monthly condo fee, and in exchange, you never have to worry about the unexpected, time-consuming pitfalls and details of home ownership. There is somebody responsible for cleaning your windows, clearing the walk-ways, taking care of mechanical problems, shining your doorknobs, heating and air-conditioning your space, vacuuming the hallways, mopping the floors, cleaning your parking space, dealing with your garbage and recycling, and bringing in your mail. It's all taken care of. It is just about the most idiot-proof way of living there is. And there is a reason this sell is particularly effective now, at a time when young people and retiring boomers alike are becoming accustomed to having every service in their lives outsourced.

This need among buyers to see their homes as a sort of affirma-tion—and as a reflection of their idealized selves—is leading condo developers to create a whole new culture of "you-centred" living. It's no coincidence, says White, that the entrepreneurs most responsible for conceiving some of the most desirable condominium residences in Manhattan got their start in the nightclub and hotel industries. "That explains everything," he says. "The condo is a mix of nightclub and hotel." He particularly identifies real estate moguls Ian Schraeger—of Studio 54 and Morgan Hotels notoriety—and Andre Balasz, who also began as an investor in nightclubs before becoming a boutique hotelier, as pioneers.

To understand what makes Schraeger's approach so seductive, you need only watch his slick on-line advertisement for 40 Bond, his super-deluxe condominium project in Manhattan's trendy NoHo neighbourhood, designed by the world-renowned Swiss architectural firm Herzog & De Meuron. "I'm always out to change things, rethink them and make them better," he tells an anonymous interviewer, documentary style. "Now, more than ever, I feel the status quo is unacceptable. This is what I did with my nightclubs and hotels and I intend to do with people's homes." Each unit of 40 Bond is, of course, "unique and original." But what will really distinguish this property is the concept of what he calls "effortless living." The building offers its residents a seemingly endless menu of services: limousine service, turn-down service, massage and spa service, personal shopping service, pet walking and sitting services, dry-cleaning pickup, computer technical support service, painting and repair service, fresh-flower service and wake-up calls. "[It's] this idea of providing, twenty-four hours a day, seven days a week, this complete level of service that makes living in the city so much easier," he says. "To say that the service we're providing is just about room service and housekeeping services is not getting the idea. It is much more than that. It is really managing one's life. Giving a person the opportunity to have a complete household staff without the expense or the work required in supervising it, to make your home a refuge and not a second career, to make it the art of living and not the job of living." In other words, here, you will not just be an anonymous resident, you'll be a VIP guest in your own home.

Condo developments are also marketed to appeal to different urban tribes. In Manhattan's financial district, for instance, at the corner of William and Beaver Streets, Andre Balazs recently unveiled the cheekily named William Beaver House, marketed as a sin-palace for sexually frustrated single men with *Wall Street* fantasies. Early ads—later pulled because of angry critics who deemed them sexist—featured Japanese anime porn-style illustrations of a woman doing a striptease for a reclining man, and another playing basketball in her underwear. The suites themselves were said to feature bathtubs with louvred walls that open onto the bedrooms and, in the building's entrance, an upward glance at the ceiling reveals the underside of a glass-bottomed Jacuzzi. The *New York Times* dubbed the project "housing rated NC-17."

Similarly, as we saw in Toronto with Bohemian Embassy Lofts, there is a building for you, no matter what brand of person you want to self-identify with. If you see yourself as the type to hobnob with celebrities, Toronto's Festival Tower, now under construction, will house the headquarters for the prestigious Toronto International Film Festival: "One part condo. One part film festival. A world first." Maybe you're a sports-loving alpha male. You might consider The Residences of Maple Leaf Square, a pair of high-rise towers located right next to the Air Canada Centre (home of the NHL's Maple Leafs and the NBA's Raptors), billed as "Toronto's first sports and entertainment condominium." Or perhaps you identify as an eco-minded sophisticate. For you, there is Rezen, a condo that apparently embodies "a new zenitude." Suites are described as "sanctuaries." "Rezen is eco-friendly and energy efficient, inside and out," boasts the promotional literature; it's designed to promote wellness of "body, soul, spirit, mind." The website graphics show a person, presumably a resident, in a yoga meditation pose—and a sand garden, ostensibly newly raked by an obliging downtown monk. Casting a wider net is the plainly named Bay Street development U. Signifying "ultimate living," U is a condo that is—you guessed it—"all about U."

All of the specifics of an individual project—the design, the layout, the interiors, and the location—act as a screening process, virtually guaranteeing that you will be surrounded by neighbours who will more or less mirror your ideal self back to you: with similar aspirations and aesthetic sensibility, and in a similar profession and stage of life. They are the kinds of people who might self-identify as having "zenitude" or "hipster edge."

As the industry becomes more competitive, ever-greater pools of money are being dedicated to harnessing all-important buzz—anything to set a new residential project apart. It didn't take long for the industry to look to celebrities—those icons of luxury living—for a boost. "Starchitects" like Daniel Libeskind, Ralph Johnson, Will Alsop, Philippe Starck, and Michael Graves are being recruited to lend their star power to ultra-lavish projects. In Manhattan, condominium grand-opening parties have featured live performances by celebrity recording artists like Seal and John Legend. Lobbies are being furnished with multi-million-dollar interiors by Armani/Casa and valuable pieces of art by Jasper Johns or actor/photographer Dennis Hopper. In early 2007, the *New York Post* reported that a new development called Atelier on West 42nd Street in Manhattan was offering to let starlet Lindsay Lohan use a suite gratis in order to lend the building additional cachet. Atelier's marketers had already used the images of model Maggie Rizer, tennis stud James Blake, volleyball babe Gabrielle Reese, and Jesse L. Martin of *Law and Order* in ad campaigns. None of them had bought in the building. Still, their images function like Heather Locklear in the L'Oréal commercials, telling you, "You're worth it." You belong among the elite.

CUSTOM YOU

Much like Dell Computers, the Toyota Scion, American Girl, and countless other brands that lean heavily on the Designer Effect, avant-garde condominium developers make a big show to prospective buyers of the many ways in which they can customize their purchase. These sorts of "personal touches" were unheard of at the average person's price point. Of course, the You Sell in housing, like everywhere else, is indiscriminate. You = anyone. Twenty years ago, condominiums were first and foremost functional, low-cost spaces. Today, forward-thinking developers will recruit the biggest names in interior design to select a limited range of standard options for buyers to choose from: three or four different hardwood stains and a few choices in the colour of tiles, backsplashes, countertops and cabinetry, for example. Buyers can also invest in upgrades—a kitchen island, maybe, slate bathroom floors, or stainless-steel appliances. They cost more, but, the pitch goes, the more money you spend, the more "unique" your home will be. Essentially, the designers serve as lifestyle editors. They eliminate thousands of decisions and variables for you, and offer you options from a very narrow spectrum of designer-sanctioned stylish selections. Even though the choices are very limited, the important thing is creating the illusion that the final selections were yours. Stylewise, the system is foolproof.

In truth, the sell is an inch deep, an exercise in co-operative self-delusion. Nobody becomes an arty bohemian or a Wall Street player just by buying into a space—and if they did, you'd have to wonder about their definition of the terms. And structurally, there is only so much even the most brilliant architects, designers, and developers can do with, say, a 700-square-foot box. They can play with ceiling heights. They can decide to add balconies or terraces onto some units. They can offer different styles of hardwood or polished concrete floors, gas for cooking, stainless-steel appliances, floor-to-ceiling windows, European cabinetry, stone countertops, and a nice, functional layout. More often than not, developers say it's the little details that hook people. Maybe it's the soaker tub that makes the sale. Or a sexy bathroom vanity. A woman might see it and imagine her future self there some morning, perhaps wearing a glamorous silk kimono, and performing her daily ablutions.

"You have a nice vanity with a nice sink and a very contemporary tap—it gets them every time," says Lamb.

Because the box is not what they're selling, anyway.

On billboards and other promotional materials, the words "luxury," "exclusive," and "prestigious" are tossed around like cheap accessories. But as the elite have always known, true luxury speaks for itself.

"A 'luxury home' is a gratifying self-indulgence even though the term itself is a kind of status giveaway," writes Marjorie Garber, a Harvard University professor and chair of the school's department of visual and environmental studies. "If you need to say it, you're not there yet." Still, the You Sell is about perception. It's about you and your need for a home that reflects the identity you wish to project to the world. In an era of "massclusivity," where anyone can shell out $150 for a Stella McCartney dress at H&M—or spend an extra $2 to get a high-end designer toilet paper—luxury has become a cheap concept. More than anything now, it's used as a means for propping up prospective consumers—to sell us on the notion that you deserve, as Burger King says, to "Have it your way."

HOME AS OPTICAL ILLUSION

If you are living alone, it is not surprising that, in theory, your space would take on a whole different sort of emotional significance. For so many of us, in lieu of family or a romantic partner, home becomes a surrogate—something to care for, to nurture and be nurtured by. It's a place that exists just for you. Garber describes how the modern home can serve all sorts of stand-in functions. "Anyone who doubts the possibility of falling in love with a house—with all that implies of fast-beating heart, sweaty palms, and waiting for the phone to ring—just hasn't met the right one yet," she writes. "In our present-day culture, the house often plays the role of lover, partner, significant other—the dream date and the dream mate—the one who will realize our desires and give a purpose to our plans and days." The idea of home as affirmation of who we've become, and what we've achieved, is a powerful one.

Moreover, because time has become such a precious commodity, home needs to serve as many functions as possible to make up for all of the activities one no longer has time to do outside the home. And so, it becomes not just home, but also gym, movie theatre, spa, gourmet restaurant, bar lounge, yoga room, and so on. We want our homes, writes Garber, to be a concrete projection of the life we imagine for ourselves, "a life that includes fine cooking, relaxing, exercising, entertaining," whether we do these things or not.

The success of condo marketing suggests that, for many of us, our homes are a projection of self, and as with all projections, there is a disconnect between the idea and the actual experience of it. More than a genuine concern, condo marketing transforms home into a fetish. This perhaps explains why the hotel aesthetic has become such a popular trope among designers. Hotel suites, much like other "customizable" consumer products, offer blank slates onto which we can project an infinite range of possible future experiences. W Hotels, Westin, Sofitel, Kimpton Hotels, James Hotels, even Holiday Inn—all have their own product lines for consumers who want to mirror the hotel experience at home. We may rarely find the time or the occasion to use our gourmet kitchens or spa bathrooms, but they provide psychic comfort nonetheless.

They conjure possibility.

"It's like that old argument about non-working women as leisure symbols," says Susan Saegert, director of the Centre for Human Environments and a professor of environmental psychology at the City University of New York Graduate Centre. "I think it's a little bit like that, where you have all of these non-working domestic appurtenances which give the impression of home even if you're not actually using them to make yourself feel at home." You may have never made a panini in your life, but your stainless-steel DeLonghi grill projects the idea that you live the life of someone who might.

THE ECONOMIC IMPERATIVE

The most significant change brought on by the influx of condo development is the sheer volume of households it has created. In 1960, there were roughly 53 million households in the United States, according to the U.S. Census Bureau. 13.1 percent of which were occupied by a single person. By 2000, there were almost double that number—105 million households—and single people made up more than a quarter of those. Atomization serves an important economic imperative—the most obvious being that it creates markets. Now, says Saegert, "each person has to have everything. It's profitable to buy into the fact that each individual should have a separate life and separate gear and express themselves through their gear and their home design and that it should be an individual kind of a thing." The U.S. Census Bureau is predicting that by 2010 there will be more than 34 million people living alone in the United States. Think of that in terms of television sets alone: in 2007, 98.2 percent of households had *at least* one.

For the economy, the spike in single-person households is a windfall. According to the 2005 U.S. Consumer Expenditure Survey, a person living alone will spend an average of $26,773 per year on personal expenditures—everything from food, clothing, cleaning supplies, furniture and appliances. A household consisting of five or more people, meanwhile, only spends a collective total of $62,618, or a maximum average of $12,524 each. Between 1999 and 2004, Research and Markets reported that household-appliance industry sales grew by 22 percent ($3.8 billion), largely because of an increased number of household units. In 1992, the average American spent $168 on home electronics and appliances. By 2005, that number had doubled.

Instead of one washer and dryer for every four or five people, we now have one for every one or two people. This holds true for everything: toaster ovens, phone service, beds and duvets, bathtubs, cutlery sets, and on and on. Not only that, but a whole new market for premium-priced, single-sized portions of everything from tomato soup to Hamburger Helper has emerged. In a report on the lifestyles of single people in the U.S., *American Demographics* magazine found that "a surprisingly large number of these singles, no matter their age, have two things in common: financial success and the willingness to spend to satisfy their desires."

After surveying this demographic, Yankelovich Monitor found that across all age groups, members of single-person households are far more willing to spend money on themselves than others their own age who are in other living arrangements.

"What sets singles apart from the rest of the population is their different focus in terms of responsibilities," Carey Earle, CEO of Harvest Communications, told *American Demographics*. "We even see this difference between single luxury-good purchasers and other luxury-good purchasers. Because even at the highest earning level, they can afford more than someone at the same level who has kids. Their prioritization is different: being single allows them to be a little selfish."

In truth, being single doesn't *allow* people to be a little selfish; the market *demands* selfishness of all of us. Where single people are concerned, it's just more evident.

PHANTOM COMMUNITIES

Despite more people spending more time alone, the *idea* of community is still important to us, a fact that smart condo developers are highly attuned to. The result is marketing concepts that emphasize the trappings of community and the potential for social interaction—in the form of health clubs, retail spaces, restaurants, performance spaces, party rooms, screening rooms and so on—but without the obligations or duties required by a real social network. The idea is one of community-on-demand—you can order it up like cable. Belonging to a condo does technically involve shared responsibilities and, to some degree, a shared fate, which might provide a sense of belonging to something. But you're under no obligation to participate in a phantom community. Regardless of whether shared spaces get used or not, the very possibility that they may get used provides residents with psychic comfort. Much like on-line communities, these are virtual social networks that replicate the feeling of connecting without the effort or the commitment. Here, participation happens entirely on one's own terms.

Part of this is a result of the fact that more young urban people in particular are thinking of their homes as temporary. An article published in early 2007 in the *New York Times* described how young people tend to think of real estate in investment terms, rather than emotional terms—that is, buying smart, borrowing large, and ultimately cashing out. Belonging to and helping to cultivate a community is a secondary concern. And if people don't stay put, neighbourhood relationships and attachments simply don't develop. "What I know from my research on residential density," says Susan Saegert, "is that if there is turnover in [residential complexes] in which there is no logical place to meet others and know who's who, then the tendency is for people to not distinguish one person from another because there are just too many of them ... It works a little bit the same as how a dorm might work. It's a transient community."

In a time-starved society in which getting to know one's neighbours is an unnatural undertaking and a perpetual source of effort, community doesn't flourish. People work longer-than-ever hours, and at the end of a draining day, they are less likely to be out in the streets, meeting their neighbours and frequenting local establishments. Everything we used to do outside the home—banking, laundry, entertainment—can now be done faster and easier from within.

"The more common outcome in cities, where people are faced with the choice of sharing much or nothing, is nothing," wrote Jane Jacobs, a warning embedded in her work that is coming true on a massive scale. "In city areas that lack a natural and casual public life, it is common for residents to isolate themselves from each other to a fantastic degree. If mere contact with your neighbours threatens to entangle you in their private lives, or entangle them in yours ... the logical solution is absolutely to avoid friendliness or casual offers of help. Better to stay thoroughly distant."

But once we are ensconced in our alcoves, the "atmosphere

amenities" aren't necessarily what they're cracked up to be presented in the sales centres and brochures.

"Once you're in these units, I think very many people experience a kind of loneliness," says Saegert, "that it's not necessarily such an easy thing to actually live." Study after study supports the sociologist Robert Putnam's claims that social networks are collapsing all around us. The condo boom is not only a symptom of this fact; it's also a driver.

A recurring theme in contemporary sociological research is the paradox that people feel as though they have fewer people to talk to, despite all of the technology available to them ostensibly designed to facilitate communication. Take, for instance, a 2006 study out of Duke University that found that Americans have fewer friends than ever. The researchers compared data from 1985 to 2004 on the number of friends the average American has with whom he or she can share personal issues. The typical American had an intimate social circle of just about three people in the mid-eighties. Over the course of nineteen years, that already-tiny number dropped to two. Moreover, the percentage of people who talk only to family members about important matters increased from about 57 percent in 1985 to 80 percent in 2004, and the number of people who said they had no one at all to confide in more than doubled, to almost 25 percent.

In fact, statistically, a person is more likely to socialize at home with a pet than another human being. According to the American Pet Products Manufacturers Association, 63 percent of U.S. households own at least one pet, up 7 percentage points over 1988. Which makes sense: dogs and cats conform more willingly to our lifestyles, tastes, and schedules in a way that people often don't. Also, they don't make personal demands or judgments. Which is why household pets have taken on a privileged role in mainstream culture. In 2006, the APPMA estimated pet owners spent $38.4 billion on everything from vet care and food to grooming, clothing and accessories, toys and treats—*double* what they were spending in 1994.

Even people who do live together in a traditional family household are being fragmented by long work hours and a growing overreliance on technology. A 2007 University of Toronto NetLab study on "The Networked Household" explained: "Household life has sped up and people multitask or rush from task to task, feeling they have too much to do and too little time to do it. Contentions between home life and work life are high. As the work day has lengthened, tele-workers do all or part of their jobs at home."

The study found that contemporary households often function as individualized networks rather than unified groups: "Each household member functions as a semi-autonomous actor, with her/his own agenda, using a variety of transportation and communications media to contact and co-ordinate with each other." The vast majority of North Americans now connect to the Internet from their homes.

"I think that technology makes home less of a retreat and that people are not as off-duty as they used to be able to be and I think it's pretty pervasive," says Saegert. "Not in all classes and not all forms of jobs, obviously. But it also means that even while people are in the home, even if it's for recreational purposes, they're psychically away from the home. So I think a lot of time is spent engaged technologically in ways that don't necessarily bond you to the space."

To determine the effects of communications technology devices in the home, the NetLab researchers surveyed an average working-and-middle-class group of 167 adults living with a partner in a community in East Toronto. They conducted lengthy in-home interviews with the couples and found that 82 percent of them go on-line between 6 and 11 p.m., after they're home from work. More than a third of them say they have more than one household computer. More than a quarter have two or more cars, and 68 percent of them carry cell phones. These devices facilitate a form of communication, as much as they also create new types of distance between people and serve as barriers between members of a household. For instance, respondents rarely reported keeping secrets from their family members (mind you, being secrets, this should come as no great surprise). Still, their cell phones, unlike their home's landlines, are personal and private. Even if family members share a computer, they often have private passwords, and users can talk, email, or chat with whomever they want with very little likelihood that family members will find out.

In any household of more than one person, this is bound to create friction. Reading a family member's email, checking their voice mail, or even scrolling through their iPod playlists starts to feel like a betrayal. A *Wall Street Journal* article by Ellen Gamerman exploring the prickly territory of "digital cohabitation" found that couples are struggling to determine how much of their digital lives—their Facebook pages, their blogs, their voice-mail access codes, their virtual gaming activities, etcetera—to share, and how much to keep separate. "Technology companies are pushing ever-more-personalized products and services," writes Gamerman, "but as things get more tailored to an individual's use, they also become less compatible with the give-and-take of married life." The proliferation of services designed to serve you at home, combined with the quality and complexity of home entertainment and media technology, continue to make it easy to access the outside world without ever having to actually wade out into it.

THE SUBURBANIZATION OF URBAN LIFE

And so, unlike Jacobs' cherished vision of Greenwich Village in the 1950s and 1960s, there is nothing organic about newly minted urban neighbourhoods. They may increase the number of people taking up residence on a particular street, but they don't generate much in the way of diversity of residents. They are not organically created, multiuse spaces that facilitate the sort of "strange and unpredictable uses and peculiar scenes" Jacobs valued so highly. Jacobs wrote that the whole *point* of cities is "multiplicity of choice." The condo boom, however, generates very little variety in residents. Quite the opposite. Urban residential environments, following the lead of the suburbs, promote homogeneity and isolation. Here is where we see the paradox of the Ego Boom at home more fully: the more people buy into the You Sell, the more uniform our lifestyles become.

In their very design—their spa bathrooms, entertainment centres, gourmet kitchens—condominiums entice residents to stay indoors. Of course, the wealthy classes have always lived in communities that lend themselves to isolation and exclusion. The significance of condos, however, is that they bring personal control and autonomy to the urban masses—just as the suburbs brought it to middle class families.

This homogeneity is discernible in the way in which people who have occupied a particular urban community for generations have become priced out of it. The installation of a Starbucks has become an early warning signal of big changes to come.

"I live in an Italian neighbourhood in Brooklyn," says Saegart, "and I've seen it go through four waves of gentrification. One of the things that's happened is that there are no more Italian fruit stores at all. There were lots of shopkeepers who were related to people in the neighbourhood and who knew them over the course of their lives and knew multiple generations and they got whooshed out of there through gentrification. Place after place after place closed."

Instead, condominiums, much like suburban neighbourhoods, collect people with similar lifestyles, similar routines, and similar work hours—which means fewer people out in the streets at all hours. People who provide services in the community vanish after closing time. Architect Mason White describes the atmosphere as "cruiseship-like": "If you think about urban life, urban life has unpredictability," he says. "It has foreign agents that occupy it . . . and condos don't really allow for that. Condos have all these little thresholds that are like buffer zones that protect you from those unpredictabilities. Even the gym on the second floor or wherever—it's all residents. So you're never going to have the unpredictability of someone else coming in." It's enough to make you ask yourself why you wanted to live in the city in the first place.

Now, all of these individual people in their individual pods are reshaping urban landscapes, both aesthetically and functionally. The result is a massive shift inward, so that external and public spaces become considerably less relevant to the average person. We have fewer and fewer reasons to be emotionally invested. "Central to the allure of condominium developments is their ability to bring qualities of seeming urbanity into the complex," says White. "However, condominium urbanity is very different from the less predictable sidewalk-bound energy of the city. Condominiums produce a kind of Petri-dish urbanity. It is contained, controlled, and always room temperature. Once urbanism is invited to the condo interior it is tamed and becomes more sterilized and homogenous. Its homogeneity is generated from the unwritten laws of economy and lifestyle."

It's almost as though we are very gradually, and collectively, forgetting what it means to co-exist with strangers—particularly those who are not "people like us."

Throughout the twentieth century, the components of city life—the markets, the libraries, the café culture, and the nightlife—evolved organically, popping up and spreading out as needed. These days, we are more apt to buy the "downtown living" concept fully formed from real estate developers. But city life isn't something you can sell in a kit. We make cities; we don't buy them. With the condominium model, the You Sell entices us with two incompatible concepts—gritty urban living *and* controlled, customizable luxury. The result is a sort of urban suburbanism: cleaned-up, cordoned-off pieces of the urban experience.

GREENWICH VILLAGE 2.0

Even Jane Jacobs' beloved Greenwich Village, that idealized haven to artists and bohemians, has not managed to stave off the economic forces of the Ego Boom that have suburbanized life in so many cities. Today, housing costs in the Village are astronomical—not prices that a struggling musician or poet, even one with a mid-sized trust fund, could readily afford. If anything, the Village has become one of New York's strongest branded communities—an area that still represents the idea of boho whimsy, even though it is instead home to wealthy socialites and hipster celebrities like Uma Thurman and Philip Seymour Hoffman. Mom-and-pop stores have been replaced with Marc Jacobs boutiques.

In concrete terms, nowhere is the Ego Boom phenomenon more evident than in the carving up of a limited amount of urban property into ever-smaller, ever-higher, ever-more-precious residential spaces. Brad Lamb and his peers were smart enough to have anticipated the coming of this social change twenty years ago. He may not have understood it as atomization, but he and others correctly intuited that this kind of high-density, low-maintenance living would eventually appeal to a huge number of people—and he stuck with it through the early days, when people derided condominiums as "crappy shoeboxes in the sky." Now, he's got millions and an unlimited stock of I Told You Sos to show for it. The rest of us, we have our forty-eight-inch, wall-mounted flat-screens, our Italian cappuccino makers, and our soaker tubs. Our suites are pristine and hermetically sealed, and we might feel glad. And yet, isn't it strange to look down the hallway to find dozens of others living the exact same, unique lifestyle as you?

CHAPTER FIVE

PERSONAL DEMOCRACY AND OTHER OXYMORONS

I f the rise of the custom economy and the triumph of the
You Sell came at the expense of our community instincts, does that
mean our communities are doomed? As each successive generation
becomes increasingly self-focused, are we moving inexorably toward
the day when the basic assumptions of our participatory democracy
will no longer hold true? Or is it possible that the power of the Ego
Boom can be harnessed to reinvigorate our governments, our institutions, and even our sense of what makes us a society?

In a darkened auditorium at Pace University in Lower Manhattan,
a couple of hundred observers sit, faces illuminated by the glow of laptop screens, listening and learning about how technology might accom-
plish what a succession of multi-million-dollar public education and
publicity campaigns have failed to do. The objective is a redefinition
of the political process for the digital age—a new approach that will
speak to a generation of young voters who feel no affinity for the familiar
and traditional institutions of the state. Up on stage, Lawrence Lessig—
Harvard professor and hero of the anti-copyright movement—is playing a few of his favourite YouTube clips.

The first is from "The Daily Show with Jon Stewart": a hapless
senator is deliberately misunderstanding the testimony of a witness
before a congressional committee so that he can make his obtuse point

about some bit of regulatory minutia. The film snaps back to Stewart with his trademark half-puzzled, half-bemused expression. "This guy is a fucking idiot," Stewart deadpans, which elicits a roar of approval from the audience. Lessig moves on to a video by Johan Söderberg in which clips of Tony Blair and George Bush have been spliced together in slow motion and set to the syrupy 1980s ballad "Endless Love" by Lionel Richie and Diana Ross. It's pretty funny, but Lessig sees an importance that goes way beyond mere yuks. This, he says, is the future of political expression in the digital age. And, he thinks, it is a very good thing.

Technology, Lessig explains, makes it possible for all of us to be Jon Stewarts. With an ordinary computer and some cheap software, anyone can grab a bit of video, edit it, rearrange it, and distribute it to the world, virtually for free. "This technique has been democratized," he enthuses, and that represents "a radical change in the opportunity for people to participate in the political process." There were no dissenters among the crowd, only occasional laughs and brief rounds of applause as Lessig spoke. The rest of the time, the air is filled with the soft clicking of a few dozen audience members posting their own thoughts and reactions directly to their blogs.

Lessig is here at the annual Personal Democracy Forum because he is one of the champions of a new emboldened public that is redrawing the political power structure and breaking the dominance of old institutions that distort the fundamental right of every person in a free society to be heard. Andrew Rasiej, the founder of PersonalDemocracy.org and lead organizer of this gathering, says it's about "disintermediation"—and though he doesn't say so, it boils down to another variation on the You Sell. Just as Chris Anderson has argued that the central problem of popular culture is the dominance of a few unrepresentative distributors who manipulate the notion of "mainstream" for their own purposes, this conference makes much the same claim about the world of politics and public policy. The central problem of today's political system is the sclerotic and stultifying dominance of mediators—the press, the parties, the fundraisers, and the bureaucracies—who insulate the public from direct action in the system. And the solution can be found in the conference's anti-authoritarian title: "Personal Democracy—The Flattening of Politics."

The name itself is a nod to another of today's star attractions, Thomas Friedman, *New York Times* columnist and author of *The World is Flat*. In that best-selling ode to free trade and unfettered competition, Friedman describes a world in which individuals are put on equal footing and the best idea wins, no matter where it originated. The book's up-with-people message, and Friedman's firm belief in the democratizing potential of the Internet, make him the perfect host to lob good-natured talking points back and forth with Eric Schmidt, CEO of Google, and, coincidentally, lead sponsor of today's events.

Friedman opens with the declaration that the Internet is "the dial tone of the twenty-first century" and Schmidt enthusiastically agrees that "if you're not online you really don't have access to the modern world." When the conversation eventually meanders around to the political process, Schmidt predicts that the "incredible phenomenon" that is YouTube "will have a significant effect on the next election." His advice to candidates and activists: put everything online (YouTube being an ideal place to start) and let the masses take your message and run with it. If you don't do it yourself, he warns, someone else "will do it to you." And then comes the really big assertion: that the World Wide Web in general and digital video-sharing sites in particular, are "the best single argument in favour of free, democratic expression, and more importantly, of personal individual freedom, that's ever been built." No wonder Google paid $1.6 billion for YouTube just a few months before. Even that stunning sum seems like a bargain for something with the power to reinvigorate our tired democracies. It's only on slightly closer inspection that the holes begin to appear in his optimistic vision.

What will this beautiful new era of free, open dialogue among unfettered individuals look like? "Well, what we know from You Tube is this: online video generally needs to rely more on humour than other media," Schmidt explains. "It needs excitement, it needs to be quicker to be effective. People lose interest quite rapidly when they see a long monotone on screen." In the 2008 U.S. election, that translated into hundreds of YouTube videos—from Sarah Palin's beauty pageant footage to the ubiquitous "Obama Girl." Not a terribly inspiring introduction to a medium that's supposed to be a quantum leap forward in communication and engagement, but the point passes by without any opposition. But nobody stands up and asks whether that is really such a good thing. Nobody seems concerned that a new medium that worships brevity, smartassery, and "excitement" above all else, might really just be taking all the worst elements of the television revolution and amplifying them. To the nodding faces in the audience, all this sounds just great.

The morning moves on to a series of upbeat presentations on how technology is revitalizing the body politic: the fact that young people make no distinction between virtual worlds and real life; the fact that more and more are turning to the Web for political information rather than "traditional" media; the fact that there are now an estimated 14 million "political content creators" (mostly bloggers) in the U.S. alone; and that candidates are replacing traditional "meet-and-greets" with "online outreach." One presenter suggests that the U.S.'s "no child left behind" educational reform agenda should be replaced with an "every child connected" effort to ensure that every grade schooler has access to the Web. Another takes that idea further and suggests the Internet should be declared a public good and distributed "like water" to every home.

This is where the Ego Boom is heading, as it branches beyond the world of consumer goods and economic development, and into the realm of political action, government, and public policy. To the organizers and presenters at this conference, digital technology and the Internet will be a bridge back to community involvement and civic engagement. Personal Democracy, it seems, means revitalizing the system one video mashup, friend list, and podcast at a time, and there are some striking success stories that lend credence to the idea that ad hoc coalitions of individuals can form the basis of a new kind of community action. But there are also problems.

Sitting in the auditorium in the blue glow of laptop monitors, it's easy to forget that we are now more than a decade into the Internet age and the trends for community action are almost all heading away from community involvement. It's easy to ignore the reality that information has never been cheaper or more readily available, yet people continue to choose political ignorance at record levels; that never has more effort been directed toward enticing ordinary citizens to engage and yet apathy and isolation continue to be the defining characteristics of most Western democracies. And despite all the sunny optimism, and a handful of hopeful exceptions, by and large things are getting rapidly worse.

NOT BOWLING AT ALL

Back in 2000, one of Lessig's colleagues at Harvard, Professor Robert Putnam, published an unlikely best-seller called *Bowling Alone: The Collapse and Revival of American Community*. Through 500-plus pages of statistics, graphs, and anecdotes, the book demonstrated the gradual decline of community institutions between the mid-1960s and the late-1990s. Information about disappearing bowling leagues and bridge clubs, shrinking Rotary organizations, even a sharp drop in the sales of greeting cards, was meticulously laid out to bolster Putnam's argument that the sometimes subtle bonds that hold communities together were being gradually melted away.

Putnam argued that as people withdraw into their own lives, it leads to a decline in "generalized reciprocity"—the intangible goodwill that both binds and lubricates social networks of neighbours, friends, colleagues, acquaintances, and strangers. The mindset of generalized reciprocity works like this: "I'll do this for you without expecting anything specific back from you, in the confident expectation that someone else will so something for me down the road," Putnam wrote. Put another way, it is the community-wide acknowledgement of the old adage "what goes around, comes around." It's not altruism, but a proper understanding that we're all better off if we look out for each other.

Putnam's work wasn't simply a nostalgic lament for the disappearance of church-hall dinners, but an attempt to diagnose what was at the root of America's deepening democratic funk, manifested most obviously in dismal voter turnout at every level of government. Our tendency to "cocoon" into our own lives—spending more time on solitary entertainment, and tasks around home and work—was literally killing our communities, he said. Rising cynicism, falling participation, and a decline in respect and trust of others—it was all symptomatic of the disease. The American public seemed all too aware of these changes. The hundreds of studies cited by Putnam included a 1992 survey in which 75 percent of respondents agreed that the decline of community and a rise in selfishness was a serious problem, and 77 percent said the nation was worse off because of the decline of community activities. And yet we appear to be unwilling or unable to reverse the decline.

Putnam's critics have frequently noted that there was an increase in voter turnout in the 2004 election that would seem to call into question his sense of pessimism about the state of civic engagement. Indeed, with the U.S. at war and two extremely contrasting figures (incumbent George W. Bush and Democratic senator John Kerry) vying for the White House, participation climbed to 55 percent—the highest voter turnout since 1972. On the other hand, turnout has hovered between 49 percent and 55 percent since 1980, so the 2004 figure hardly represented a popular uprising. And the fact that just over half of eligible voters bothered to cast a ballot in an election that amounted to a national referendum on the U.S. war effort isn't much of an endorsement on the health of American democracy. In fact, when you look at the underlying trends and attitudes behind that participation, the picture is even less encouraging.

Since 2000, the state of civic participation and social engagement has continued to deteriorate by almost every significant measure. The "cocooning" that Putnam decried is increasingly the central feature of urban and suburban life in the major cities of North America. As we've pointed out, we excel at clipping the ties that bind us to our neighbours, but as we do so, our discontent with the state of society at large is cresting. In a 2006 Gallup poll, 81 percent of respondents said they believed society's moral values are getting worse. In 2002, only 67 percent expressed that same opinion. In the same poll, 74 percent of people said they are dissatisfied with the general level of honesty and standards of behaviour in society. A Pew Research Center poll in 2005 found 74 percent think people are less moral and honest than they used to be. And a CBS News poll in the summer of 2007 found that 72 percent of Americans believe the country's founding fathers would be disappointed to see how the country had turned out.

That sense of despair has translated into widespread disenchantment with the central pillars of the system. In June 2007, Gallup reported that 70 percent of Americans were now dissatisfied with the direction of the country, and respect for the major institutions of civil society had tumbled to the lowest levels since the aftermath of Watergate. Public confidence in organized religion had fallen from 64 percent in 1977, to 46 percent. Confidence in the public school system had dropped from 54 percent to 34 percent. The Supreme Court held the confidence of 54 percent of Americans thirty years ago, but now had fallen to just 33 percent. And Congress's approval had gone from 40 percent, to a pathetic 14 percent. Perhaps most telling, in light of our central value in the age of the Ego Boom—more than half of Americans said that the political system just isn't responsive enough to their individual demands.

Not surprisingly, the "social capital" that Putnam considers so essential to a working society continued to show signs of rapid erosion. The National Conference on Citizenship issues an annual report on America's civic health, and in 2006 it was entitled *Broken Engagement.*

Despite an uptick in voter turnout for the 2004 presidential elections, the NCC enumerated a litany of indicators showing that Americans continue to drift away from electoral politics and community participation. Attendance at public meetings, membership in community groups, trust in fellow citizens, even family dinners—all key indicators of robust social capital—have eroded significantly since the turn of the millennium, and the trends are more extreme among the youngest cohort of citizens.

The Center for Information and Research on Civic Learning and Engagement (better known as CIRCLE) revealed in its annual report that young adults between the ages of eighteen and twenty-five are the least likely to describe themselves as regular voters (26 percent compared to 56 percent in the general population); the least likely to belong to a political group (just 16 percent, compared to 23 percent for Americans as a whole); and they appear to be getting less likely to engage in basic forms of political activism, such as signing petitions or taking part in boycotts. Similar findings have been reported in polls across virtually every major western democracy from the U.K. and France, to the U.S. and Canada, and the most vivid results can be seen in waning party memberships, consistently weak voter turnout, and a shocking degree of ignorance when people are quizzed about the basics of public policy and government.

So what's behind this steady erosion in both interest and knowledge? The most commonly cited culprits are failures of education and of the institutions themselves. The pat answer goes like this: institutions of government simply have to do a better job satisfying people, and our schools need to do a better job educating kids about the importance of those institutions. Peter Levine is a research scholar at the University of Maryland, a director of CIRCLE, and a passionate advocate for renewed civic engagement. He makes the case that a lack of experience is at the root of declining civic engagement among young people, and calls for a massive reinvestment in civics lessons, both in the regular school curriculum and also through after-school programs aimed at getting kids involved with their communities. And while all of that may indeed be lacking, it seems a stretch to suggest that we could reverse three generations of political estrangement by making civics a compulsory course in middle school.

The rough outline of a more fundamental explanation began to emerge in 2003 at a little-known public forum held at the University of Alberta entitled "Escape from Politics." Panelists took turns describing what they saw as a "crisis in representative democracy" and discussing familiar ideas for various institutional reforms. But Professor Reg Whitaker suggested that the problems were more deeply ingrained in the way ideas are disseminated and sold in the modern world. "New communications technologies are fragmenting the community," he said. "Marketing these days is no longer about mass marketing, but micro marketing. Multiple TV channels pander to specialized entities, Internet communication draws people of like interests together. Political parties no longer broadcast, but narrow-cast their ideals." What Whitaker was describing was the process by which the central elements of the You Sell are being gradually adopted in the political realm. Rather than promoting common values, politicians and parties and associations engage in a form of niche pandering, designed to maximize appeal to a collection of voting blocs, rather than advancing any coherent vision for society. And while this may have yielded short-term results, the overall effect is as far-reaching as it is corrosive because it reduces politics to a consumer marketing effort like any other.

As Putnam makes clear, a functioning political system rests on personal responsibilities, mutual obligations, and uncertain rewards. But for a generation constantly reassured that the world revolves around them, those kinds of intangible civic virtues run counter to everything they've come to value and believe.

The solution most often endorsed by academics is a call for more education and a renewed focus on civics lessons in schools. They often interpret declining participation among young citizens as a backlash against a broken system, and suggest that young voters are registering their anger and contempt by staying away. If only young people could see how important the system is, if only the system were more attentive to the needs and aspirations of young people, then everything would be okay. Or so the thinking goes. But when you actually ask young voters what they think, you get a very different answer. Young people are neither angry nor confused. They just aren't particularly interested in the product on offer.

It's easy for older generations to wag their finger at younger voters and complain about that kind of apathy, but the truth is, there is a logic underlying the disinterest—it's the logic of the retail industry. As Anthony Downs demonstrated in his groundbreaking 1957 work on "rational ignorance," *An Economic Theory of Democracy*, voting is, in essence, an irrational activity since the chance of any one voter significantly affecting the outcome of an election is so low. Why spend a lot of time listening to boring debates and reading confusing news articles, not to mention going to the trouble of voting, when each individual vote is negligible in the grand scheme of things? Simply put, the effort required to engage in political life and representative government seems like a lousy investment of effort and energy to each successive generation of increasingly me-centred citizens.

PORTRAIT OF A CIVIC NARCISSIST

The youngest cohort of North American adults, otherwise known as the immediate future of our democratic system, is feeling pretty sweet these days. Yes, there's a war on, oil prices are high, jihadists are plotting against the West, and our inner cities remain rife with poverty and drug abuse. They know all that. They go to the movies and watch "24." It's just that none of it has them particularly disturbed.

Thanks to Mom and Dad, your typical 18- to twenty-four-year-old is flush with cash and has a pretty good education under their belt.

They know the economy needs them, so they can afford to be choosy about which jobs they accept. They've got a cell phone, an iPod, a sweet ride, nice clothes, a PVR, and a flat screen. They have little of their parents' generation's moral indignation at the state of the world, nor Gen X's angst about meaningless McJobs and empty consumerism. Ask them what they're rebelling against, and if you get an answer at all, it's most likely to be "boredom."

Life is good.

Near the end of 2006, the Pew Research Center for People and the Press compiled their own research, with massive sample sizes, and culled various other published surveys to assemble what may be the most comprehensive snapshot of what it called "Generation Next." What it found was a generation of young Americans reared in peace and plenty that is a hotbed of social rest. Fully 84 percent of young people rated their quality of life as "excellent or good"—the highest score of any age group. Asked about their general frame of mind, 93 percent said they were "very happy" or "pretty happy"—again the highest score by far. Breaking down the results further, 93 percent were satisfied with their family life, 82 percent with their housing situation, 82 percent were content with their job, and 81 percent felt they had enough free time. And while many expressed some concern about the direction the country was headed (only 43 percent were satisfied) the youngest cohort was again the most sanguine (among older Americans, only 31 percent were satisfied).

But it's not just the present that young people are happy with, they're generally pretty optimistic about the future, too. Asked whether they thought their life would be better or worse five years from now, 74 percent said things were looking up. By comparison, among those older than twenty-six, only 59 percent expected their lives to improve. Asked whether today's children will inherit a world as good as theirs, young optimists outnumbered the pessimists by 45 percent to 39 percent. Among older Americans, it was just the opposite: a majority predicted a decline in quality of life for children being born today. This pattern held across virtually every area of questioning. On education, jobs, sexual freedom, and financial security, young adults feel they've inherited a golden age, and they generally predict things will just keep getting better. This sunny outlook seems to have contributed to a very open and tolerant set of values and beliefs, as young voters are, by far, the most likely to be accepting of different lifestyles and cultures, and most suspicious of government attempts to legislate in areas of personal freedom and morality.

From this same wellspring of open parenting, focused on fostering self-esteem, has come a generation of profound self-regard. Pew dubbed this the "look at me" generation, and when it comes to matters of politics and community, its members spend little time looking beyond the confines of their own limited life experience. Among eighteen to twenty-four-year-olds, 64 percent believe they belong to a "unique" generation, and yet a majority said they think the generation just ahead of them (people now in their thirties) is not unique at all. Ask these same people what worries them, and just about all of them will talk about something directly in their lives as opposed to some broader social concern. To be fair, this is true of almost all Americans— when asked about their worries, just 8 percent of all respondents referred to the economy, or the war, or terrorism, or poverty—but the trend is especially prevalent among young people. Just 2 percent of Gen Next mentioned a broad social concern. Their biggest worries, in order, were: money (30 percent), their education (18 percent) and their job (16 percent).

That focus on money came to the fore, and vividly illustrates the me-first tendencies of young adults, when Pew asked about their goals in life. Young people were substantially more likely than older respondents to say their highest ambitions include getting rich (81 percent of young adults gave this answer compared to 62 percent of people aged twenty-six to forty). Young people were also far more likely to say they want to be famous (51 percent compared to 29 percent in the older age group). Generation Next was substantially less likely than the older group to include helping people (30 percent), being a community leader (22 percent), or becoming more spiritual (10 percent) among their goals in life.

It will come as no surprise, by now, that these response patterns—broad self-satisfaction and confidence, combined with a conspicuous lack of concern for others—perfectly fit the profile used by psychologists to diagnose narcissistic personalities. It also stands to reason that none of these values—a pursuit of wealth and fame, and ambivalence toward the fate of those around you—is particularly conducive to political and community engagement. What's striking is how quickly those values seem to be falling by the wayside. A few years ago, a major U.S. Census survey of Generation X—people now in their thirties and early forties—found a strong latent desire to be more involved in their communities, but they were turned off by various aspects of the institutions. In the same survey, respondents regretted that life had "come to be dominated by an 'I' mentality, rather than a 'we' mentality." But that lament doesn't seem to have even occurred to the newest generation of adults. As Putnam demonstrated, and countless surveys have since confirmed, that deep ambivalence shows up in the aging membership and failing health of our community institutions—from churches and Rotary clubs to political parties and activist groups.

The mistake that many observers repeatedly make, however, is to equate this ambivalence with disaffection. Generation X and its hippie parents may have been, on some level, rebelling against old forms of civic engagement, but that's not true of today's new voters. According to Pew, young people are far less likely than adults, and less likely than young people twenty years ago, to express contempt for government as wasteful and inefficient. They're also generally less cynical about the political system, with the vast majority (72 percent) agreeing that a vote gives people "a say in how government is run." What emerges is a picture of a generation that is not angry or disillusioned, but uninterested—a fact confirmed by numerous studies measuring the political literacy of young adults throughout the Western world.

Pew conducts an annual survey of political knowledge and in 2006 found, for example, that only 69 percent of American respondents could name the vice-president, compared with 74 percent in 1989. The same poll found that only 36 percent could name the president of Russia, compared with 47 percent who came up with the right answer in 1989. Again, the younger you were, the more likely you were to score badly. Pew reported that 56 percent of respondents aged eighteen to twenty-nine were considered to have low political knowledge, compared with just 15 percent who scored high. Similarly, Canada's Institute for Research on Public Policy issued a report in the summer of 2005, suggesting that the country is in the midst of a worsening epidemic of civic illiteracy. In 1990, a government survey found that abut 56 percent of eighteen to twenty-nine-year-olds could correctly answer no more than one out of three basic political knowledge questions (questions like "Who is the leader of the federal Liberal Party?"). That result was rightly considered dismal, but when the test was repeated in 2000, 67 percent of young voters could answer one or none of the three questions. By 2004, the results were still getting worse. For example, in the final days of the 2000 election, after more than a month of constant headlines and blanket television coverage following the campaign, only 60 percent of respondents under thirty could name Paul Martin as leader of the federal Liberals; fewer than half knew that Stephen Harper was leader of the Conservatives.

The author of the IRPP report, Henry Milner, diagnosed what he saw as a rising plague of "political dropouts" among young potential voters throughout the major Western democracies. This phenomenon, he said, is distinct from the non-voting "political protesters" of previous generations. Whereas the hippies and anarchists of the baby boom generation were often well informed but registered their discontent by staying away from the polls, today's political dropouts know little about politics and the idea of voting rarely occurs to them. "Political dropouts are of special concern, because they constitute a growing group among young people in established democracies who, despite being better educated on average, are less attentive to, and thus less well informed about, available choices than were young people in earlier generations," Milner wrote. In the words of a 2002 report on civic engagement in Canada, penned by researchers at the University of Montreal, University of Toronto, and McGill, "The problem seems to be one of disengagement rather than active discontent." The most obvious result is a steady decline in voter turnout, especially for municipal votes and by-elections that receive scant media attention. And these declines are evident in practically every major developed nation. After steady increases in voting rates between 1945 and the late 1980s, the Netherlands, Italy, Portugal, Finland, Austria, Japan, Canada, and the U.K. have all experienced near-record-low voter turnout in elections held post-2000.

Obviously, political dropouts are staying away from ballot boxes in droves, but it's not just casting a vote that leaves them cold. They also seem uninterested in many of the underlying ideas that foster community action, and those ideas seem to be falling out of vogue extremely quickly. For instance, every year in the U.K., the Henley Centre, a public sector consultancy, conducts a survey measuring Britons' attitudes toward certain social and political ideas. One question they ask every year is whether the quality of life in Britain is best improved by a) looking after community interests before their own or b) looking after themselves, which will raise standards for all. Back in 1997, 70 percent favoured a focus on community interests. Each successive year, the margin narrowed, until 2006 when, for the first time, a majority of 52 percent said it's better to look after yourself first.

It should be noted also, that this isn't just symptomatic of old democracies falling prey to the complacency born of stale institutions and taking democratic rights for granted. In China—just two decades removed from the bloody pro-democracy demonstrations in Tiananmen Square—many experts have noted the rise of that country's own "Me Generation." In the fall of 2007, Simon Elegant of *Time* magazine spent time with a group of young, urban Chinese adults and described a generation increasingly fixated on the gadgets, fashions, and status symbols of Western-style affluence, but utterly estranged from questions of politics or social justice. The writer branded their outlook as staunch "self-interested, apolitical pragmatism." These are young men and women, millions of whom were raised as only children thanks to China's one-child policy, who've seen their earning potential and wealth skyrocket in just a few years, and they see politics as irrelevant to their life aspirations. "Survey young, urban Chinese today, and you will find them drinking Starbucks, wearing Nikes and blogging obsessively," Elegant writes. "But you will detect little interest in demanding voting rights, let alone overthrowing the country's communist rulers. 'On their wish list,' says Hong Huang, a publisher of several lifestyle magazines, 'a Nintendo Wii comes way ahead of democracy.'"

That description, it turns out, could pretty much apply to young people in any Western country now swept up in the affluence and ideology of the digital age. In 2000, University of Pennsylvania researcher Peter Buckingham argued that much of the blame for this pragmatic lack of interest rests with the news media. "Young People today are postmodern citizens—cynical, distracted, no longer possessed of the civic virtues and responsibilities of older generations," he writes. "For them, conventional politics is merely an irrelevance: the personal has become the political, the private has become the public, entertainment has become education." He urged the major news organizations to heal themselves for the sake of the future. But in an era of unfettered choice, how do you reach an audience steeped in the ethos of personal gratification once it has decided it isn't interested in the message you're selling?

TAKING THE MASS OUT OF MEDIA

Back in 1976, Richard Salant, the stubborn idealist who ran CBS News for almost twenty years in the sixties and seventies, set down to codify the principles and values that guided the network's thousands of re-porters, editors, producers, and photographers. The eighty-page doc-ument covered everything from the use of anonymous sources to the proper way to cover a riot, and is still regarded by many news veterans as the defining manifesto of responsible journalism. Salant empha-sized fairness, honesty, and open-mindedness. But what he could not abide is the notion that a newsroom should be slavishly dedicated to the interests and demands of its audience.

"To the extent that radio and television are mass media of enter-tainment, it is entirely proper to give most of the people what most of them want most of the time. But we in broadcast journalism cannot, should not, and will not base our judgments on what we think viewers and listeners are 'most interested' in, or hinge our news judgment and our news treatment on our guesses as to what news the people want to hear or see."

Later in life, Salant became a little less diplomatic and a whole lot more blunt about what he saw as the responsibilities of modern media and distilled his thoughts this way: "Our job is to give people not what they want, but what we decide they ought to have." Nowadays, that quote is frequently dredged up by various opponents of the so-called "mainstream media" as prima facie evidence that news organizations have always been in the business of manipulating reality and jamming it down the throats of a gullible public.

Those close to Salant, however, knew better. They saw him lead one of the world's most important and influential news organizations through two of the most turbulent decades of the modern era, cover-ing presidential assassinations, the Pentagon Papers, the Watergate scandal, Vietnam and the Arab Oil embargo to name just a few. Salant was no manipulator, but he was patriarchal. There was stuff the public needed to know, and the public, he realized, often didn't know what it needed until it was told. He believed that the media were an essential window on democracy, that news and reliable information had a social value that couldn't be measured simply through public demand, and that potential for profit is a poor measure of journalistic merit.

It was a monopolist's view, and a naïve one. It was fine to insist on upholding standards and ignoring the pull of popular entertainment as long as 80 percent of the American public was tuning in to one of three national network broadcasts, all of which shared the same basic set of values. Under those circumstances, the audience was essentially captive, and the profits were practically guaranteed. But with the arrival of cable, and the rapid fragmentation of the audience, Salant's vision of the media as a bulwark against the tyranny of popular opinion inevitably began to erode.

Salant died in February 1993, only a short time before the Internet arrived to pound the final nail into the coffin of his ideals. Today's media environment is more vibrant and chaotic than ever, and it is almost entirely beholden to that force Salant held in such deep contempt: ratings and readership. Today, the news agenda is driven almost entirely by popular interest, and the fastest-growing news services are those that put the role of news editor in the hands of the audience. And traditional news organizations—with their lofty values, far-flung correspondents and commitment to "hard news"—are in crisis.

In 2005, American news outlets slashed about 9,500 jobs even as the U.S. economy was growing nicely. In 2006, that number rose to almost 18,000, and in 2007 another 11,700 got pink slips as major organizations like the *New York Times, Boston Globe, Baltimore Sun,* and *Time* magazine all downsized their operations. The cuts were worst in the print media, but they were certainly not confined there. Each of the four major U.S. TV networks has cut staff over the past few years.

But even with that torrid pace of cost cutting, the industry couldn't seem to keep pace with its deteriorating economics. According to the Washington-based Project for Excellence in Journalism, overall revenue in the American news media was roughly flat in 2006 from the previous year, but for the first time in a non-recession year, industry-wide profits fell, by 8 percent. In 2007, newspaper revenues fell by another 5 percent and Wall Street finally hit the panic button, driving down media stock prices by 42 percent on average, after a decline of 11 percent the year before. Not surprisingly, major media organizations came under heavy pressure for sweeping changes. Investors demanded management change from the family-owned *New York Times*; Rupert Murdoch wrested control of the *Wall Street Journal* from the Bancroft family, which had owned it for generations; the venerable Knight Ridder chain of newspapers was sold off piece by piece at the insistence of angry investors; and Tribune Co., owner of Chicago's most esteemed old newspaper, put itself up for sale, only to discover a severe shortage of interested buyers. Overall, the value of newspaper stocks shed $15 billion between 2004 and 2007. The year ended with the closure of the *Cincinnati Post* newspaper, which ceased publication after 126 years in business.

The story in broadcast industry was almost as bleak. Over the past twenty-five years, the total audience for evening network newscasts has shrunk from a little over 51 million per night, to about 26 million. Those who are watching tend to be older. Even cable news channels, which long bucked the trend of declining viewership, have seen steep declines in recent years, with the median prime-time audience slipping by 8 percent in 2006. For the first time in its history, Fox News saw its average audience decline.

The drop in ratings for traditional news outlets has corresponded with a steep decline in public respect and trust for the fourth estate. Just like every other mass market brand, the dominant icons of the news industry have been laid low by a public no longer willing to passively accept the authority of so-called "experts" to dictate what is worth knowing and why. As the Project for Excellence in Journalism reported last year, trust and respect for journalists, media companies, and the institution of the fourth estate have been in a steady decline for more than twenty years. "Since the early 1980s, the public has come to view the news media as less professional, less accurate, less caring, less moral and more inclined to cover up rather than correct mistakes." A study by the Pew Research Center for People and the Press found that

32 percent of the public considers the press to be "immoral," up from 13 percent in 1985. The number of respondents who consider journalists "unprofessional" has doubled, to 22 percent in the past twenty years. Perhaps most surprising, more than a third of Americans (36 percent) expressed the opinion that the mainstream news media "hurts democracy." Asked who they would trust to give a more accurate impression of what's happening in the war in Iraq, a majority (52 percent) favoured the military over the press (42 percent).

This trend crosses national borders, and is true of both private news organizations and the public national broadcasters supported through taxes and licensing fees. A poll last year found that 59 percent of Britons reported that they now have less respect and trust for the once-revered BBC than they used to. And a Canadian survey found that less than half of those polled said they trust journalists (roughly on par with the score for lawyers and insurance salesmen). Undoubtedly, a string of high-profile journalistic scandals has contributed to the decline, but several polls have demonstrated a long-term slide in public trust across almost every major public institution. The same 2007 Pew study found that respect for the U.S. Supreme Court, Congress, and both major political parties had all declined sharply over the past twenty years. A Gallup poll in September 2007 found that barely half of the American public expressed confidence in the ability of the federal government to handle international problems. In domestic problems, the score was even worse, with just 47 percent expressing confidence in the federal government. To get a sense of just how far that confidence has fallen, consider that in 1968 (CBC/Ekos poll), approximately 60 percent of both Canadians and Americans said they trusted government to do what was right at least most of the time. By 2002, that number had slipped to below 30 percent on both sides of the border.

As public faith in both government and media has crumbled, North Americans have put more and more faith in their own native instincts, and the power of popular opinion. While traditional news organizations have watched their audiences and profits evaporate, a new breed of news service has burst onto the scene, one perfectly suited to the demands of me-centred consumers. We are now in the age of the news aggregator sites: Google, Yahoo!, MSN, and others simply collect content from other major news organizations, organize them according to popularity, and pass them along to readers who have customized their Web settings to weed out all but what most interests them. Such sites reduce the role of news judgment to a simple algorithm, adjusted to match the pre-set preferences of you, the reader. If that's not enough control for you, then there are the so-called user-moderated sites like del.icio.us, Reddit, Newsvine, and Digg—the fastest-growing information sources in cyberspace—relying purely on the wisdom of the online masses to determine what has news value, and what does not.

Digg.com began in 2004 as a site dedicated primarily to technology news. It invited users to submit articles to the site and asked registered readers to vote on whether or not the story was useful, interesting, or worthwhile. If you liked what you read, you clicked "Digg." If you thought it was lame, you voted to "bury" it. The more Diggs a story gets, the more it rises in the rankings. In the years since Digg burst onto the scene, it has become a cultural and commercial phenomenon, making its thirty-year-old founder, Kevin Rose, an overnight multi-millionaire. The site has since branched far beyond its tech-news roots, today offering pretty much a full-service news site with stories on everything from technology and business to politics and entertainment, and there are plenty out there who argue that the mob rule of Digg is far superior to the authoritarian, top-down model espoused by the much-derided "MSM" (mainstream media). But spend much time at Digg and you'll soon remember why the words "mob mentality" connote something bad. On one random day in the late summer of 2007, while the *New York Times* was reporting on the latest from Iraq, and there were allegations that Russian fighters had bombed a village in Georgia, and as thousands of Americans were losing their homes due to toxic mortgages and rising interest rates, Digg's top stories were as follows:

#1 was a blog posting about a pornographic image that purportedly flashed onto the screen for 1/24th of a second during a debate of Democratic presidential hopefuls, hosted by CNN.

#2 was a piece from Cracked.com decrying six common Hollywood movie formulas.

#3 was a story reporting that story #1 was a hoax.

#4 was a story about a British reality show allegedly rigged by the producers.

#5 was a story about President George W. Bush's falling approval ratings.

#6 was a story about the falling U.S. dollar, which reported, incorrectly, that the greenback had fallen below the value of the Canadian dollar. (It wouldn't actually fall that low for another three months.)

To Rose and his acolytes, the eccentric and unpredictable nature of Digg's coverage is not a weakness but a virtue. There is no old white guy deciding what matters. And besides, what could be more democratic than voting on what's important? As one contributor to Digg recently posted on the site: "if the majority decides something is true, then it's the truth. Majority rule." The comedian Stephen Colbert coined the term "truthiness" as a satirical dig at the creative use of facts in politics. But to hear some tell it, truthiness is no joke. To some, reality can be bent to conform with one's own opinion. And that mindset, a quintessential by-product of the me-centred world, may already be redefining what "news" means.

Last year, a study by researchers at the John F. Kennedy School of Government at Harvard University found that the young people who make up the core of audience for sites like Digg.com aren't just uninterested in politics, they generally shy away from anything traditionally defined as "hard news." And though the younger generations are spending more time than ever immersed in media—especially TV and the Internet—almost none of their attention went to learning about major world events, according to the Harvard study. Wars, the economy, policy debates, civil liberties—none of these are of any particular interest for the majority of viewers under age thirty. Instead, their interests run more to celebrity divorces, video gaming, fashion, and movie reviews. And so, major news events often pass them by completely.

Ironically, it may be that as the sheer volume of available information has increased, the typical level of awareness of news events has fallen. How can it be that more information is increasing ignorance? The researchers concluded that the culprit is unfettered choice. Looking at news consumption over time, the study found that the proliferation of choice has created options that allow people to avoid the stuff they consider boring or confusing—and with each passing generation, people are choosing more and more to do just that. "For 150 years the daily news audience had been expanding," the authors explain. But, starting in the 1980s, "the news audience began to shrink, with young adults in the vanguard . . . the same media system that provides a rich array of news content also makes it possible for citizens to avoid the news with ease."

That, of course, helps explain why the annual list of top 10 Google and Yahoo! searches is invariably dominated by celebrities and performers, and why traditional news outlets have given over more and more of their coverage to so-called "soft news." A whole generation of consumers has come to believe that their interests and opinions are as valuable as anything the *New York Times* has to say, and major media outlets, faced with dwindling subscriber numbers and stagnant advertising revenue, feel increasing pressure to let the online masses dictate the news agenda.

Now, in theory, one might have expected that the sudden surge in competition from online aggregators might have sharpened the competitive instincts and the quality of big-name media institutions. The proliferation of news sources and the fragmentation of the audience might have sparked a battle for top talent, and a determination to hold on to their most valuable content, rather then letting online interlopers give it away for free. But that is not how the media industry has reacted to rising competition throughout its history. Faced with a fragmenting marketplace, most major newspapers have essentially given up the expensive and risky fight to be the last media outlet still trying to speak to a mass audience that isn't listening. Instead, news outlets have retreated into the world of niche marketing, and resigned themselves to a future of diminished ambitions.

In 2005, two Harvard economists, Sendhil Mullainathan and Andrei Shleifer, undertook the first systematic examination of this phenomenon in a paper they called "The Market for News." In it, they demonstrated that competition results in lower prices and more polarized coverage. Rather than trying to be a large tent, trusted and respected by mass audiences across the board, news outlets have instead narrowed their coverage to appeal to a core audience, reinforcing their connection by serving that audience what it wants to hear and see. As we've already seen, one result has been a marked increase in "soft news"—entertainment, lifestyle features, sports, and society gossip—subjects that tend to generate the most interest among all readers, but especially young readers. And when it comes to "hard news"—crime, politics, business, and public policy—the researchers found that competitive outlets "segment the market and slant toward extreme positions."

Duke University professor James Hamilton describes the modern-day Catch-22 that faces the news business as it grapples with the unmitigated market forces that place a premium on buzz over substance. The vast majority of news is delivered by private, for-profit companies which rely on advertisers for most of their revenue. Advertisers demand not just large audience numbers, but desirable audience demographics in return for their ad dollars. And so, Hamilton says, Salant's patriarchal model is out the window, replaced with a new "five-Ws" of modern reporting: "Who cares about a particular piece of information? What are they willing to pay to find it? Where can media outlets or advertisers reach these people? When is it profitable to provide the information? Why is this profitable?"

In other words, popular interest has become *the* defining characteristic of news value, as major media outlets have been forced to bend to the will of a public that expects to be catered to at all times. And as more and more of the audience, particularly the younger and wealthier ones, migrate toward online services that let them personalize their information sources, pre-selecting the news they want to receive, the mass market in news is replaced by an ever-more-fragmented array of niche media. In Joseph Pine's vocabulary, every person becomes a news market of one: vast legions of readers and viewers undisturbed by subject matter or perspectives that don't comfortably mesh with their pre-set worldview, and untroubled by questions they haven't thought to ask.

The founders of Digg and other services defend this evolution as yet another triumph of free will and consumer empowerment, but there is a more straightforward commercial motive at work too, and some potentially far-reaching effects. "There is an old saying in educational programming for children that you have to reach before you teach," Hamilton says. "That meant that educational programming for children had to always balance entertainment with instruction. At many outlets now, however, the focus is on audience numbers." In other words, it's all reach, no teach. As for those people who are out there demanding more substance, they can get it if they want, but they have become a niche market unto themselves. Does that matter? Only if you think the mass media plays an important role in the building of a healthy society and responsible government. "My personal opinion is that right now you can see areas of coverage in the U.S. where media failures help contribute to highly costly policy failures," Hamilton says. "A prime example being the Iraq war."

Of course, it's impossible to know if a more popular mass media could really prevent a policy mistake like the invasion of Iraq. The world has changed enormously. The news business Salant remembers had the luxury of focusing on its responsibility to inform citizens and act as a watchdog of government. There were only a few channels to choose from, and a dominant paper or two in each city, so commercial concerns pretty much took care of themselves. And yet, there was still no shortage of public policy disasters and government scandals. Salant's principles and huge network ratings didn't prevent Vietnam. But the fact remains that today we have more information more readily available to more people from more sources than at any time in our history, and yet we have never been so broadly uninformed about the state of our world, our communities, and our government. Is it because we've been trained to follow our base desires as consumers over our high-minded ideals as citizens? Or is the problem more about how we've come to view ourselves?

OF CONSUMERS AND CITIZENS

It's not really possible to say exactly when, but sometime in the late 1960s, years after John F. Kennedy was assassinated, "consumer" began its inexorable slide toward dirty-word status. Of course, consumerism didn't stop, or even slow down. But the word itself became synonymous with gluttony and selfishness. Along the way, a robust canon of academic analysis developed on the evils of consumerism. Everything from the breakdown of traditional "family values" and obesity to urban sprawl and the environmental crisis has been blamed, at one time or another, on the Western world's obsession with material consumption.

The latest, but by no means the last, contribution to the flourishing anti-consumerist genre came from University of Maryland professor Benjamin Barber in his 2007 bestseller, *Consumed*. In Barber's view, our "radical consumerist society" is responsible for the "infantilization" of adults and the destruction of citizenship in practically every major Western nation. Barber argues that the market economy and capitalism used to be okay when it emphasized production and virtue, but it has since been distorted into a philosophy focused solely on consumption and vice. Anyone looking for the root causes of a decline in general morality; the boom in cosmetic surgery; the rise of video gaming; the popularity of *Harry Potter, Lord of the Rings,* and *Spider-Man;* obesity; and the decline of proper business attire can find it here. All of this and much more, Barber argues, is the result of thinking adults becoming enslaved by their desire to buy stuff. Marketers and merchandisers, "these avatars of consumer capitalism" are "seeking to encourage adult regression, hoping to rekindle in grown-ups the tastes and habits of children so that they can sell globally the relatively useless cornucopia of games, gadgets, and myriad consumer goods for which there is no discernible 'need market' other than the one created by capitalism's own frantic imperative to sell."

Like most critics, Barber equates the rise of consumerism with a right-wing political philosophy tied to the dark powers of big business. But the roots of this mindset are more nuanced than that, according to Harvard University historian Lizabeth Cohen. The American president who put consumers on the political map wasn't some fulminating right-wing free marketer, doing the bidding of his deep-pocketed Wall Street backers. It was John F. Kennedy, still seen as a hero to the liberal American middle class, and he did so over the screaming objections of big business. In 1960, campaigning for the White House against Richard Nixon, Kennedy framed his candidacy around protecting the rights of consumers against the big industrial and commercial interests just then gaining steam in the U.S. economy. "The consumer is the only man in our economy without a high-powered lobbyist. I intend to be that lobbyist," he said.

Two years later, he sent the first-ever Consumer Bill of Rights to Congress. It amounted to a declaration that American buyers have the right, in Cohen's words, "to safety, to be informed, to choose and to be heard." Cohen calls this the spark of the modern consumer movement, and it would ultimately prove even more influential than Roosevelt's New Deal. Kennedy's decision to champion the needs of consumers stretched far beyond his death and was responsible for much of the American regulatory framework that still exists today—a system of checks and official oversight that has been emulated and extended around the world. The strengthening of the Federal Trade Commission and Food and Drug Administration; the establishment of the Highway Safety Bureau; the National Commission on Product Safety; the Environmental Protection Agency; and a host of legislation covering everything from air quality to flammable fabrics, toxic chemicals, and truth in lending can all be traced back to the ascendancy of consumerism in the political process.

Like many academics, Cohen makes it clear that she is no great fan of the way consumerism has evolved in the years since Kennedy. She laments consumerism's drift away from the pursuit of a more just and responsive system. But to observers like Michael Schudsen, a distinguished professor at the University of California at San Diego, this distinction between virtuous citizens on the one hand and venal consumers on the other, is both false and misleading. In reality, it is impossible to separate the evolution of a consumer economy from the development of democratic institutions. The American Revolution began as a commercial revolt against unjust consumer taxation imposed by Britain on its American colony. The civil rights movement was, in important ways, a fight by black consumers for the right to more fully participate in American society. It was, of course, a struggle for fundamental equality. But many of the most immediate expressions of that injustice, the everyday things that actually mobilized people, existed in the realm of consumer rights: the right to eat at the same restaurants, to swim in the same pools, and to sit in the same bus seats as their white counterparts. In both the American Revolution and the civil rights movement, people had currency before they had full democratic liberty. The exercise of one helped bring about the other.

Nevertheless, the demonization of consumerism has been a recurrent theme in Western culture for generations. In his essay "Citizens, Consumers and the Good Society," Schudsen quotes one-time presidential nominee John Dewey, way back in 1927, blaming the decline of responsible citizenship on the newfound financial freedom of American shoppers. "The movie, radio, cheap reading material and motor car" all served to divert attention from the sober and serious business of government and politics, he said. But this enduring perspective "offers a narrow and misleading view of consumer behaviour as well as an absurdly romantic view of civic behaviour," Schudsen writes. Consumers have long used their buying power to articulate political values— avoiding products from certain countries, favouring some merchants over others. At the same time, people have used their votes and their political influence for nakedly selfish objectives, such as ad hoc "Not In My Back Yard" movements that mobilize to keep halfway houses and garbage dumps confined to less affluent counties. "Nimbyism and blatant pandering to political elites, while civic in nature, are every bit as self-centred as the most vain consumerism," he says.

But, as Schudsen concedes, both "consumer and civic behaviour and styles are in flux." And that is important. We are all both consumers and citizens and our approach to both roles is being redefined with each passing generation of new adults. And that shift is being reflected in the way we buy, as well as the way we vote. In 2002, Swedish sociologist Li Bennich-Bjorkman suggested that political life in the West had entered a "post-collective phase" and that governments have begun to act "post-institutionally." In practice, this means people are no longer willing to settle for simply "having a voice" in some large, impersonal state apparatus. They expect action on their individual priorities, in keeping with their rights as a sovereign consumer. This can be seen in the subtle change in the meaning of being "a taxpayer." Whereas people used to invoke that phrase to convey that they had, like good citizens, made their contribution to the greater good, people today tend to interpret it as a statement that they can expect to be catered to, as someone buying services from the state. They have a right to expect satisfaction, regardless of what impact that might have on others. It's this shift that people really have in mind when they talk about citizens versus consumers—it's a more fundamental and far-reaching tension between "the self-centred and the public spirited," Schudsen says.

That struggle is at the root of what W. Lance Bennett has called "a generational shift" in what it means to be a citizen. Western voters are transforming from what he calls the "dutiful citizen" model of earlier generations, to the "actualizing citizen" model, best exemplified by young adults and teenagers throughout North America and Europe. Simply put, people in their late teens and twenties, as well as many in their thirties, reject the notion that they have an obligation or a duty to participate in the political process and to contribute time and energy to community organizations. They favour what Bennett calls "loosely-networked activism to address issues that reflect personal values."

This is explicitly confirmed by a trove of polling data collected over the past few years. The Pew study of Generation Next revealed that just 62 percent of the American population now believes it is their "duty as a citizen to always vote." Among voters twenty-five and under, just 42 percent agree. Among that youngest group, just 50 percent said they feel guilty for not voting—the least likely of any group to feel that way. A similar result emerged from Henry Milner's 2005 study for the Institute for Research on Public Policy. Among Canadians under twenty-five, only 18 percent said they feel guilty for not voting. Among fifteen to twenty-five year olds, "only 38 percent say that citizenship entails special obligations, while 58 percent say simply being a good person is enough." In Europe, too, young people consistently rate voting as less important, and less of a duty, than older people do, Milner says.

To the "actualizing citizen" described by Bennett, the responsibilities all belong to the government, and the rights belong to the individual. Politics is not a means to achieve common goals on behalf of a community, but a system in which individuals express personal preferences and advance individual priorities. This attitude is not wrong, but it is a fundamental reinterpretation of civic life.

The gradual rise of the self-centred, at the expense of the public-spirited, is not about consumerism but narcissism, and the distinction is an important one to recognize. Contrary to what so many cultural critics maintain, we are not voiceless, powerless victims, manipulated by forces beyond our control to do things that we otherwise wouldn't. Our world is shaped by the priorities expressed and the decisions made by independent, educated adults, raised with better access and understanding of the political system than any previous generation. We are the authors of these changes, and both business and government are responding to the new demands of an increasingly fragmented, inward-looking political and commercial marketplace.

PUBLIC POLICY, MADE TO ORDER

In the winter of 2004, Tony Blair's Labour Party government was in the midst of a sweeping set of changes to the way that country's public services were structured. The prime minister put out the call to various interest groups, inviting input on what the future of social services in Britain should look like. Perhaps the most definitive and revolutionary recommendation came from the National Consumer Council's Policy Commission on Public Services.

"Traditional concepts of citizenship are problematic," the council concluded. "Engagement and trust in the electoral process is declining and voting rights confer limited influence over the direct provision of services ... If public services are to respond to the plurality and diversity of consumer demand, the catch-all term 'citizen' is unhelpful when it assumes there is a homogeneous 'citizen interest' ... It is more helpful to think about the plurality of individuals as consumers, stakeholders and individuals."

The NCC was suggesting, in effect, that government abandon the notion of a monolithic public interest, and focus instead on the millions of individual priorities and needs, each of which must be treated with the same weight. Decades ago, this might have been shocking, but by the time the council made its recommendations public, this line of thinking was already well established in British politics. Back in 1987, Margaret Thatcher was already well into her battle to strip down the U.K.'s mammoth and creaky social support system, when she told the London *Sunday Times* that, henceforth, government would work on behalf of the individual. "There is no such thing as society," she said. "The quality of our lives will depend upon how much each of us is prepared to take responsibility for ourselves."

Back then, the Labour party railed against Thatcher. Just over a decade later, those same ideas had become the driving philosophy behind the Labour government's new vision of social services. The mantra for New Labour's public sector reforms was "choice" and flexibility and the introduction of more flexibility and more private commercial involvement in the system. As far back as 2000, Blair had promised to reform the National Health Service from a "get what you are given" service, to one dedicated to a "get what you want" commercial mindset. The NHS dedicated itself to publishing more information so people could decide which hospitals they could use, even which doctors would treat them and how.

Emboldened by a resounding re-election win in 2001, Blair resolved to push his desire to "personalize" public services even further in his second term. No more would government offer a one-size-fits-all social safety net, Blair said. From now on, hospitals, schools, employment offices, licensing bureaus, and regulators would be "customer focused" and the whole public sector would be "re-branded."

"Choice puts the levers in the hands of parents and patients so that they as citizens and consumers can be a driving force for improvement in their public services," Blair said in 2004. "We are proposing to put an entirely different dynamic in place to drive our public services; one where the service will be driven not by the government or by the manager but by the user—the patient, the parent, the pupil and the law-abiding citizen."

The You Sell had most definitely come to the public sector. Just as Dell was inviting people to design their own computer; TiVo was putting people in control of their TV schedule; iPod was urging people to overturn the structure of the music business; and L'Oreal was assuring people that "you're worth it," world leaders were turning the reins of the public sector over to the infallible judgment of millions of individuals. As John Clarke and Janet Newman of the U.K.'s The Open University noted in a 2005 paper on the subject, "the imagery that pervades New Labour discourse on public service reform is derived directly from the market model (competition between providers; choice exercised by a 'sovereign' consumer in pursuit of individual wants.)" So popular was the program that Britain's Conservative party soon adopted essentially the same mantra—a vocabulary of self-sufficiency that was now spreading through the political discourse of virtually every developed nation.

Around the same time that Tony Blair was championing choice in Britain's social services, U.S. president George W. Bush embarked on an overhaul of the American social security system, part of a wider domestic policy initiative dubbed "the ownership society." The White House proposed to phase out the system of providing guaranteed social security benefits to retirees, instead giving Americans the option to divert part of their payroll taxes into personal retirement savings accounts, which they would control. Rather than government's cumbersome system and its paltry returns, individuals would be able to direct their social security investments like a personal stock portfolio. In early 2005, Bush embarked on an aggressive cross-country promotion tour, saying the reforms would "modernize" social security, telling audiences he was offering "a retirement iPod"—personalized and designed for the twenty-first century.

Beyond social security, the ownership society involved broad tax cuts, incentives for home ownership ("helping families help themselves") and tax-free health savings accounts ("more choices in health care"). In essence, the whole agenda revolved around a shift of emphasis away from the State and onto the individual—a road map for smaller government and increased personal responsibility.

Aside from the massive tax cuts that were enacted starting in 2001, the key elements of Bush's plan ran aground in 2006 when the

Democrats won control of both branches of Congress, but not because the ownership society was wildly unpopular with the American public. In fact, most polling showed deep divisions over the plan, with most people supporting the idea of increased control, but fearful of the erosion of the social safety net that went along with it. It's worth noting, however, that the plan tended to be most popular with young voters—a 2005 poll of several thousand young adults found that 74 percent of those under twenty-five supported Bush's plan to privatize social security. Nevertheless, the social security agenda mainly fell victim to its enormous price tag (it would have required more than a trillion dollars of funding in the early years) and because the White House was forced to focus energy on the war in Iraq. Many elements of the ownership society, however, remain integral to Republican party policy, and the mindset behind that agenda continues to flourish.

Since 2000, a long line of developed countries, including France, Germany, Sweden, Canada, Japan, and Mexico, has elected governments focused, to varying degrees, on tax cuts, a reduction in the size of the state, and policies aimed squarely at "actualizing citizens." In every instance, the You Sell has been integral to the message. For example, in late 2005, the Canadian federal election was fought largely on two competing visions for providing Canadians with better access to child care. On the one hand, the Liberal party was advocating a centralized multi-billion-dollar national system that would open public daycares and would license private operators to provide a standardized early-childhood curriculum. It was an old-school, collectively funded institutional answer to a social problem—exactly the kind of sweeping program Western governments are increasingly hesitant to offer these days. The response from the Conservative party was to offer parents a monthly $100 cheque for every child under age five. It was a policy made of what Bennich-Bjorkman called the "post-institutional" world, and it had the You Sell written all over it. The Conservatives said, in effect, "Hey, parents, nobody knows what's best for your kid better than you do. So, whether you choose to put your child in daycare, or to stay home, or to leave the kids with family during the day, the government is going to send you $100 a month to help defray the costs. How you use the money will be up to you."

Not only was the Conservative plan cheaper and easier to understand, it appealed simultaneously to the narcissism of the electorate and popular disenchantment with large-scale government programs perceived as social engineering. Soon there were rallies taking place across the country in support of the Conservative plan under the banner "Fund the child (not the system)." What was, arguably, the defining moment of the child care debate came during a TV news program when a Liberal strategist said that the centralized plan was superior because it's irresponsible to send monthly cheques to parents with no control over how that money would be spent. The money, he said, would be blown on "beer and popcorn." The Conservatives leapt on that quote and used it to portray the Liberals as arrogant and disdainful of the individual judgment of parents. It was political suicide to tell a narcissistic electorate that government knows better, especially so bluntly. By emphasizing the idea that Canadians should be free to keep more of their hard-earned income and to choose how that money is spent, without big-government interference, the Conservatives pulled off what had been seen as a highly unlikely election victory.

That central message—that government should cater to the beliefs of individuals and should not tell taxpayers how to live their lives—has become paramount in modern political campaigning and in the design of public services. Parents know best, so school boards from Edmonton to New Orleans are building specialized schools to cater to the special skills and needs of different children, some focused on the arts, others on math and sciences, others on athletics. The U.K. is now considering developing hospital league tables: ranking different hospitals on patient outcomes so that "health care consumers" can decide where they want to have their knee replaced. And throughout the West, public services increasingly rely on user fees rather than taxation. In every case, "choice" is the watchword.

Even in the rare cases when a politician boldly champions a large-scale government initiative, it must be couched in the vocabulary of the You Sell. Thus, when Hillary Clinton was looking to strike just the right populist note, she turned to an Internet vote to select her campaign song. The winner was Celine Dion's "You and I." When Clinton made a mandatory national health insurance program the centre-piece of her presidential campaign platform, it was dubbed "The American Health Choices Plan" and she rushed to assure supporters that what she proposed "is not government-run health care." Instead, she insisted, government would provide tax subsidies for Americans to buy the type of coverage that best suited their needs. Everyone would be required to have it, just as all drivers are required to have car insurance, but Americans could choose their provider and their level of coverage. Not surprisingly, when Clinton was defeated as the Democratic nominee for the 2008 presidential election, it was by a rival who had made even better use than she had of You Sell principles to brand his campaign.

Early in 2008, conservative commentator Rush Limbaugh mocked Barack Obama's lack of specific policy proposals, saying that the Illinois senator was attempting to be a "blank canvas upon which anyone can project their fantasies or desires." Limbaugh meant it as an insult, as a suggestion that Obama was not prepared for the difficult choices involved in running the country. In reality, Limbaugh's assessment was a perfect description of Obama's success at employing the central strategy of the You Sell—and a direct echo of the stated goal of companies like Dell Computer, to be the "blank canvas" on which people project their lives. Obama was successful, not by promising any specific policies, but by talking about "change" and "restoring hope"—themes that allowed people to see themselves in him. It was an expansive promise to be "different"—whatever "different" happens to mean to you.

TAKE YOUR PICK

In the era of the You Sell, promising greater choice and avoiding any suggestion of rigid rules is absolutely essential to political success. No politician in their right mind would suggest that government, with approval ratings hovering in the teens, knows better than individuals. But is greater choice and personal control really the highest ideal of civic life in the modern era? And is the explosion of information, options, and alternatives really likely to make for more satisfied citizens in the long run?

A few years ago, two graduate students from Columbia University and Stanford tested that very question. Sheena Iyengar and Mark Lepper noted that "the human ability to desire and manage choice is infinite." The supposition that "the more choices the better...pervades our economics, norms and customs." The question was this: Is there such a thing as "choice overload"? Put another way, people may think they want to control every facet of their lives, choosing from a huge array of alternatives, but does choice reach a point when it is self-defeating?

To test the limits of our choice obsession, the researchers designed three experiments. In the first, they set up a tasting booth at a fancy grocery store, and offered people samples of various jams and a coupon to buy the one they liked most. Half the group was offered six alternatives, the other half got to choose from twenty-four flavours. In the second study, students in a university class were offered the chance to write a short two-page essay as an extra-credit assignment. Half the students were offered six topics to choose from, and the other group could pick from a list of thirty potential essay subjects. The final experiment worked much like the first, except the subjects were offered chocolates and were split into three groups. One group got to sample six chocolates and were offered a coupon to buy their favourite, another group got the chance to choose from thirty alternatives, and a control group was given no alternatives: they just got a chocolate randomly selected on their behalf and were given a coupon to buy more if they wanted.

What the studies found was a startlingly consistent pattern: first, and not surprisingly, we are attracted to greater choice. People were a lot more likely to stop at the tasting booth when they saw lots of jams to pick from instead of just a few. However, having more options didn't lead people to sample more options—whether there were six or twenty-four jams on the table, people typically sampled just one or two. The really important discoveries, though, had to do with buying behaviour. In both the food studies, the people who were given many choices were far less likely to buy *any* jam or chocolate than those who were picking from a smaller range of alternatives. The authors concluded that when people are presented with a wide array of choices, they are far more likely to feel overwhelmed and simply walk away. What's more, when the people with more choices did decide to buy chocolates, they ended up less satisfied with their selection than those who had just a few options. The more we have to choose from, the more we wonder whether we made the right choice. When it came to the essays, a similar pattern emerged. Again, students were more likely to complete the assignment when they had just a few topics to choose from. Just as fascinating—the students with more limited options tended to produce higher-quality work.

This is where the effect of choice differs from the designer effect identified by Frank Piller's watch studies. As we've seen, people are very attached to and place a high value on things we feel we *made*. But the same doesn't necessarily hold true for things we have *chosen*. As Iyengar and Lepper pointed out, a few limited choices are better than no choice at all, but when it comes to offering unlimited freedom of choice, there is a gap between what we say we want and what we actually respond to. In fact, it may be that more choice is actually de-motivating because it exposes our lack of expertise. Confronted with many options, we put pressure on ourselves to make the right call, and that anxiety—always wondering if we did the right thing—drains away much of the satisfaction that comes from a feeling of control.

All of that, of course, has huge implications when considered in the context of politics, "control," and the You Sell. Could it be that, in the rush to put individual citizen choices at the forefront of our public policy, we are actually discouraging people from active involvement? Does the You Sell, though superficially appealing, actually help make our lives too complicated to easily navigate? And if that is contributing to the decline of our public institutions and encouraging people to be political dropouts, is technology, information, and the impulse to focus even more on a narrow vision of "personal democracy" really the answer?

ALL IN OUR ECHO CHAMBERS

Back in the darkened auditorium of Pace University, the discussion remains firmly rooted in the goal of individual empowerment and the potential for technology to personalize the democratic experience. The Web, it is said, lets everyone engage on their own terms, making us all the stars of our own political movements. Above all, the Web is a tool for connecting with the like-minded. And in the search for the precious common ground that yields true political power, it serves as an elaborate sorting filter, keeping out everything except what we invite into our sphere of influence.

All the talk of virtual receiving lines and political outreach through Facebook is infused with an infectious optimism and a self-righteous confidence that these people are involved in reclaiming democracy on behalf of the people. Their faith is refreshing, and understandable. Throughout history we've held to the belief that if we're ever going to find the perfect realization of our democratic impulse, and achieve world peace, social justice, and universal prosperity—it'll be through the wonders of innovation and technology. In his book *The Victorian Internet*, Tom Standage recounts how political and social elites expected the telegraph would make wars a thing of the past. The idea was that wars were largely a function of miscommunication. They were certainly irrational, almost always costing all parties involved far more in blood and treasure than they could ever hope to achieve through victory. So, with the ability to communicate clearly and quickly across great distances, enlightened leaders would avoid war by finding more civilized means to resolve their differences. Just as the telegraph was reaching the height of its technological power, World War I came along and shattered their optimism, demonstrating that wars are often fought between rivals that communicate perfectly well.

The advent of radio and television triggered a similar wave of optimism about the impact that wide and reliable dissemination of information would have on the political process. It's much the same argument advanced here at the Personal Democracy Forum regarding the Internet. But all that is based on the belief that good citizenship rests on access to information, and the Web is a phenomenal tool for accessing information. But evidence continues to mount that suggests the Web (and all the various communications technologies that go along with it) is not having the impact on civic participation that its proponents expect.

Bruce Bimber, a former director of the Center for Information Technology and Society at the University of California–Santa Barbara, was among those who had predicted a decade ago that the "information revolution" would crack the dominance of mainstream media and political parties, leading to viable minor party campaigns and more effective grassroots organizing. But in 2001, he released the results of a study showing that there was no connection between the use of information technologies and political engagement. Echoing the conclusions of previous studies by the likes of U.C.–San Diego's Michael Schudsen, Bimber agreed that an analysis of voting patterns "fails to support the thesis of a positive correlation between the evolution of informational and communicational resources and levels of citizen engagement. If any correlation exists, it may actually be negative," he wrote. "Neither access to the Internet nor use of the Internet to obtain campaign information is predictive of voting or other forms of political participation." In 2003, Bimber published a book titled *Information and American Democracy*, in which he threw cold water on the notion that the Internet would spark a renaissance of informed citizenship and community involvement. The Internet "doesn't generate interest in politics," he said at the time. "It satisfies an interest in politics. Those who are disinterested and disengaged aren't going out and poking around."

So, the information revolution isn't likely to draw legions of political dropouts back into the system, but that's not to say it's having no impact, Bimber says. On the one hand, he says, technology is making it easier for interest groups to organize and get their message out, but at the same time "the technology is intensifying narrow-interest politics. While it makes it easier for like-minded people to find each other, it also makes it easier for them to avoid people and information they don't agree with." In other words, just as our cities and our consumer products facilitate our desire to withdraw into our own cocoons, the rapid advances of the Web are facilitating a kind of intellectual withdrawal into a world dominated by preconceived notions and unchallenged biases.

The first prominent person to warn of this phenomenon was Cass Sunstein, a legal scholar and professor at the University of Chicago, who wrote the 2001 book *Republic.com*, in which he described the tendency of Web users to filter unwelcome information, creating a "daily me" compendium of news sources and message boards that already fit neatly into a pre-built world view. This echo chamber effect means that "the increased power of individual choice allows people to sort themselves into innumerable homogeneous groups, which often results in amplifying their pre-existing views ... a system of 'gated communities' is as unhealthy in cyberspace as it is in the real world."

Sunstein's subsequent work suggested that when like-minded people get together to discuss and deliberate on the issues of the day, with little or nothing in the way of dissenting views represented they tend not only to reinforce each other's ideas, but to amplify them. In effect, liberal-minded people will emerge with even more staunchly liberal ideas and even more contempt for conservatives than they had going in. The same is true of those on the other side of the political spectrum. If Sunstein is right, then the emerging world of Internet echo chambers will not only fail to produce a more meaningful and productive public discourse, it may actually be contributing to the intense polarization of politics seen in recent years.

Sunstein's warning about withdrawing into our proverbial gated communities seems increasingly pertinent given the explosion of millions of personal weblogs, or blogs, in recent years. Troll through any of the major political blogs attracting bigger and bigger audiences today, and you'll find more intense and naked partisanship than even the most opinionated of the traditional media. Comments are typically resounding endorsements of the blog's dominant ideology, or vitriolic denunciations—and have the effect of virtual "keep out" signs to anyone who might want to disagree or calmly contradict. As for YouTube and the other meccas of user-generated material on the Web, even Google's Schmidt acknowledges that these new media are primarily geared toward simple, punchy, emotional, and humorous messages. Complexity, nuance, and moderation—these are the endangered commodities of the "information age."

But in the era of the political You Sell, in which the masses are being urged to grab control of everything, the purveyors of personal democracy aren't about to get caught up in a self-defeating argument over whether democracy was ever meant to be a solo endeavour, much less whether technology spreads ignorance as efficiently as enlightenment. "We don't make value judgments about how people choose to personalize the service," Schmidt says as the hushed personal democrats in the audience type his words into cyberspace in real time. "Of course people shouldn't have a narrow point of view. Obviously, Google can be used to make people more narrow, and that's not a good thing. But narrow-minded people will be narrow-minded with or without Google. But as long as you're searching you're learning. And I would *hope* people will choose to learn as broadly as possible."

That may sound like a cop-out, but in Schmidt's defence, he is the CEO of a huge corporation with public shareholders expecting the company to grow and turn a profit. He is not the guardian of democracy and he is not the authority charged with forcing people to use the Web for the greater good. This phenomenon is bigger than Google, bigger even than the Internet. The forces driving us into our personal bubbles, prompting us to dispense with civic literacy in favour of light entertainment, to value freedom of choice above all else, and to abandon all the subtle but important connections that amalgamate groups of individuals into true communities—these impulses come from within us, and they've been building since long before the Internet came along.

Schmidt and his associates at Google are at the vanguard of the Ego Boom, and they're making a fortune by giving people what they want, when they want it. Still, all this rapturous talk about the triumph of free expression and limitless curiosity seems a little disingenuous from a guy who knows better than anyone that the top search on GoogleNews in 2006 was Paris Hilton, followed by Orlando Bloom.

Does it matter if people opt out of political participation, go their own way, and base their lives around the question "What's in it for me?" There are certainly many who would argue that the public interest is best served when all individuals simply pursue their own self-interest and pretty much let the chips fall where they may. But it's worth remembering that two of the earliest advocates of Western democracy would have cautioned against that line of thinking. John Adams, one of the founding fathers, and the second president of the United States, wrote that freedom rests on two cornerstones: the knowledge and virtue of its citizens. We've already seen what's becoming of our political knowledge, but virtue is more complicated. Adams defined it, in the words of historian Robert Bresler, as "the capacity of a people to place limits on their appetite, respect the rights of others, and be willing to put the interests of the country before their own." It was this delicate balance between knowledge, virtue, and self-interest that made a free society possible, without devolving into anarchy and civil war.

Even Alexis de Tocqueville, one of the earliest admirers of Republican democracy, worried that the allure of individualism might be our undoing one day. In their 2000 translation of de Tocqueville's classic *Democracy in America*, Delba Winthrop and Harvey Mansfield noted that the author was fearful that a culture of self-absorption might one day undermine self-government. "With unlimited choices, unsure of everything and passionate about little else but securing their comfort, people will be tempted to surrender responsibility for making their own decisions." With participation rates plunging, in a time of unprecedented wealth, exploding choice, and unfettered access to information, Tocqueville's warning seems to have come true.

As always, we've put our faith in technology to save us. But while "personal democracy" is most definitely part of a booming growth industry, it's still not clear that it is the solution to our democratic funk. The evidence so far suggests it's only a symptom of it.

CHAPTER SIX

THE QUEST FOR THE PERFECT QUEST

"You are the Michelangelo of your own life. The David you are sculpting is you."

—*The Secret*

"Narcissism: When one grows too old to believe in one's uniqueness, one falls in love with one's complexity."

—John Fowles

"**A**re you an inspiration to others?"

This is The Secret Expo, Toronto's inaugural trade show and speakers series devoted to all things related (and, in many cases, tangential) to *The Secret*, the record-shattering, Oprah-endorsed book and film by Australian reality-TV producer Rhonda Byrne. First released on the Internet as a ninety-minute film in February 2006, *The Secret* was passed around via word of mouth, and within a matter of months it became one of the greatest viral marketing success stories of all time. In November 2006, Atria Books, a division of Simon & Schuster, turned the film into a book which, according to the *New York Times*, was cobbled together in less than a month. Echoing the aesthetic of the film, the book was packaged *Da*

Vinci Code–style, with faux parchment paper, a hodgepodge of symbology, and a big red wax seal on the cover, conveying something ancient and revelatory inside. By March 2007, *The Secret* had been featured on the covers of *USA Today*, *Newsweek*, and the *New York Times* "Sunday Styles" section, and secured spots on ten different bestseller lists in the U.S. alone. Major retailers couldn't keep it in stock, to the point where Judith Curr, the executive vice-president and publisher of Atria, put a rush on two million more copies, and entreated booksellers to please, please be patient. People couldn't get enough of the message.

Simply put, the *Secret* in question is "The Law of Attraction"—the idea that if you think positive thoughts, you will attract positive things into your life. If you think negative things, you will attract negative things. "Thoughts are magnetic and they have a frequency," *The Secret* tells us. "As you think, those thoughts are sent out into the Universe, and they magnetically attract all *like* things that are on the same frequency. Everything sent out returns to the source. And that source is You." In other words, Intelligent Design does indeed exist—only what you may not have realized is that the Designer is not "out there." He or She is staring right back at you in the mirror. "It's like having the Universe as your catalogue," says Dr. Joe Vitale, one of *The Secret*'s featured teachers, a former Amway executive who now works as a certified hypnotherapist, metaphysical practitioner, ordained minister, Chi Kung healer, and is, according to his bio, "one of the top marketing specialists in the world." Just place an order and wait for your delivery. People have used *The Secret* to bring about vast fortunes, beautiful homes, great romances, dream jobs, expensive cars, fine jewellery and the best parking spot in the lot—every time! The world, according to the Law of Attraction, is your playground, existing solely for the purpose of making your every dream come true—that is, if you know how to wield your power. "If you see it in your mind," *The Secret* reads, "you're going to hold it in your hand."

Rhonda Byrne, the woman behind the mania, is something like the

J.K. Rowling of self-help. An attractive, middle-aged, blue-eyed blonde of mysterious mien, she has an apparent gift for spinning fantasy, and a personal rags-to-riches story propelled by magic. Legend has it Byrne was inspired to create *The Secret* after a particularly trying period in her life. Her world was in shambles. She was deeply in debt. Her father had died. Then one day, her daughter gave her a chin-up note, along with a book called *The Science of Getting Rich* by Wallace D. Wattles, a classic self-help text written in 1910, and just like that, everything changed. In this book, Byrne caught her first whiff of the Secret, and so she began manically—actually quite breathlessly, as it is re-enacted in the film—tracing it back through time, and was stunned to discover that "the greatest people in history" had all known it: Shakespeare, Plato, Newton, Hugo, Beethoven, Lincoln, Emerson, Edison, Einstein, and many others! (Byrne's sheer enthusiasm is almost enough to compensate for an utter lack of supporting evidence.) "In a few short weeks," she says, "I had traced the Secret back through the centuries, and I had discovered the modern-day practitioners of the Secret." Which would seem to suggest that either Rhonda Byrne is one of the most proficient researchers and speed-readers of all time, or that the Secret in question really wasn't that cunningly concealed after all.

Still, in early February 2007, Oprah Winfrey—the Midas of mainstream legitimacy—gave *The Secret* her seal of approval by featuring it on her show for the first of two times. The week after the first hour-long segment aired, Nielsen Book Scan reported that weekly sales of the book jumped from 18,000 to 101,000 copies. The following week, 190,000 copies were sold. By May 2007, 3.8 million copies were in print in the U.S. alone, and an estimated 1.5 million DVDs had been sold, not including those downloaded from *The Secret*'s elaborate website. It was a bestseller in the U.S., Canada, England, Australia, and Ireland.

Back in Toronto, riding the momentum of Byrne's commercial success, The Secret Expo is "dedicated to bringing *The Secret* of Health, Wealth and Happiness" to the city. Wandering around, visitors are invited to stop in at dozens of booths offering goods and services ostensibly designed to facilitate the Law of Attraction—everything from financial services to organic teas, anti-aging and weight loss treatments, aromatherapies, inspirational music, love-finding services, and natural migraine and snoring treatments. On hand are chiropractors, biofeedback experts, psychic mediums, and personal consultants, all pushing some vague interpretation of *The Secret*'s philosophy. Downstairs, lectures are taking place. Dr. Ben Johnson, one of many doctors featured in *The Secret* (but "the only actual M.D!"), is there to speak about something called "The Healing Codes." Jack Canfield, author of the *Chicken Soup for the Soul* books and *The Success Principles*—who has emerged as the *pater familias* of *The Secret* clan of teachers—is answering questions via satellite at the "Ask Jack Tele-clinic."

In one of the large beige conference rooms, Marcia Martin is giving a speech called "The Secret in Action" to a crowd of about 120, mostly women. Martin, an attractive, vivacious woman in her early sixties—who is described first and foremost as a "good friend of Rhonda Byrne" in the event marketing material—has been involved in the New Age movement for decades. She is a co-founder of Erhard Seminars Training (EST), a training and educational company which grew out of the human potential movement in the seventies and later became the Landmark Forum. She has been giving training seminars on the Law of Attraction for decades to everyone from the debt-ridden, the love-lorn, and the health-challenged to corporate executives from Chase Bank, Capital One, and Remax. Behind the scenes, Martin played a pivotal role in creating *The Secret* phenomenon.

In 2004, Martin, along with her long-time friend Jack Canfield, co-founded the Transformational Leadership Council, an organization of teachers, trainers, thought leaders, authors, moviemakers, and coaches of "personal and organizational transformation." "It was so that we could get together and hang out and have fun and learn from each other and kind of have a colleague experience together," says

Martin in a post-seminar interview. The TLC started out with about thirty members, and in its short life it has expanded to include over one hundred "thought leaders," including John Gray of *Men are From Mars, Women are from Venus* fame, and other best-selling self-help authors, such as Wayne Dyer and Marianne Williamson.

Amid all the *Secret* hype, one thing more or less overlooked about the story was the symbiotic relationship the franchise enjoyed with the Transformational Leadership Council, and by extension the entire spirituality industrial complex. In 2005, the TLC was planning to descend on Aspen for an official meeting of minds to compare paradigms and swap tales of transformation. One day, Martin, who was in charge of programming for the meeting, received a phone call from Byrne, then a stranger, saying she was making a documentary about the Law of Attraction. Almost every one of the "living teachers" Byrne wanted to interview would be at this meeting, and she wanted to know if she could pop in with a film crew.

At first, Martin says, Canfield advised her to decline, believing a film crew would be too distracting. But Marcia's inner voice told her that it was important for Byrne to come. "I called Jack back and I said, 'You know, if you give it the go-ahead, I promise the meeting will run perfectly and it won't be a distraction. We'll set it up so it runs great.' So he says, 'Ok, I guess so,' which I always laugh about because he became a really wonderful big star. A lot more people know about him as a result of *The Secret* than any of the things he's done." And so the bulk of *The Secret* was filmed at the posh Snowmass Club in Aspen in July 2005 in a small executive office outfitted with a green screen. All the special effects and the overwrought dramatizations were added later. The total cost of the film was $3 million.

In January 2006, the TLC hosted another official meeting and Byrne turned up to give a special advance screening of her film to the group. "It was really funny because we all sort of said to each other, 'This is going to be a very boring film,'" says Martin. "I mean, what can you do with a bunch of heads talking?" But they were "stunned and amazed," she says. "In ninety-five minutes, we realized that this was going to change humankind. We were so inspired. Because you have to understand, we're a group of people that has spent thirty or forty years of our lives changing mindsets and creating new paradigms and having people wake up and become more enlightened and here was a film that did it in ninety-five minutes." The TLC members are also a group with influence, with a combined network of millions of people, Martin says. "If we make a recommendation, people actually usually do what we say." Each person in the screening room that day, says Martin, was a top trainer and teacher with decades' worth of loyal graduates. "We were so impressed with the film that of course we got right on the computer and sent out messages, 'You have to see this movie!' So it became an Internet sensation really overnight. It became a number one bestseller on the Internet *way* before Oprah."

Byrne became a multi-millionaire off the TLC members' teachings and in return many of them were lavished with more press coverage than they'd ever been able to manifest on their own. Attendance at their seminars swelled. And although a critical backlash did ensue, *The Secret* whetted the public's appetite for cosmic short-cuts. An avalanche of spinoff books was released: *The Secret: Universal Mind Meditation*; *Law of Attraction: The Science of Attraction More of What You Want and Less of What You Don't*; *The Law of Attraction: The Basics of the Teachings of Abraham*; *The Secret: Unlocking the Source of Joy and Fulfillment*; *The Secret: What Great Leaders Know—And Do*; *The Secret Gratitude Book; Bliss: Tribute to the Secret Movie*. And of course, events like The Secret Expo were organized, where the *Secret* philosophy could be taken to its logical and illogical extremes—hence the Oxylift Facelift in a Box, and something called a Geopathic Stress Eliminator. "You deserve all good things life has to offer," *The Secret* blasts. "Welcome to the magic of life, the magnificence of YOU!"

BYE, BYE, AMERICAN PIETY

On the surface, the outrageous success of *The Secret* should have come as a greater surprise than it did, particularly in the U.S., a country widely considered to be the most pious nation in the Western world. Eighty-two percent of Americans self-identify as Christians—either Catholic or Protestant—and a third of those, 100 million, identify as evangelical Protestant. In 2006, the Institute for Studies of Religion at Baylor University in Waco, Texas, published the most extensive and broad-ranging study of American religion ever conducted. Among their findings, researchers discovered that 85 to 90 percent of people routinely respond "yes" when asked, "Do you, personally, believe in God?" Nearly three-quarters pray at least once a week, and almost half attend church at least once a month. The survey also found that, while the number of Americans who are not affiliated with any religious tradition is steadily climbing (currently the number is around 11 percent), the vast majority of these people (63 percent) still say they believe in God or some higher power. Americans are a deeply Christian lot, or so it would appear.

But what the success of *The Secret* suggests is not that the *quantity* of believers has changed, but that the focus and content of their beliefs and practices have shifted. Radically. Historically, people went to church because their families went to church. And their families went because their communities went. Values were shared and externally defined. But as community values have been supplanted by an ethos of "live and let live," "be true to yourself," and "discover your inner voice," external expectations are no longer enough of an incentive to get us to church or synagogue or temple, especially early in the morning on a day off. Instead, though people still claim a religious identity, they often understand it more as an accident of birth than a conscious choice. "'I happen to be' religion is common in the United States," notes Wade Clark Roof, chair of the department of Religious Studies at the University of California at Santa Barbara. "That is, a person may have a family-based religious identity but not really claim it in any deep way as his or her own."

In fact, research by the Barna Group, a California-based Christian research marketing firm, concluded that fewer than one in five adults firmly believes that a congregational church is a critical element in their spiritual growth, and just as few strongly contend that participation in some type of community of faith is required for them to achieve their full potential. The majority of the public talks a big game when it comes to devotion, but even among those surveyed who regularly attend a Christian church, the Barna Group found that only 15 percent ranked their relationship with God as their top priority. Most tellingly, the Barna Group found that one-third of the adult population, 76 million, had not attended any type of church service or activity, except a funeral or a wedding, in the last six months.

"Although more than four out of five adults say they are Christian," says George Barna, the founder of the Barna Group and a former pollster and campaign manager in the Massachusetts state legislature, "[they] are more likely to see themselves as Americans, consumers, spouse and parent, and even employee than to describe themselves primarily in terms of their faith commitment." Which also likely explains why, when we delve a little further, we find all sorts of inconsistencies and apparent contradictions in American belief systems. For example, while Americans are, as a group, strong consumers of mainstream Christian merchandise and media (approximately 20 percent of the U.S. population has read a book in the *Left Behind* series, the Baylor Religious Survey says, 20 percent have read *The Purpose Driven Life* by Rick Warren, and more than half have watched "Touched by an Angel"), many self-identifying Christians also claim to hold paranormal beliefs that are decidedly at odds with the traditional tenets of the church. Twenty-eight percent believe it is possible to influence the world through telekinesis, for instance; 37 percent believe in haunted houses; a quarter believe in UFOs; and over half believe that dreams can foretell the future.

Barna chalks up the bizarre state of Christian values in America to people's "soft commitment" to God: "Americans are willing to expend some energy in religious activities such as attending church and reading the Bible, and they are willing to throw some money in the offering basket," he says. "Because of such activities, they convince themselves that they are people of faith ... We want to be 'spiritual' and we want to have God's favor, but we're not sure we want Him taking control of our lives and messing with the image and outcomes we've worked so hard to produce."

We point this out not to advocate a mass return to the church. But there's an important point of continuity to be made here. Just as the You Sell can sell us on cars, housing, and political candidates, it can be used to sell us a way of looking at life, the world, even God, that is entirely of a piece with our personal consumption habits. In a culture gone the way of mass customization, the You Sell intimates, why submit yourself to someone else's God—with all of His rigid rules and expectations—when you can just customize a belief system, a God, of your own, one that won't quash your whims or cramp your lifestyle?

THE SECRET AND THE YOU SELL

The beauty of a book like *The Secret* is that, interpreted the right way, it doesn't necessarily conflict with traditional religious values. It just reframes them. God still exists. Only instead of being something external—something greater than any one individual—God is inside you. In one form or another, the idea of "God on the inside" is one that religious scholars say dates back centuries. "Movements like theosophy in the late nineteenth century very much pushed this idea that all religions are essentially the same in their core—that their esoteric teaching is the same—and this teaching is said to be a notion of our inner divinity," says Richard King, a professor of religious studies at Vanderbilt University in Nashville, Tennessee, and the co-author, with

Jeremy Carrette, of *Selling Spirituality: The Silent Takeover of Religion*. What *is* unique to the modern era, however—and not surprising in an era of endless "Your Burger, Your Way" messaging—is *The Secret's* particularly consumerist approach. The teachings of *The Secret*, and reams of similar texts, can, and *should*, be used not just for salvation or for some greater good, but for selfish and material gain: riches, cars, jewels, and yes, parking spots. There is no higher authority than You, it says, and You were meant to live in abundance!

The Secret's authors have been accused of circular logic, hyper-materialism, faux-spiritualism, quack science, and anti-intellectualism—and it is, arguably, all of those things and worse. But its brilliance lies in how it was able to tap into the You Sell and elevate it to a cosmic level at a moment in history when research tells us that religious connections are already tenuous at best and spiritual beliefs are increasingly amorphous. Our overall receptiveness to the You Sell—the promise of our inherent worthiness—enables us to engage easily in the kind of magical thinking that *The Secret* demands: Anything you want, you deserve if you think you deserve it! In the text, metaphors for how powerful You are come fast and furious. (You, my friend, are like Aladdin with his magic lamp. Like a powerful magnet. Or better yet, a "genius beyond description.") Its approach is in effect very similar to the "I'm Special" self-esteem colouring books that began flooding kindergarten classrooms in the early eighties. Only here, your power is not just relegated to the profane. You are omnipotent! "You are the most powerful transmission tower in the Universe!" the book says. "Your transmission creates your life and it creates the world. It reverberates throughout the entire Universe. And you are transmitting that frequency *with your thoughts*!" In a narcissistic culture, that is the ultimate expression of hubris.

The Secret, of course, is only one cog in a multi-billion-dollar spirituality industry that has been catering to restless, disenchanted spiritual seekers, experimenters, and adventurers since the sixties. It is a business that is expanding just as fast as traditional allegiances are shrinking, filling the voids that religious institutions are leaving behind, with seductive promises of instant transformation, self-discovery, and abundance-as-you-understand-it. Marketdata Enterprises, a Florida-based independent market research firm, values the overall "self-help" industry—in which it includes holistic institutes, books and audiocassettes, motivational speakers, the personal-coaching market, and weight loss and stress management programs—at $12 billion.

In an increasingly homogenous and relentlessly materialistic consumer culture, products with a spiritual "theme" have become so many more props at our disposal for the purpose of differentiating ourselves. Most of these products have until recently been telling us that we are missing something, or that we need to improve in some way. But as the Ego Boom has taken off, the messages have become increasingly affirmational, telling us that we are fine just as we are—that the products only function as enhancements to our inherently divine nature.

And so we have yoga gear and Kaballah-sanctioned votive candles, meditation music, Zen-influenced home furnishings, Hindu-inspired fashion accessories, organic drinks, and aromatherapy bath oils—all of which provide new opportunities for individuals to pronounce to the world, "I'm spiritual!" The beauty is that, even if you don't have the time or energy to actually *be* spiritual, you can still convey spiritual-*ness* by surrounding yourself with products that seem to contain an inherent spirituality. Not only does the You Sell brand of personal transformation require little or no exertion, it can actually occur *in spite* of our actions and behaviours, even when they are selfish or flat-out unethical. "Anytime you look at yourself with critical eyes," *The Secret* says, "switch your focus immediately to the *presence* within, and its perfection will reveal itself to You."

TRUTHINESS

In his legendary rant on "truthiness"—a word now forever enshrined in the pop cultural lexicon, and tied to the George W. Bush administration's unique communications approach—the Comedy Network's satirical super-pundit Stephen Colbert outlined the distinction between this concept and truth itself. "Face it, folks, we are a divided nation," he told his audience of "heroes." "We are divided between those who think with their head, and those who know with their heart." Books, with all of their "facts," Colbert says, are smug and elitist. "Who's Britannica to tell me the Panama Canal was finished in 1914?" he asks. "If I want to say it happened in 1941, that's my right. I don't trust books. They're all fact, no heart." Sure, he says, "facts" might suggest that the U.S. invasion of Iraq was ill conceived, but he counters, didn't it "feel" good to have "taken out" Saddam Hussein? And so he pledges to his audience: "The truthiness is, anyone can *read* the news to you. I promise to *feel* the news at you."

With truthiness, Colbert was illustrating how the You Sell works in the political sphere (if it *feels* good, do it. If it doesn't, do something else). But he could just as easily have been talking about the modern approach to belief systems. Much in the same way political rhetoric spins hard truths into pleasing platitudes, the spirituality movement breaks down the firm moral codes, rules, and beliefs of traditional society into vague, comforting notions, moral relativism, and lifestyle props divorced from their historical meaning. As a result, in the same way we're seeing an explosion of political misinformation in the public realm, religious illiteracy is becoming an epidemic. According to Stephen Prothero, chair of Boston University's religion department, America is both the most religious nation in the developed world (in terms of claiming belief in God, the Virgin Birth, heaven, hell, and angels) and also the most religiously ignorant, not only in regard to world religions, but to its own traditions as well.

Prothero reveals that fewer than half of U.S. citizens can identify

THE EGO BOOM

205

Genesis as the first book of the Bible, and only a third know that Jesus delivered the Sermon on the Mount. Among other choice examples, he points out that one in ten adults believe that Noah's wife was Joan of Arc, only half can name even one of the four Gospels, and a whopping three-quarters of adults, he writes, falsely believe that the Bible (and not Ben Franklin) teaches that "God helps those who help themselves."

Of course, spirituality and faith are extremely powerful selling tools, and there have been religious entrepreneurs since the beginning of time. In any forum, we often don't bother to question the medium if the message sounds good. It is, after all, the oldest marketing trick in the book. ("Our scientists have finally cracked the code of soft shiny hair!" It certainly sounds promising.) But in the era of the Ego Boom, we've become particularly receptive to "truthy" sales pitches, because we want our spiritual quest to conform to our chosen lifestyle. The You Sell tells us what we *want* to hear, rather than what we *know* to be true.

In this way, *The Secret* and other spirituality brands exploit the vagueness of the word "spirituality," calling upon great minds—Jesus! Buddha! Shakespeare!—to bolster the authenticity of the message they're selling. In one passage, *The Secret* makes this suggestion to readers: "If you grew up thinking being wealthy is not spiritual, then read *The Millionaires of the Bible* by Catherine Ponder. She says Abraham, Isaac, Jacob, Joseph, Moses, and Jesus were all prosperity teachers, and millionaires themselves, with more affluent lifestyles than many present-day millionaires could conceive of!" Of course, unless you redefine a millionaire as being someone rich in goodness, Christian scholars will tell you this is preposterous. (What about the time Jesus said it was harder for a rich man to enter the kingdom of Heaven than it was for a camel to pass through the eye of a needle? they'd probably wonder.) Still, the idea that God wants you to be rich sure is appealing.

SHORTCUTS TO MEANING

As people pull away from the restrictive, sometimes oppressive influence of traditional religious institutions, a massive industry has cropped up to fill the presumed void that millions feel in their search for meaning beyond the here and now. In the Ego Boom era, what it comes down to, what we all want to hear, and what spirituality entrepreneurs are happy to tell us, is that we are okay, just as we are. That God—or the Universe, as the case may be—wants you to relax! Enjoy! Dig in! The spirituality business continues to grow by leaps and bounds in large part because of the spectacular profits to be reaped from telling people this very thing. Whether it's Jack Canfield's *Chicken Soup for the Soul* books, Wayne Dyer's *Meditations for Manifesting: Morning and Evening Meditations to Literally Create Your Heart's Desire*, or Deepak Chopra's *Growing Younger: A Practical Guide to Lifelong Youth*, these messages sell because they give people something they're hungry for—affirmation, reassurance, validation, permission.

But more than any other consumer "theme," the You Sell as applied to spirituality betrays a sort of widespread modern malaise, what Wade Clark Roof and others have described as "wholeness hunger." Despite their often painfully outmoded teachings, the traditions we used to collectively adhere to functioned to provide contexts—even certainties, for many—for understanding the world and your place in it. Without these framing devices, as Roof writes, talk of finding "balance," "harmony," and "connectedness," once relegated primarily to New Age discourse, has become a staple of everyday conversation. "Modernity," he says, "severs connections to place and community, alienates people from their natural environments, separates work and life, dilutes ethical values, all of which makes the need for unifying experience so deeply felt." It is no wonder the You Sell as applied to belief systems is so effective. These days, we seek guidance from "lifestyle gurus" who appear to have created a template that works and can be easily reproduced with the right set of tools, whether they be self-help books,

Martha Stewart linens or baking tins, or the items listed every month in the "Things I Love" section of Oprah's *O Magazine*.

As Oprah herself said about *The Secret* on her show, the phenomenon was touching a nerve "because so many people are hungry for guidance and meaning." Our eroding desire or ability to connect to community and religious groups has been thoroughly documented by Harvard sociologist Robert Putnam in *Bowling Alone* and others. Countless studies point out to us our own broad dissatisfaction. We are, science tells us, anxious, overworked, over-drugged, and addicted to technology. We are lonely and disconnected, stressed out beyond help, and obsessed with sensationalistic twenty-four-hour news networks and seedy celebrity scandals. Who knows if that's true or not? Happiness—hard to quantify, let alone define—is ultimately subjective. But one thing we do know is that the spirituality industry, propped up by the You Sell, generates billions of dollars every year. Just as we buy individuality, sophistication, glamour, and sex appeal with the swipe of a credit card, we are eager to buy a piece of connectedness, transcendence, and meaning to soothe our bruised spirits—be it in the form of an aromatherapy candle or a cash-for-healing donation to Jimmy Swaggart's "Hour of Power."

The rush of simplify-your-life products to hit the market in the past decade seems to suggest that even consumption-fatigue itself can be transformed into new ways of consuming. Savvy marketers have managed to package and sell the idea that we should consume *less* and "get back to our roots" in the form of organic foods, all-natural cosmetics, magazines, and spa products, all packaged in warm, muted earth tones.

Through a traditional lens, the credit-card approach to solving an existential crisis might seem rather futile, but the You Sell warmly invites and encourages the instant gratification of desires. It woos us, and in an unexpected way consumer culture has evolved as a perfect system of generating and managing this so-called "wholeness hunger." In fact, this very dynamic has itself become a marketing strategy. In the view of marketing consultant John Grant, following the breakdown of traditional society, individuals are hungry for traditions and "ideas to live by." Brands, he says, have become "the new traditions." "Culture and media's main role has become meeting this hunger for meaning and order." And so the spirituality industrial complex sells us material remedies to modern ills which, ironically, to the extent they do indeed exist, the You Sell helped to create in the first place. Products to soothe mind, body and spirit. The genius of it is, these products have no real or self-sustaining benefits—if they did, why would we need to buy keep buying them in perpetuity?—and so we wind up with a closed, self-perpetuating, and highly lucrative cycle of creating and temporarily soothing spiritual angst.

WE'RE ALL SHEILAS NOW

In the mid-80s, Berkeley sociologist Robert Bellah and his colleagues explored the role of individualism and commitment in American life. During the course of his research, which consisted largely of interviews with Americans about their faith, Bellah came across a young nurse named Sheila Larson, who described her own very personal type of religion—which she called "Sheilaism"—as an example of new-style religious individualism. "I believe in God," Larson said. "I'm not a religious fanatic. I can't remember the last time I went to church. My faith has carried me a long way. It's Sheilaism. Just my own little voice." Sheilaism was hailed as controversial, shocking, even blasphemous. It was seen as emblematic of a cultural shift to a me-centred way of understanding the universe, one that has only become more pronounced in the decades since. In fact, twenty years later, it is the standard, encouraged approach to spirituality. Instead of belonging to a greater whole, people have come to see themselves as being on a personal journey, a Quest—not unlike the central character of a first-person video game—cobbling together clues and bits of ideas that promise to lead them where they want to go. In Quest culture, spiritual authority lies with you alone, and you are the only person it serves. Not surprisingly, writes Roof on the phenomenon, "How can I feel good about myself?" emerged as a far more pressing question to many Americans than "How can I be saved?"

Scholars are quick to trace Quest culture or "seekerism" back to the Baby Boomers. According to Roof's research, around two-thirds of those born in the decades leading up to World War II claimed a "strong" religious preference; only about 40 percent of those born afterward did. The percentage of mainstream and conservative Protestants and Catholics born between 1955 and 1962 who felt the church rules on morality were too strict more than doubled from the beliefs of those born between 1926 and 1935. After the countercultural revolutions of the sixties and seventies, writes Roof, "so widespread were the religious defections, in fact, that mainline Protestant churches began to experience a noticeable downturn in membership and influence, beginning in the mid-sixties and continuing until now." Moreover, the Baby Boomers came of age at a time when personal therapy was broadly seen as a progressive, newfangled way of approaching personal problems. Humanist psychology—most notably Maslow's hierarchy of needs, gained popularity in the fifties and sixties, and pointed people in the direction of self-actualization (defined as the innate drive among humans to reach their fullest potential) as the highest order of personal evolution.

Others trace the privatization of religion even further back—to the eighteenth-century European Enlightenment—where the founding principles of liberalism were born. "In challenging the traditional social, moral and philosophical authority of the Church," write King and Carrette in *Selling Spirituality*, "European intellectuals sought to establish a framework for society and politics that avoided the religious conflicts of previous centuries. The solution, outlined most notably by philosophers such as John Locke, was to relegate the religious to the private sphere of life—to clearly demarcate it from the public realms of politics, science and philosophy." In other words, from the moment spiritual belief systems were relegated to the private sphere—allowing for an unprecedented degree of freedom to explore and experiment—they were destined to become individualized.

And so, with each passing generation, just as we're scoring higher on the Narcissistic Personality Inventory, studies suggest we are becoming more me-centred in our approach to beliefs. The You Sell steps in to fill the holes it helped to create, nudging us to explore aspects of our personal faith through consumption. According to a multi-faith-sponsored report called "OMG! How Generation Y is Redefining Faith in the iPod Era," spearheaded by Reboot, a nonprofit project devoted to helping Jewish youth address questions of cultural and religious identity, young people born between 1980 and 2000 top out as the most secular and me-centric generation in history. Reboot teamed with a range of organizations, including CIRCLE, Carnegie Corporation, and MAPS (Muslims in American Public Square), and surveyed Catholic, Protestant, Jewish, and Muslim youth, ages eighteen to twenty-five, across racial and ethnic lines, and found that religious communities are not "inured from this generational expectation for personalization and customization" that we see in everywhere from fashion to new entertainment technologies. Only 27 percent of young people, they found, define themselves as "Godly"—that is, traditional religion and God are a central part of their lives. An equal percentage define themselves as "God-less"—meaning that God and religion play little part in their lives, even though they may have spiritual or ideological aspects to their identity. The bulk of them, 46 percent, form the "undecided," who'd generally rather practise spirituality in an informal and personal way. "Anecdotally, and now scientifically," the study concluded, "we are seeing overall that members of Generation Y have individualized world views, an apparent lack of interest in traditional religious institutions and emphasize diversity." Of course. They are a generation reared on the You Sell.

The good news is, young people display an unprecedented degree of open-mindedness and tolerance for multiple viewpoints. But, the study found, the bad news is that they don't really believe in anything greater than themselves, and don't much care about anything that doesn't directly affect their lives. "Older Americans are more likely to 'believe' that God exists, younger Americans to have 'beliefs about the possibility of believing,'" writes Roof. "The latter is a means of keeping open the range of outcomes in the world of belief without having necessarily to commit, a strategy much in keeping with a popular quest mentality." Overwhelmingly, the OMG! survey's "God-less" youth say they don't believe that people need to believe in God to be moral or have good morals. "The God-less are individuals, and strongly believe people should do their own thing, even if others think it is strange," the researchers concluded. Besides, young people of today have more pressing things to think about. When the survey asked them to list their top concerns in life, a relationship with God (or anyone else, for that matter) fell pretty far down the list. Instead, the number one concern young people are "very worried" about is getting a sexually transmitted disease (35 percent), followed by finding a job after school (23 percent), grades (26 percent), friends (19 percent), and parents (18 percent). God was beat out only by deciding who to vote for, contributing to the community, and finding a life partner.

Again, the link between religious disengagement and civic apathy is striking, but not surprising: both are products of the Ego Boom. "Among the less religious, religion is not supplanted by a stronger ascribed or achieved characteristic," the OMG! survey concludes. "In fact, less religious youth are less strongly identified with anything at all." As boundaries in all facets of life become more fluid, people's beliefs have become more shallow and diffuse. We expect our value systems to conform to us, not vice versa. Spirituality, as a vague concept, allows for this sort of me-focused customization. On the one hand, this is clearly a good thing: it frees us up to think for ourselves. The problem, King and Carrette point out, is that spirituality has been overtaken by hyper-individuality and accomodationist beliefs that are not compatible with a socially engaged perspective: "Such closure, establishing the impermeable boundaries of the modern, individual self, undermines an awareness of interdependence and erodes our sense of solidarity with others."

PU PU PLATTER RELIGION

Beliefnet, a popular multi-faith online community—and a darling among online advertisers—was designed to help individuals meet their personal religious and spiritual needs. Like Dell Computers, it is in the business of mass customization. Launched in 1999, Beliefnet has become "a mainstream mass-market media outlet" for spirituality, according to its website, collaborating with *Newsweek*, ABC "World News Tonight," and others, and syndicated by Religious News Service. The website attracts 3.1 million unique monthly visitors, and sends out over 343 million email newsletters to subscribers every month on a range of subjects including Religious Jokes, Angel Wisdom, Buddhist Wisdom, Bible Reading, Weight Loss, Muslim Wisdom, and Saint of the Day. "We are independent," the site says. "We are not affiliated with a particular religion or spiritual movement. We are not out to convert you to a particular approach, but rather to help you find your own." It does this by providing information, community, inspirational messages, and, of course, products for helping people cobble together their own faith. One particularly popular tool they offer is a personality quiz called the "Belief-o-Matic™. Answer twenty questions about your concept of God, the afterlife, and human nature and the Belief-o-Matic™ will crunch the data and spit out an analysis of what type of religion you practise, "or ought to consider practising."

But, unlike mass customization in computers or hamburgers or condominiums, mass customization in spirituality affects how we understand our own traditions. Spirituality entrepreneurs can only establish their business by plundering what's already there—traditions that are thousands of years old. What we've begun to see over the past two decades is what academics have labelled "a wholesale commodification" of religion in which spirituality entrepreneurs divest the traditional religions of their most appealing cultural assets—their symbols, practices, texts, and colourful rituals—then dilute them of their historical meaning, rebrand them, and sell them off in attractive packaging. In this way, the spirituality industry assigns itself the authenticity of historical traditions and the cachet of vague, mystical associations, while separating itself from any negative restrictive connotations with the religion. Divorced from any historical context, spirituality has become much like fashion—we borrow, pilfer, and mix-and-match influences from all different eras and parts of the world. Like clothing, we're encouraged to try it on and accessorize as befits our mood. A particular spiritual style might be trendy one minute, dated the next. If it makes you look fat, throw it away.

YOGA INC.

The yoga industry is perhaps the best example of the Disney-style transformation of an ancient tradition into a modern consumer trend. Overnight, it seems, yoga—a 5,000-year-old spiritual philosophy designed to promote strength and balance of the body and mind—has become a multi-billion-dollar industry in North America. As a mass fitness trend, it was perhaps first popularized by celebrities like Madonna, Sting, and Gwyneth Paltrow, who raved about its life-altering effects in magazines and on late-night talk shows. In 2005, *Yoga Journal*—North America's largest yoga publication—released the results of its second annual yoga market survey, in which it announced that upward of 16.5 million people practise yoga in the U.S. alone. Overwhelmingly, enthusiasts are multi-tasking twenty- and thirty-something women, stoked by the idea of a workout that burns calories and induces spiritual well-being in a single shot. But its appeal runs far deeper than stretching and toning. The broadly defined element of spirituality—absent from, say, the manic aerobics trend of the eighties—is what has taken yoga from a fitness trend to a full-blown lifestyle in North America.

As spirituality entrepreneurs go, Lululemon Athletica may be the most successful and thoroughly conceived yoga brand in North America. In 1998, Chip Wilson opened the first Lululemon store in Vancouver's Kitsilano neighbourhood, showcasing the brand's rather sparse selection of brightly coloured yoga tanks, bras, hoodies, pants, and accessories made from Luon, its signature fabric, a nylon and Lycra blend that wicks away moisture, but feels like cotton. Wilson also developed a brand manifesto—a list of New-Agey tenets to establish the brand's underlying ideology: a perceptive blend of fashion, spirituality, athleticism. ("Children are the orgasms of life," reads one rather icky commandment. "Friends are more important than money," reads another.) Self-help is a central part of the culture. Employees are strongly encouraged to take Landmark Forum training and study the Law of Attraction.

Hype surrounding the brand spread quickly through word of mouth and before long hipster women were showing up at urban gyms and an ever-growing number of yoga studios branded with the Lululemon logo—a stylized "A" that looks like some sort of cultish hieroglyph. Soon, to be seen sporting one of Lululemon's colourful Mandarin-collared "Whisper tanks" ($52) or booty-contouring "Groove pants" ($93) became a conspicuous sign that said, "I'm spiritual," something traditionally hard to convey without a nun's habit or a monk's robe and a beggar's bowl (after all, traditionally, devoutness involved the renunciation of material goods, not their acquisition). Lululemon started introducing clothing made of appealing, unusual materials purported to have wide-ranging health benefits, including seaweed and bamboo fibre (claims that were called into question by the federal Competition Bureau in 2007). By the end of 2007, the company had seventy-eight locations spanning North America as well as in Australia and Japan.

Perhaps more than any other spiritual philosophy, yoga is susceptible to You Sell marketing because its teachings are non-religious, non-threatening, and can be so widely interpreted. In the past few years, there's been a race to slap the word "yoga" onto anything—clothing, bags, mats, books, CDs, videos, and designer incense—hike up the price, and watch the profits soar. Critics have dubbed the phenomenon "McYoga." As a fashion trend, yoga works brilliantly because it's the easiest way to announce to the world in a concrete way that you have adopted yoga consciousness into your life (without having to do any yoga!).

The word "yoga" itself is derived from the ancient Sanskrit for "unity." But in North America, legal squabbles over who can claim ownership of the ancient tradition have created extreme divisions within the yoga community. At the forefront of a series of recent trademark battles is Bikram Choudhury, the Calcutta-born, Beverly Hills–based guru-to-the-stars who developed Bikram Yoga—a popular program consisting of a sequence of twenty-six traditional postures, performed in a room heated to 41 degrees Celsius—which he copyrighted.

In 2002, upon learning that his eponymous technique had been adopted by yoga instructors not sanctioned through his training and franchising program, Choudhury—a multi-millionaire who travels in chauffeured Rolls-Royces, wears a diamond-encrusted Rolex, and was once hailed in the *Yoga Journal* as "Yoga's Bad Boy"—sent out over 100 angry cease-and-desist orders, accusing these studio owners of stealing his intellectual property. ("I have balls like atom bombs, two of them, 100 megatons each," he told *Business 2.0* magazine of the situation. "Nobody fucks with me.") In 2003, he sued a studio in Costa Mesa, California, and won a private settlement, which he trumpeted on his website as a warning to others.

The outcome created a ripple of anxiety across the yogascape, primarily among small, independent yoga studio owners, fearful of being bullied out of business. In July 2003, a San Francisco–based collective of yoga enthusiasts, called Open Source Yoga Unity (OSYU), filed a countersuit against Bikram, arguing that *asanas* (classic yoga postures) cannot be copyrighted by anyone. "Any attempt by an individual to own a yoga style runs counter to the general spirit of yoga," lawyer James Harrison wrote in a statement. In early May 2005, the lawsuit was dismissed after Bikram and OSYU reached an undisclosed "mutually satisfactory" agreement.

Still, the word "yoga" is used liberally in the private sector. In Vancouver, the heart of Canada's yoga community, companies like Karma Athletics and Lotuswear (which names its garments after Hindu goddesses) are cropping up. Mainstream brands like Danskin, Adidas, Roots, and Aritzia have added yoga lines to their collections. Celebrities and fashion designers have gotten into the mix. Nuala by Puma is a line of yogawear designed by supermodel Christy Turlington. Marc Jacobs has designed a $400 Yoga Mat Bag. Even Gucci, a brand synonymous with material excess, has produced a luxury yoga mat for $870. Yoga tourism—theme cruises, retreats, and spa vacations—is already an overcrowded industry. Instruction of yoga has morphed into hybrids: yoga aerobics, yoga spinning, pre- and post-natal yoga. Hip-hop impresario Russell Simmons released a series of urban-themed yoga videos, set to original hip-hop music. It's safe to say we're on the sorry side of a yoga glut.

SPIRITUAL BUT NOT RELIGIOUS

These days, a whopping 20 percent of Americans describe themselves as "spiritual but not religious." And yet, funnily enough, there is no universally agreed-upon definition of what "spiritual" means. It is a vague and infinitely malleable term, and in this way, it conveniently comes with none of the social, historical, and geopolitical baggage of "religion." Spirituality is an umbrella term that has come to encompass everything vaguely related to self-actualization and wellness. In effect, it means nothing and anything. In his studies in the late eighties, Roof found that "talk about spirituality was often rambling and far-ranging." One theme, however, always stood out—that of a self-authored search, a journey, a Quest.

Rather than functioning at odds with consumer culture, spirituality aligns beautifully with it by offering for-profit solutions for Questers. An endless stream of self-help books, meditation tapes, and accoutrements like henna tattoos, bindis, jewellery, vessels, and Buddha statues, ostensibly help to propel us forward on our journey. Explorer, Voyager, Pathfinder, Discovery, Odyssey, and Quest, Roof points out, are all names of 1990s cars, trucks, and vans. Everything becomes just a brand, or just a logo, so the crucifix or the peace symbol have no more cultural resonance than the Mercedes symbol or the Nike Swoosh. We have perfumes called Samsara and Eternity. We have clothing lines with names like True Religion, Jesus Jeans, and Buddhist Punk.

It's not just symbols and artifacts that are being co-opted by the You Sell, but living spiritual practices as well. Severed from their point of origin, they are rendered meaningless in every way except the ways we choose. Eastern cultures are particularly vulnerable to our mucking around because their "exoticism" lends them additional romance. And so, Indian meditation practice is retooled and set to vaguely exotic-sounding music. Feng Shui becomes a popular home decor trend, the Kama Sutra a Valentine's Day gag gift. Deepak Chopra, one of the masters of reformatting Eastern traditions for a Western capitalist audience, has made fortunes selling Buddhist and Hindu–tinged books on attaining spiritual success, harnessing instant wealth, and staying young forever.

Globalization is pushing this phenomenon further and further afield: with the explosion of commerce in China, the same sort of cultural repurposing is even starting to happen there. In an article for the Jewish cultural publication *Moment Magazine*, journalist Susan Fishman Orlins described how, on a trip to Beijing, she noticed that in the business section of bookstores, titles like the *Jewish People's Bible for Business and Managing the World* and *The Wisdom of Judaic Trader* were becoming popular, due to a widespread and apparently hazy notion that Jews are masters of commerce. The latter, she says, is filled with illustrations of big-nosed caricatures. In many of these books, she writes, "the content is simply fabricated, highlighting, for instance, the success of financier J.P. Morgan (who was Episcopalian, not Jewish)."

In corporate North America, in light of the strict separation of church and state, spirituality has become an efficient tool for making the whole culture of capitalism seem meaningful from the inside out. Billions of dollars are spent every year on New Age consultants and coaches, tasked with teaching leadership, assertiveness, and creative-thinking techniques. According to the market research firm Market-data Enterprises, the top twelve motivational speakers grossed $303 million in 2003, via public seminars and private workshops for exec-utives, and increasingly, personal coaching. In bookstores, we find the "Tao" of everything from *The Tao of Leadership* to *The Tao of Warren Buffett*. In his book *Corporate Religion: Building a Strong Company Through Personality and Corporate Soul,* the Danish branding expert Jesper Kunde writes that companies that want to succeed in the modern era need to find ways to "bind people together in belief," much like a religion. "Spiritual management," he writes, "is set to become the most important management tool of the future, because it provides the only protection against the complexity of new products and the speed of market change."

A LITTLE LESS GOD-Y, PLEASE

Not only is the corporatization of religion happening on the "believer" end, it's happening within traditional religious institutions as well. In early 1994, when Reverend William Tully, an expert in church growth and communications, took over at St. Bartholomew's Episcopalian in New York City, the institution was dying of attrition. And so the minister decided to introduce a policy of "radical welcome"—where people of all stripes would not feel bound to worship by traditional rules. He introduced a new service called the "Come As You Are" Eucharist, which he defined as "a venture in postmodern, seeker-sensitive liturgical worship." Tully implemented pioneering interfaith programming and modern musical accompaniment. Soon, membership swelled and other institutions began knocking on his door, desperate to understand his formula, a form of liturgical mass customization. In 2003, the church hosted its first of five popular annual conferences called "Reinventing Church" to teach lay and clergy leaders how to implement attention-grabbing programs and grow their membership. What they realized, although they might not define it in these terms, is that the climate in the Ego Boom demands that they accept people as individual consumers, and speak to them in the language of the You Sell.

It is not uncommon now to find traditional institutions working with professional marketing firms to cultivate brand identities and marketing strategies, and to pander to desirable demographic groups, much like brands. Churches have realized that in order to survive, they need to adapt. But they can't place demographics and market research at the heart of their programming strategies and not irrevocably change the nature of their institutions. The You Sell has become so powerful that the only way the church can compete is to adopt it. In particular, churches increasingly cater to the demands and "felt needs" of churchgoers as consumers, rather than challenging the integrity of a self-interested lifestyle, a bothersome message even to many traditional adherents. "In a sense," write Richard King and Jeremy Carrette, "the most troubling aspect of many modern spiritualities is precisely that they are not troubling enough ... What is being sold to us as radical, trendy and transformative spirituality in fact produces little in the way of a significant change in one's lifestyle or fundamental behaviour patterns." In many ways, the church is becoming another instrument for reinforcing the Ego Boom.

The Barna Group has conducted market research—or taken the

spiritual temperature of the nation—for thousands of para-church ministries, Christian churches, and corporations ranging from the Ford Motor Company to Walt Disney and VISA. Barna has written more than thirty-five books on the subject of spiritual trends and church strategies, including *Grow Your Church from the Outside In* (formerly titled *Re-Churching the Unchurched*), which takes a strong business-minded approach to attracting new congregants. There are nearly 100 million "unchurched" people in the U.S. right now, and in this book, Barna set out to explore their world. Armed with this information, churches might better connect, attract, and retain these strays. "Once you understand the values, attitudes, beliefs, religious practices, demographics, life goals, and spiritual expectations of the unchurched," the publisher promises, "you will have a better chance of relating to them in meaningful ways."

Without a doubt, the marriage of church and commerce has been successful in bringing pieces of the church to the people. According to a 2006 survey by the CBA, the Christian Business Association, the industry is now a $4.63 billion business. The CBA, based in Colorado Springs, is the trade association for the Christian retail channel, with 2,055 member Christian stores—and 570 associate member book publishers, record companies, gift companies, and other product suppliers—which sell everything from bibles and other Christian-themed books to videos, music, gifts, software, greeting cards, toys, apparel, and other materials. The average Christian shopper spends roughly $300 per year on books alone (compared to $200 a year among the general public). Every summer, the industry gathers for the International Christian Retail Show, a networking and buying event with representatives from all fifty states and more than sixty countries around the world to showcase the "latest and greatest" in Christian paraphernalia. The combined displays of products occupy six acres of exhibits, the equivalent of six football fields.

Bringing people to church, however, is a different story. To keep services "relevant" and palatable, religious leaders are learning to integrate "exciting" new media and marketing techniques to recast their teachings as more me-centred and less God-centred. In order to reach as broad a market as possible, they're easing up on the hardcore God-talk, which might turn people off. Hell, Satan, the wrath of God, and sinfulness are all dialed down. Instead, religious themes tend to be couched in humanist psychological terms—notions of "spirituality," "inner peace," and "self-discovery" are integrated wherever possible. "Marketing principles are becoming the arbiter of truth. Elements of the message that don't fit the promotional plan are simply omitted," writes John MacArthur, the pastor of Grace Community Church in Sun Valley, California, and host of a nationally syndicated radio show on spiritual issues. "Marketing savvy demands that the offense of the cross must be downplayed. Salesmanship requires that negative subjects like divine wrath be avoided. Consumer satisfaction means that the standard of righteousness cannot be raised too high. The seeds of a watered-down gospel are thus sown in the very philosophy that drives many ministries today."

Perhaps most notably, the past two decades have seen the invention of the Protestant megachurch (generally defined as having a weekly attendance of more than 2,000). Geared to "seekers" or "questers" looking to customize a form of Christianity that speaks to them, megachurches—which doubled in number to 1,210 in the U.S. between 2000 and 2005, according to a Hartford Institute for Religious Research survey—have state-of-the-art facilities, celebrity preachers, and more amenities (cafés, daycare, food courts, sports grounds, social networking groups, bookstores, etc.) than your average small town. Relying heavily on feel-good rhetoric, contemporary music, multi-media entertainment, and even humour, mega-churches allow congregants the freedom and flexibility to customize a form of Christianity that serves their needs. In the '90s, Denver's conservative Full Gospel Chapel took over a $7.8 million shopping mall space and changed its name to the Happy Church. "It draws people," the pastor told reporters.

The bells and whistles have become particularly important in the effort to attract young people, with their mythically short attention spans, back into the fold. In a Barna Group research report entitled "The Buster Report: A New Generation of Adults Describes Their Life and Spirituality," researchers honed in on young people's spirituality "style" and how it differs from their parents'. "It is important for churches to understand the natural skepticism of Busters as well as their desire for spiritual and conversational depth," concluded Barna Group vice-president David Kinnaman. "Young adults do not want to hear on-the-stage monologues about moral regulations. To earn access to their hearts and minds, you have to understand each person's unique background, identity, and doubts, and must tangibly model a biblical lifestyle for them beyond the walls of the church."

And so, in order to make church feel less "churchy" to young people, alt-ministries are moving away from traditional settings in favour of coffee shops or skate parks. Jay Bakker, the son of Jim and Tammy Faye Bakker, started his own ministry in the mid-nineties called Revolution, whose members meet in bars, punk clubs, empty warehouses, private homes, or anywhere else they feel comfortable. To appeal to teenagers musically, you can now find Christian music in every category: punk, pop, reggae, jazz, gospel, hip-hop. The Hassidic Jewish Reggae star Matisyahu is a best-selling artist. There are "street slang" bibles, Christian, Muslim, and Jewish teen magazines and romance novels.

ANTI-INTELLECTUALISM AND MAGICAL THINKING

For its part, the spirituality movement has sought credibility by cultivating a widespread atmosphere of ornate pseudo-intellectualism, quack-scientific jargon, and quasi-mystical mumbo-jumbo. There are plenty of credible teachers out there, to be sure. But the industry is also a natural home for supreme practitioners of Stephen Colbert–style truthiness. In an interview with *Share Guide*, a holistic health magazine, *The Secret's* Jack Canfield makes the absurd pronouncement that, "We now have research to indicate that at the very least, our thoughts can travel 250,000 miles." How do we now know this? Well, he says, "That's the result of experiments that were done with astronauts that were up on the moon or in a lunar module. They had students at the parapsychology department at Duke University sitting in their laboratory. They would close their eyes and focus on what shape the astronaut was sending them—a square, a triangle, a circle, a pentagon, etc. The students had an uncannily high rate of accuracy, which would indicate that the thoughts could travel that far." With the words "Duke University" thrown in there, it sounds like a very credible and important experiment. In fact, the institution where the research in question was conducted is called the Rhine Research Center Institute for Parapsychology, a facility that promotes the research and investigation of paranormal phenomena such as extrasensory perception (ESP), hauntings, and poltergeists. Though it is located on Duke University property, the university cut all its ties to the institute back in 1965.

The spirituality movement is shameless in its use of fake information—and *The Secret*, the number-one-selling book and audiobook of 2007, according to the Nielsen Company—is a premier example of bald-faced "truthy" marketing: everything you want now, without the pesky evidence. In relation to health matters, *The Secret*'s authors offer advice that is outlandish to the point of being delusional. In a post-AIDS culture, it tells its audience, "You cannot 'catch' anything unless you think you can, and thinking you can is inviting it to you with your thought." It says you can cure yourself of cancer by renting funny movies and laughing it away with a positive attitude. If you are overweight, and a medical doctor tells you that you have a slow thyroid or hereditary weight problems, ignore him. These are "fat thoughts," *The Secret* says. "A person cannot think 'thin thoughts' and be fat," the book says. "It completely defies the Law of Attraction." So keep eating those Krispy Kremes, and think yourself thin. Gratify yourself now, *The Secret* says, and let the universe clean up the mess.

JUST ANOTHER IDEOLOGY

The great irony of modern secular spirituality is that it appears to bring great freedom and choice, but much like traditional religion, it comes with profound limitations—it, too, is rather narrow. It encourages irrational judgments and a limited world view. Quest culture—the heralding of a never-ending spiritual journey that is the central practice of modern spirituality—leads by necessity to a spiral of self-absorption and consumption, and obsessive focus on a brighter future that will never come.

A quest is about "getting there." Where "there" is is almost beside the point. Nevertheless, being spiritual today is one big, never-ending process of preparation for the trip. The only surefire way to do this properly—and to convey our spiritual diligence to others—is to outfit ourselves with the right gear. A proper quest will always require more inspirational books, more DVDs, more meditation classes, more yoga gear, more spa treatments, and more issues of *Body + Soul* magazine. "It's like fast food," says Richard King. "You eat it and it's kind of fun when you have it but a few minutes later you're hungry. It doesn't nourish you in a longer sense." But pushing spirituality as a means for self-actualization is a powerful use of the You Sell in that it prompts a narcissistic loop on the most profound level: the more spirituality-themed stuff we buy, the more anxious and depressed we become over their ultimate inadequacy, and in turn, the more we cling to the next affirmational message that comes along, and buy the attendant stuff. Ultimately, the You Sell only ever feeds itself.

HARNESSING THE BOOM

C all it ego, or narcissism, or simply individualism, the unquenchable human need for self-fulfillment, personal expression, and autonomy lie at the root of the greatest achievements in modern Western society. These things are also the fuel for the most dynamic economic awakening since the industrial revolution. In a society that has it all, feeding the perpetual motion machine of prosperity and growth means tapping into consumer desires that can never be truly satisfied. The need to be different, and to express that difference in everything we do, fits the bill nicely.

We are living in a land of non-fat soy milk and artisanal honey. For individuals, there has never been so much on offer for those yearning to express themselves, and hold the rest of the world at bay. Your clothes, your home, family, faith—all things that once signalled a sense of belonging are now just extensions of the essential You. And since you are constantly evolving, all of it is always negotiable, and easily disposable. For every person who has ever felt stifled by the expectations of society (and, really, who hasn't?) the ties that bind have never been so easy to clip. We don't just accept the heightened inward gaze and self-indulgence of each new generation, we celebrate it like never before.

The rewards of this boom are everywhere around us. We have wealth, prosperity, opportunity, and rights, and for all of it we can thank our individual liberty. There can be no freedom without individualism, no individualism without freedom. And over the past generation, as we have married this ideology to technological innovation, the digital age has unleashed our power for self-expression in ways never before imagined.

Less clear are the costs.

For one, the affirmational mentality—the need to constantly prop up a self-constructed image of oneself—requires constant tending. It's both time-consuming and addictive. Trapped by the You Sell, individuals live in a constant state of dissatisfaction that can have a corrosive effect on everything from intimate relationships to broader social ties to one's comfort in one's own skin.

On a larger scale, if there is one overwhelming malaise pointed to again and again in modern society, it is the sense of isolation and alienation that comes up perennially in public opinion polls and epidemiological studies looking for the root causes of rising rates of depression and anxiety, among other modern plagues. It's been more than thirty years since epidemiologist Lisa Berkman at the Harvard School of Public Health established a link between feelings of social isolation and overall health. Her work, and dozens of studies since, suggest that there are real physical consequences that come from feeling disconnected from the world and people around you. As Berkman told the *Los Angeles Times* in 2006, isolation "accelerates the way people age," increasing stress hormones, compromising the immune system, even distorting our judgment and perceptions of the world around us.

To put it bluntly, humans are pack animals, and thriving within a pack often requires the ability to sublimate one's own ego and to keep at least some focus on one's place in the greater scheme of things. But that particular sociological muscle is one that seems to be atrophying as we hone our ability to customize the tiniest details of our own world.

Of course, there's nothing wrong, or unduly selfish, with enjoying your own iPod, or wanting a computer that's a little different from everybody else's. The trouble arises when that me-centred mindset becomes so powerful that it metastasizes into every part of one's life, changing not only the way we consume, but the way we live, love, vote, learn, and pray.

The danger is when the ascendancy of "You" crowds out any sense of "us."

The You Sell works because we are so deeply attracted to the promise of control. The Designer Effect exists because of our natural affinity for the ideas that spring from our own imaginations. And if we are ignorant about politics, current affairs, and history, and indifferent to the fate of those beyond our shrinking circle of friends and family, it's because we have found other things that are more entertaining, more fun, more immediately rewarding to occupy our minds. This is not the product of mind control, but of wilful self-delusion.

To borrow a phrase from acclaimed anthropologist Jared Diamond, the Ego Boom and the me-obsessed culture it has created are "auto-catalytic"—the product of a virtuous, self-feeding cycle. The more we customize our lives, the more we consume, and the more we are willing to pay for the privilege of consuming products that are ostensibly of our own design. The more we pay, the more we create opportunities to customize. On and on the cycle goes, as long as we participate blindly.

The Ego Boom, therefore, is something to be managed, not destroyed. The only way to manage it is to be able to recognize the You Sell when we see it and to arm ourselves with an awareness that will allow us to clearly examine our own motivations and make informed decisions—and to prevent that impulse from subsuming all sense of what is affordable and healthy. Once we begin to recognize it, we are more likely to start asking ourselves a few important questions: Do I really need to spend an extra hundred bucks on something that is "Just For Me"—especially when it is Just For Everyone Else, too? Suddenly the sell doesn't seem so flattering.

At the same time, some are seeking to find out whether the Ego

Boom can be harnessed for anything other than profit and a fleeting sense of control. Nascent movements within consumer culture suggest that it can. What is perhaps most amazing (and encouraging) about the autocatalytic triumph of individualism is the fact that it has never completely squelched our positive belief in things like community, cooperation, and generosity. Despite the fact that we are, demonstrably and profoundly, a self-centred society, and getting more so all the time, we still see selfishness as a moral failing. Ego drives our behaviour to an enormous extent, but that is not something we easily admit to. And that suggests that the power of the You Sell, if properly aimed, could help bring our collective priorities back into a healthier balance.

Earlier this year, market forecasting agency TrendWatching.com discussed the rising desire of image-conscious consumers to convey more than just affluence and taste in their wardrobe, accessories, and gadgets. "As mature consumer societies are increasingly dominated by (physical) abundance, by saturation, by experiences, by virtual worlds, by individualism, by participation, by feelings of guilt and concern about the side effects of unbridled consumption, status is to be had in many more ways than leading a lifestyle centred on hoarding as many branded, luxury goods as possible." The world is breaking down into "status spheres"—groups in which people try to articulate their values through what they buy. One of the most powerful "status spheres," they say, is the "eco sphere" in which people try not only to buy goods that are more environmentally friendly, but that communicate to the world, "I care about the Earth." (Consider London handbag designer Anya Hindmarch's must-have canvas tote, which pronounced righteously "I am not a plastic bag," and sold out in a matter of hours.) As eco-friendly businesses try to exploit the positive image of green products, they are finding that the You Sell is a powerful tool.

These kinds of products don't just appeal to committed activists and well-informed environmentalists. They appeal to that far larger market of people who want to communicate that they sympathize with hardcore greens, or at least want to be *seen* as sympathizing—especially if it doesn't involve any truly painful sacrifices. Is it narcissism? Sure it is. But it's narcissism put to some useful purpose.

The same impulse is driving charities, non-profit groups, and political campaigns to embrace political consumerism however they can in hopes of luring back the young, wealthy, and uninterested demographic into a non-threatening struggle for social change. In recent years, this has meant aligning themselves with celebrities like Bono, Angelina Jolie, Brad Pitt, and other glamorous altruists with whom the public are eager to identify themselves.

Oprah Winfrey made use of the You Sell in her ABC reality-TV game show, "Oprah's Big Give," a series "that [defied] television convention with the bold idea of people competing to give rather than get." The show consisted of ten contestants vying for the role of "Biggest Giver" in a competition to give away (Oprah's sponsors') money to those in desperate need—and to revel in their gratitude. The show sold the glory of self-interested altruism in the hopes that viewers at home would be inspired to want to claim a bit of that glory for themselves in their own lives. The winner of the show received a million dollars for his troubles as well as the admiration of millions of viewers for his goodness.

Are such individuals driven as much by their own narcissistic impulses as they are by concern for, say, the environment or impoverished children? Probably. Does it matter? Maybe not. The goal is persuasion, and whether you're selling a product, spreading a message or organizing a movement, the principles of the You Sell apply. That lesson is slowly seeping into even the most traditionally earnest non-profit endeavours.

Last year, London-based consultancy nfpSynergy issued a report entitled "The 21st Century Volunteer." It was commissioned by the Scout Association and offered advice for non-profit groups and community organizations around the world that find themselves struggling to attract the community support and participation essential to stay afloat. The fifty-three-page document by authors Elisha Evans and Joe Saxton ended with a conclusion entitled "Harnessing Selfish Altruism." The message is a stark one for all traditional charities that issue desperate and heartfelt appeals to our generosity. According to Evans and Saxton, today's volunteers want to know what they will get out of the experience. They want to be made to feel generous, but they also want their time to be rewarding. To succeed, they say, charities must start thinking of their volunteer positions as a "product" to be sold by promising "an opportunity, a privilege, and a stride toward greatness." The path to success, in other words, is a blatant appeal, not to our kindness, but to our self-regard.

That will undoubtedly strike many as wrong—true, but wrong. It's unsettling to realize just how far we've wandered from John F. Kennedy's admonition to "ask not what your country can do for you...." It is a speech so familiar, and yet so distant, that it has all the ideological resonance of a children's nursery rhyme. Then again, solutions are solutions regardless of what motivates them, and as we look out at the major challenges of the next generation we're not in a position to quibble about motives.

How will Western societies cope with aging populations without bankrupting the institutions that form the social safety net? How will we cope with changes to the global climate? How will we defuse the rising tension and violence stemming from our diminishing natural resources and the spread of global hunger? All of this and more will require us to understand that it is in our self interest to rediscover common interest, cooperation, and yes, even some sacrifice—all things that have fallen out of vogue, but are due for a comeback.

The good news, to put it in the only terms that really matter in the midst of the Ego Boom, is that community is still a strong brand, almost as strong as individualism. And these two sides of our nature need not be mutually exclusive. Indeed, if we're to avoid Teddy Roosevelt's dark warning from almost 100 years ago about the dangers of too much and too little individual freedom, we must remember that neither side can be allowed to snuff out the other.

Chapter One

American Girl Corporate Website www.americangirl.com/corp/index.php.

Acosta-Alzuru, Carolina. "The American Girl Dolls: Defining American Girlhood through Representation, Identity and Consumption." Ph.D. dissertation. University of Georgia, 1999.

Baumeister, Roy F., Jennifer D. Campell, Joachim I. Krueger and Kathleen D. Vohs. "Does High Self-Esteem Cause Better Performance, Interpersonal Success, Happiness, or Healthier Lifestyles?" *Psychological Science in the Public Interest.* Vol 4, No. 1, April, 2003.

Bushman, Brad J. and Roy F. Baumeister. "Threatened Egotism, Narcissism, Self-Esteem, and Direct and Misplaced Aggression: Does Self-Love or Self-Hate Lead to Violence?" Journal of Personality and Social Psychology, Vol. 75, No. 1, 1998.

Belk, Russell W. and Richard Pollay. "Images of ourselves: The Good Life in Twentieth Century Advertising." *Journal of Consumer Research*, March, 1985.

Chaudhry, Lakshmi. "Mirror, Mirror on the Web." *The Nation*, January 11, 2007.

Côté, James E. and Anton L. Allahar. *Ivory Tower Blues: A University System in Crisis.* University of Toronto Press. 2007.

Emler, Nicholas. *Self-Esteem: The Costs and Causes of Low Self-Worth.* A report from the Joseph Rowntree Foundation. November, 2001.

Gregory Thomas, Susan. *Buy, Buy Baby: How Consumer Culture Manipulates Parents and Harms Young Minds.* Houghton Mifflin, 2007.

Hira, Nadira A. "Attracting the Twentysomething Worker." *Fortune Magazine Online.* May 15, 2007.

Hyman, Peter. "Porn for the People." *Radar.* June/July, 2007.

Jayson, Sharon. "Are Social Norms Steadily Unraveling?" *USA Today.* April 12, 2006.

Katz, Lilian G. Self-Esteem and Narcissism: Implications for Practice." *ERIC*

Clearinghouse on Elementary and Early Childhood Education. August, 1993.

Kilbourne, Jean. *Can't Buy My Love: How Advertising Changes the Way We Think and Feel.* Free Press, 2000.

Lasch, Christopher. *The Culture of Narcissism: American Life in an Age of Diminishing Expectations.* WW Norton & Company, 1979.

Lowen, Alexander. *Narcissism: Denial of the True Self.* Macmillan, 1984.

Markus, Hazel Rose and Shinobu Kitayama. "Culture and the Self: Implications for Cognition, Emotion, and Motivation." *Psychological Review.* Vol. 98, 1991.

Myers, David G. "The Inflated Self." *Christian Century.* December 1, 1982.

National Association for Self-Esteem, www.self-esteem-nase.org.

Putnam, Robert D. *Bowling Alone: The Collapse and Revival of American Community.* Simon & Schuster, 2001.

Sacks, Peter. *Generation X Goes to College: An Eye-Opening Account of Teaching in Postmodern America.* Open Court Publishing Company, 1996.

Schor, Juliet B. *Born to Buy: The Commercialized Child and the New Consumer Culture.* Scribner, 2005.

Schufelt, Tim. "To Attract Youth, Firms Learn to get in their Facebook." *The Globe and Mail.* July 18, 2007.

Slater, Lauren. "The Trouble with Self-Esteem." *The New York Times.* February 3, 2002.

Twitchell, James B. "Lux Populi." *The Wilson Quarterly.* Winter, 2007.

Twenge, Jean. *Generation Me: Why Today's Young Americans are MoConfident, Assertive, Entitled—and ore Miserable Than Ever Before.* Free Press, 2006.

Wallace, H.M. and Baumeister, R.F. "The performance of narcissists rises and falls with perceived opportunity for glory." *Journal of Personality and Social Psychology,* 2002.

Yankelovich, Daniel. *New Rules: Searching for Self-Fulfillment in a Worth Turned Upside-Down.* Bantam Books, 1982

Young, S. Mark and Drew Pinsky. "Narcissism and Celebrity." *Journal of Research in Personality.* Vol. 40, No. 5, October, 2006.

Zaslow, Jeffrey. "Blame it on Mr. Rogers: Why Young Adults Feel So Entitled." *The Wall Street Journal.* July 5, 2007.

Chapter Two

DeBord, Guy. *The Society of Spectacle,* 1967, translated by Ken Knabb, Rebel Press, 1992.

Piller, Frank and Franke, Nikolaus. "Toolkits for User Innovation and Design: exploring user interaction and value creation in the watch market," *Journal of Product Innovation Management* #21 (Nov. 2004).

Pine, Joseph. *Mass Customization: the new frontier in business competition,* Harvard Business School Press (1993).

Chapter Three

Anderson, Chris. *The Long Tail: Why the future of business is selling less of more,* Hyperion (2006).

Garfield, Bob. "The You Tube Effect" *Wired,* December, 2006.

Goldstein, Patrick. "Hollywood is seeing fans pull a power play." *Los Angeles Times,* January 23, 2007.

Chapter Four

Bruegmann, Robert. *Sprawl: A Compact History,* The University of Chicago Press, 2005.

Carter, Steven and Julia Sokol. *Men Who Can't Love: How To Recognize a Commitmentphobic Man Before He Breaks Your Heart.* Berkley Books, 1987.

The Economist. "The World Goes to Town." Special Report. May 3, 2007.

Gamerman, Ellen. "Til Tech do us Part." *The Wall Street Journal.* August 4, 2007.

Garber, Marjorie. *Sex and Real Estate: Why We Love Houses.* Anchor Books, 2000.

Haughney, Christine. "Young Buyers, Prepared and Fearless." *The New York Times.* February 4. 2007.

Jacobs, Jane. *The Death and Life of Great American Cities.* Random House, 1961.

Joint Center for Housing Studies at Harvard University. "State of the Nation's Housing 2005."

Kennedy, Tracy L. M. and BarryWellman. "The Networked Household" Forthcoming in *Information, Communication and Society.* April, 2007.

Morrow, James. "A Place for One." *American Demographics.* January, 2004.

McPherson, Miller, Lynn Smith-Lovin and Matthew E. Brashears. "Social Isolation in America: Changes in Core Discussion Networks over Two Decades." *American Sociological Review.* June, 2006.

The National Marriage Project at Rutgers University. "The State of Our Unions: The Social Health of Marriage in America." Annual Report, 2007.

PewResearch Center Publications. "Not Looking for Love" Feb 13, 2006.

Roberts, Sam. "51% of Women Are Now Living Without Spouse." *The New York Times.* January 16, 2007.

U.S. Census Bureau 2008 Statistical Abstract. "Population: Households and Families."

Chapter Five

Bennett, W. Lance. "Changing Citizenship in the Digital Age" *Civic Life On-line: learning how digital media can engage youth.* The MIT Press (2008).

Bimber, Bruce. "Information and Political Engagement in America" *Political Research Quarterly* Vol. 54 No.1 (2001).

Bimber, Bruce. *Technology in the Evolution of Political Power.* Cambridge University Press (2003).

Cohen, Lizbeth. *A Consumer's Republic: The politics of mass consumption in post-war America.* Vintage Books (2003).

De Tocqueville, Alexis. *Democracy in America.* Translated by Harvey C. Mansfield and Delba Winthrop. University of Chicago Press (2000).

Elegant, Simon. "China's Me Generation," *Time Magazine.* July 26, 2007.

Hamilton, James T. *All the News That's Fit to Sell: How the market transforms information into news.* Princeton University Press (2003).

National Conference of Citizenship. *America's Civic Health Index: Broken Engagement.* A report by the NCC (Sept. 2006).

Levine, Peter. *The Future of Democracy: Developing the next generation of American citizens.* University Press of New England (2007).

Patterson, Thomas E. *Young People and the News.* A report by the John F Kennedy School of Government, Harvard University. July, 2007.

Putnam, Robert. *Bowling Alone: The collapse and revival of American community.* Simon & Schuster (2000).

Schudsen, Michael. "Citizens, Consumers and The Good Society" in *The Annals of the American Academy of Political and Social Science*. Vol. 611 No. 1 (2007).

Sunstein, Cass. *Republic.com*. Princeton University Press (2001).

Chapter Six

Bellah, Richard et.al. *Habits of the Heart: Individualism and Commitment in American Life*. University of California Press, 1985.

Byrne, Rhonda. *The Secre*. Atria Books/Beyond Words, 2006.

The Baylor Religion Survey. Selected findings: www.isreligion.org/research/surveysofreligion/surveysofreligion.pdf.

The Barna Group. www.barna.org.

Carrette, Jeremy and Richard King. *Selling Spirituality: The Silent Takeover of Religion*. Routledge, 2004.

Despres, Loraine. "Yoga's Bad Boy: Bikram Choudhury." *Yoga Journal*. Mar/Apr, 2000.

Fishman Orlins, Susan. "A Portrait of the Jews Through Chinese Eyes." *Moment Magazine*, January, 2008.

Grant, John. *The New Marketing Manifesto: The 12 Rules for Building Successful Brands in the 21st Century*. Texere Publishing, 2001.

The Hartford Institute for Religious Research http://hirr.hartsem.edu/.

MacArthur, John. *Ashamed of the Gospel: When the Church Becomes like the World*. Crossway Books, 1993.

McGee, Micki. "The Secret's Success." *The Nation*. May 17, 2007.

"OMG! How Generation Y is Redefining Faith in the iPod Era." www.rebooters.net/index.php?site=reboot&page=rbt_usethesetools.

Prothero, Stephen. *Religious Literacy: What Every American Needs to Know—And Doesn't*. HarperOne, 2008.

Roof, Wade Clark. *Spiritual Marketplace: Baby Boomers and the Remaking of American Religion*. Princeton University Press, 1999.

Share Guide, May/June. "Understanding 'The Secret': On the Law of Attraction." An interview with Jack Canfield.